W9-AEL-989

Japan's Political Marketplace

Japan's Political Marketplace

With a New Preface

J. Mark Ramseyer
Frances McCall Rosenbluth

Harvard University Press
Cambridge, Massachusetts
London, England

For our parents

First Harvard University Press paperback edition, 1997

Library of Congress Cataloging-in-Publication Data

Ramseyer, J. Mark, 1954–
    Japan's political marketplace / J. Mark Ramseyer, Frances McCall Rosenbluth.
        p.   cm.
    Includes bibliographical references and index.
    ISBN 0-674-47280-2 (alk. paper) (cloth)
    ISBN 0-674-47281-0 (pbk.)
    1. Japan—Politics and government—1945–   2. Political parties—Japan.
  3. Policy sciences.   I. Rosenbluth, Frances McCall.   II. Title
JQ1631.R36 1993   92-33647
320.952—dc2C   CIP

Preface, 1997

Since the early 1990s, change has dominated Japanese politics, and the apparent stability of decades past has vanished. In 1993, the Diet hounded the long-time ruling Liberal Democratic Party (LDP) from power. The next year, it swept out its multimember districts and installed an electoral structure that pooled three hundred seats from single-member districts with two hundred seats from proportional representation (party-list) districts. Several years, perhaps several elections, will pass before the implications of these changes become clear. At least potentially, however, the implications are profound.

In the book that follows, we propose an explicit theoretical framework for understanding the consequences of these changes. Consider their impact on the four principal-agent relationships that structure this book: the relations between voters and politicians, between the party rank-and-file and party leaders, between politicians and bureaucrats, and between politicians and judges.

Voters and politicians. The new structure will reduce the level of intraparty competition and shift electoral competition toward issue-based politics. In the short run, many incumbents will continue their pork-barrel strategies. In the longer run, the cost of these strategies will favor candidates with more issue-based appeal.

Rank-and-file leaders. Within the parties, the new electoral rules will weaken factionalism, strengthen party leaders, and increase the importance of party platforms. A crucial intervening variable will be the way each party selects its candidates. To the extent that local party organizations control endorsements, the national leaders will find it hard to hold candidates to a party platform. To the extent that they use local primaries, they will reinforce the very intraparty competition that the new rules would otherwise reduce.

In time, however, local party organizations should increasingly cede authority to the central party leaders. For large parties with a reasonable chance of winning a legislative majority, delegating power over candidate selection to party leaders makes sense. Although smaller parties on the political fringes may behave differently, even they may find that more coherent leadership enhances their ability to play the "swing party."

Politicians and bureaucrats. Bureaucrats will generally remain loyal. Granted, those LDP legislators who were most closely tied to various bureaus will no longer be there to monitor bureaucrats as directly as before. Yet majority politicians can still rely both on indirect monitoring by their constituents and on the power of their *ex post* veto to produce strong *ex ante* incentives toward loyalty.

We do not suggest that nothing will change. If politics becomes more issue-based and perhaps parties even begin to alternate in power, then the politically driven character of Japanese regulation will become obvious even to the most obstinate critics of rational-choice theory (witness the recent deregulatory initiative). If backbenchers cede more policymaking authority to party leaders, bureaucrats will less often be whipsawed between the conflicting interests of the two groups. And if political parties begin to alternate in power, politicians may find it advantageous to intervene more directly in bureaucratic personnel matters.

Most fundamentally, bureaucrats will find their discretion more tightly constrained. Under LDP rule, those with LDP sympathies disproportionately self-selected into bureaucratic careers and, once there, found themselves with broad discretion. Under alternating majorities, these bureaucrats will now receive alternating policy instructions. Given the risk of regime change, moreover, constituents may also demand statutorily specified (rather than administratively designed) programs—programs that a later administration can change only through legislative amendment.

That said, Japanese bureaucrats will still retain more apparent independence than their American counterparts. Ultimately, the parliamentary organization of government in Japan will continue to induce politicians to give bureaucrats wider berth. The reason is simple: a parliamentary majority can safely grant bureaucrats more discretion than can a legislative majority in a presidential system. It can grant that discretion because it can supervise more closely—for it need not contend with an executive who has a different constituency interest and may even come from a different political party.

Politicians and judges. Judges will probably seem to act more independently. First, if parties alternate in power, politicians will have an incentive to choose younger justices for the Supreme Court. These younger justices, in turn, will have more time to develop distinctive philosophies. Second, politicians may find it advantageous to agree (perhaps implicitly) with their rivals to minimize their losses while out of power by intervening less in the courts while themselves in power. If either occurs, courts will appear more independent than under LDP rule.

Necessarily, all these predictions are preliminary. Crucially, however, they are falsifiable hypotheses that follow directly from the theory we outline below. The changes taking place in Japan do not overrun our book. Far from it; rather, they test it. By changing the political constellation and electoral rules in place, they provide the data with which to test the arguments we develop below.

Acknowledgments, 1993

We wrote this book primarily for two groups: for the rational-choice scholars interested in the basic principal-agent relationships in politics and for comparativists interested in Japan. In the process, we have incurred a large intellectual debt to several Japanese political scientists upon whose pathbreaking work we draw heavily. Our citations should make this debt clear, but lest there be any doubt we gladly acknowledge it here. In alphabetical order, with (as we shall do throughout the book) given names first and family names last, they are Takashi Inoguchi, Tomoaki Iwai, Sadafumi Kawato, Shin'ichi Kitaoka, Tetsuhisa Matsuzaki, Ichirō Murakawa, Michio Muramatsu, Hideo Ōtake, Seizaburō Satō, and Yasunori Sone.

We received financial support from a number of sources: the National Science Foundation (NSF grants no. SES 9113795 and SES 9113738), the UCLA School of Law Dean's Fund, the UCSD IR/PS Dean's Fund, the UCLA Center for International Business Education and Research, and the UCSD Chancellor's Summer Fellowship Fund.

We have been planning this book for a long time. Over that period many friends at many institutions shared their ideas with us, both in conversation and through their gracious comments on our drafts. Those who were particularly generous with their time and thoughts include Hans Baerwald, Gary Cox, Gerald Curtis, Frank Easterbrook, Harry First, Daniel Foote, Peter Gourevitch, John Haley, Philip Heymann, Masumi Ishikawa, David Johnson, Avery Katz, William Klein, Masaru Kohno, Leonard Lynn, Percy Luney, Lisa Martin, Mathew McCubbins, Setsuo Miyazawa, Minoru Nakazato, Greg Noble, Hugh Patrick, Eric Rasmusen, Tom Roehl, Arthur Rosett, Gary Schwartz, Paul Sheard, Matthew Shugart, Michael Thies, Frank Upham, Detlev Vagts, Arthur von Mehren, John Wiley, and Stephen Yeazell. In addition, we received many helpful comments from participants in workshops at Harvard University, Stanford University, the University of California, Los Angeles, the University of California, San Diego, the University of Chicago, Hokkaido University, the University of Michigan, the University of Tokyo, and Yale University, and at presentations at the Japanese Law and Society Association, the Pacific Research on Industry, Society and Management, and the Public Choice Society.

It has become industry custom to pause here and thank secretaries, children, and spouses. We would be happy to thank our secretaries if they had typed this manuscript, but they didn't. We would love to thank our children if we had any, but we don't. We are delighted to thank Jim Rosenbluth and Norma Wyse, though not for feeding the cat (neither of us have one), for washing the dishes (a machine does it), for forgiving the many weekends lost writing this book (they were usually too busy themselves anyway), or for any of the other academically irrelevant tasks generally appreciated in this paragraph. Instead, we thank them for their unflaggingly critical sense; for persistently refusing to be impressed and—thereby—persistently driving us to try harder. Any royalties to this book are all theirs.

Finally, we happily acknowledge that we would never have had the nerve to be as intemperately polemical about Japanese rationality if our parents had not raised us as children in Japan. They inspired this book. To them, we affectionately dedicate it.

Contents

1
Introduction

Every discipline has its fables. They may be true, they may be false; no one really knows. Given the pedagogic points they make, no one really cares. Take this one in economics, attributed to Steven Cheung:

> Between the cities of Chongqing and Wuhan, the Yangtze River wends its way through a series of gorges. Although the water runs fast, modern diesel-powered ferries breeze up the river with dozens of tourists. Modern tug boats plow their way up too, even with the tons of coal that metropolitan Chongqing needs. But it was not always thus. Decades ago, crews of coolies moved the tourists and coal. Locked into rope harnesses, they climbed narrow paths carved into the mountain, and hauled the boats and barges upstream. Overseers whipped them on.
>
> The spectacle horrified occasional American passengers. But ultimately, whether the overseers whipped the coolies was not for the Americans to decide. When one American woman ordered her boat captain to stop the whipping, he simply refused. "The coolies own the right to pull these boats," he replied. "They chose to hire the overseer because they decided they needed one. They chose to give him whips because they decided they needed them. How they choose to earn their living is none of my business. And it's certainly none of yours."[1]

Acting collectively as principals, the coolies hired supervisors with whips to prevent each other from free-riding. Acting collectively, modern principals often do much the same. Problems of collective action concerted among many principals are central to political organization, and so too is the solution of hiring a common overseer as agent. Voters, for example, find it hard to act collectively, so they elect legislators and give them the power to mitigate their problems. Legislators appoint party leaders to solve theirs. And party leaders select bureaucrats and judges to see the job through. Agreements between multiple principals and their agents are endemic, occasionally obscure, and central to this book. In the chapters that follow, we trace the shape of the agreements between agents and principals in Japanese government. Throughout, we explore their implications—both for understanding the contours of government in Japan, and for developing a positive theory of politics.

Culture in Japanese Politics

Not so long ago, scholars began their accounts of Japanese politics by invoking the peculiarities of Japanese culture. One anthropologist made a minor splash when she "explained" all of Japanese politics (all of Japanese society, really) by positing that Japanese shared an obsessive need to organize themselves hierarchically into cliques. A psychiatrist "explained" just as much when he announced that all Japanese had a pathological desire to be dependent on powerful individuals. Scholars lavished praise on the theories and elaborated on them in essays about Japan's need for consensus, about its rejection of individualism and open conflict, about its Confucian fascination with loyalty, and about its patriarchal legacy.

To their credit, many Japan specialists eventually recognized the circularity of much of this work. James Q. Wilson (1989, p. 308) and others may still explain Japanese politics and bureaucracy through a "pervasive communalism in Japanese life." But many modern political scientists and legal scholars use these general notions of culture less pervasively, if at all. After almost two decades since he said it, Clifford Geertz still put it most accurately (if a little circuitously) in his paean to Talcott Parsons: "And Parsons, insisting in his grave and toneless voice that to interpret the way a group of human beings behave as an expression of their culture while defining their culture as the sum of the ways in which they have learned to behave is not terribly informative, is as responsible for [the] passing [of the concept of culture as learned behavior] as any single figure in contemporary social science."[2]

Institutions and Organizations, Principals and Agents

We are no fans of either Geertz or Parsons, but we do take their critique of culture to heart. Hence we abandon any notion of a peculiar Japanese culture and use the standard choice-theoretic approach to principals and agents instead.[3] At least in the abstract, our argument should not be controversial. In essence, we argue: (1) that the institutional framework of government—the rules of the game among political players—decisively shapes the character of political competition in Japan; (2) that the players in this competitive political market try to build organizations adapted to that framework; and (3) that these players also try to manipulate the framework to their private advantage.[4] The rest is detail.

Take an example from the business world. The regulatory rules of the game (the institutions) alter the incentives of the various parties and the costs of alternative transactional forms (Bates, 1989, ch. 1). In the process, they change the way people do business. Firms (organizations) are more apt to survive if they adapt to that regulatory structure. Car companies, for instance, are more likely to prosper if they anticipate federal mileage regulations. Firms are also more apt to do better if they manipulate the regulatory framework to their private advantage. Car companies, again, are more likely to survive if they can use the regulatory structure to disadvantage foreign competitors.

At this level, there is so far nothing original. We have known analytically since Coase (1960)—and intuitively for centuries—that institutions matter. We have known from hundreds of studies in law and economics and the "new" (or neo-) institutional economics that successful firms manipulate and adapt to institutional rules. And we are beginning to learn from recent work in choice-theoretic political economy that a similar dynamic drives competitive political markets.

In the chapters that follow, we provide the detail. Although the detail is more controversial, we still focus on the three "obvious" propositions above. First, we trace the effect that institutional rules have on Japanese politics. This institutional framework both creates the incentives for voters, politicians, bureaucrats, and judges, and determines the transactions costs of political exchange. We describe its effects on the nature of political competition, on the organization of political parties, and on the policies implemented.

Second, we trace the way Japanese political parties adapt to that institutional environment. On the basis of the Japanese election rules, for example, we examine how the majority Liberal Democratic Party (LDP) organizes itself internally to maximize its electoral success. Given the structure of government set out in the Japanese Constitution, we examine how the LDP enforces its policy preferences on bureaucrats and judges.

Third, we trace the way Japanese organizations manipulate the institutional environment itself. Within the statutory rules governing property rights, we examine how business firms buy advantageous statutes. Given the candidates' need for private goods in order to get elected, we examine how party backbenchers lobby for pork-barrel statutes. In view of the role electoral rules play in determining who controls the legislature, we examine why the LDP has not yet changed (but may soon change) those rules.

The detail thus reveals a dialectic between institutional and organizational structure—in this case, a dialectic that determines the basic contours of government. Within the dialectical process we focus primarily on the character of the various principal-agent relationships involved: on how closely politicians represent voter preferences, LDP leaders represent the preferences of the other LDP legislators, and bureaucrats and judges represent LDP preferences.

Political Entrepreneurs and Agency Slack

Although monitoring and policing costs ensure some residual "agency slack" in these principal-agent relationships (that is, some gap between what the principal expects and what the agent delivers), political entrepreneurship might nonetheless reduce the slack. In economic markets, for example, an enterprising firm may reduce the "slack" between consumer tastes and the products sold by marketing new, more responsive products. This is how it takes business away from its rivals. Presumably, the same can and does happen in political markets. Enterprising candidates or parties can reduce the slack between voter preferences and incumbent policy by marketing new, more responsive programs. They do it because they thereby obtain more votes.[5]

Yet political entrepreneurship only incompletely eliminates agency slack. Whether an entrepreneur succeeds in a political market will often depend not just on the candidate's own abilities and policies, but also on the candidate's ability to field a majority coalition.[6] However much voters like an entrepreneur, they will often select a rival instead if they think the rival's party will win control. After all, majority parties can (and in Japan sometimes do) redistribute wealth from constituents represented by opposition legislators to their own. Absent a realistic chance that an entrepreneur will assemble a majority coalition, many voters will reject the political challenger. In turn, would-be entrepreneurs may recognize the probability of that rejection ahead of time and desist. Without enough entrepreneurs, significant agency slack may remain.

As we proceed to locate that residual slack, we confirm a basic theme in the political principal-agent literature on the correlation between agency slack and transactions costs. According to Randall Calvert, Mathew McCubbins, and Barry Weingast (1989), the magnitude of slack in a principal-agent relationship should correlate with the magnitude of the transactions costs at stake. More colloquially, agency slack should be greatest where principals have the worst information and find it hardest to constrain their agents. The slack should be smallest where the principals have the best information and can control their agents most cheaply.

The location of agency slack in the Japanese government illustrates this correlation. Slack is highest between the Japanese voters and their legislative agents—for the LDP has exchanged interest-group policies for cash contributions. As the theory suggests, this is also where the principals (the voters) find it most costly to organize, where the peculiar Japanese electoral rules give the agents (the politicians) large incentives to ignore unorganized voters, where voters have the least incentive to acquire the information they need, and where (given the advantages of a large party) political entrepreneurship is least likely to succeed. By contrast, slack is lower where transactions costs are lower: between legislators and their party leaders, between party leaders and bureaucrats, and between party leaders and judges.

Implicit Agency Contracts

We draw up a sequence of relationships for the implicit agency
contracts that Japanese political actors negotiate between voters
and legislators (chapters 2 and 3); between LDP backbenchers and
their party leaders (chapters 4 and 5); between LDP leaders and
bureaucrats (chapters 6 and 7); and between LDP leaders and judges
(chapters 8 and 9).

On the face of it, the parties to these contracts could have radically
inconsistent incentives. What maximizes a voter's utility need not
maximize that of his or her legislators. What LDP leaders want
bureaucrats to promote (generally, the party's electoral interests)
need not be what the bureaucrats themselves want to promote. And
much the same conflict occurs between LDP leaders and judges.

To achieve a better alignment of these inconsistent interests,
Japanese political actors negotiate implicit agency contracts. Within
each of these relationships, one of the parties (the principal) tries
to make it worth while for the other (the agent) to promote the
principal's wants. Matters would be simpler if the principal either
knew what kind of person the agent was or could monitor the
agent's behavior cheaply. But political actors are no more likely
than economic actors to have full information. Lacking that information, they use implicit contracts to try to readjust the agent's
incentives.

The contracts these parties employ are straightforward, but for
clarity we outline them here. First, the parties often permit a settlement of accounts after the facts—depending on how the agent
behaves, the principal often keeps the right to punish the agent
later (what Rasmusen [1989, p. 148] calls a "boiling-in-oil" contract). Even if the principals do not have full information about the
agent's actions during the course of the job, they can often obtain
it afterward.[7] They can then use the information to punish the
agent. LDP Dietmembers can punish their leaders through a no-
confidence vote. The leaders can refuse to promote bureaucrats
who ignore party preferences. And LDP leaders can relegate judges
who indulge their preferences to provincial branch courts.

Second, by announcing their policy of punishing disobedient
agents, principals often induce agents to sort themselves out beforehand. By threatening to punish bureaucrats who implement leftist

policies, LDP leaders can cause leftist applicants to self-select *out* of government jobs. They can do the same with judges. And because Dietmembers demand that their leaders raise funds, those who cannot do so stay clear of leadership positions.

Third, principals sometimes require their agents to "post bonds" (Williamson, 1985). Thus LDP leaders constrain bureaucrats by paying them below-market wages for much of their career, and making the shortfall contingent on the quality of their lifetime performance (Lazear, 1979, 1981). Similarly, LDP backbenchers constrain their leaders by paying them "efficiency wages"—by entitling them to a steady stream of large rents which they would jeopardize by ignoring the party's collective interests.[8]

Last, the parties devise ways to generate information that the principals can use to select and monitor their agents more effectively. Competitive electoral markets, for instance, produce information about candidates, since the candidates have incentives to extoll their own virtues and to disclose the vices of everyone else. Tournaments among LDP backbenchers for leadership positions produce information about the fund-raising abilities of the potential leaders. Competition among ministries for LDP support likewise produces information, since bureaucrats have similar incentives (Lazear and Rosen, 1981). And LDP leaders can offer to support bureaucrats in their future political careers if the bureaucrats report any agency slack they see among their present colleagues.

The Results

If Japan scholars find the detail below controversial, we suspect that will be because we proceed from the premise that Japanese political actors rationally maximize subject to institutional constraints.[9] Both rational maximization and institutional constraints have become red flags in the field. Some Japan scholars, for example, routinely assert that the standard choice-theoretic models of constrained maximization could not apply to that country. Yet if individuals do not maximize, neither will political market competition lead to any determinate pattern of institutional adaptation or manipulation. Japan scholars also assert that institutional structures—the rules of the game—do not matter. Many purport to demonstrate, for instance, that Japanese consistently ignore legal rules.[10] Yet if the rules that comprise the institutional structure do not matter, then—again—neither will political market competition drive people to adapt to that structure or to manipulate it. Hence the ad hoc nature of orthodox Japanological research. We hope our choice-theoretic approach generates a more coherent and systematic set of findings.

Voters and Legislators

If nothing else, the LDP has won elections. Since its formation through a merger between two conservative parties in 1955, it has consistently controlled the powerful Lower House of the Japanese national legislature (the Diet). Few parties in modern democracies can claim as much. The LDP has done so, moreover, within a fiercely volatile political market. Despite its aggregate success rate, individual LDP representatives regularly lose seats in what must seem—at least to them—alarming numbers. Indeed, Japanese incumbents lose in larger percentages than do their counterparts in the United States, Great Britain, or Germany (Calder, 1988, pp. 68–69).

In any given electoral district, Japanese voters select several representatives. Although each voter has only one nontransferable vote, in each district voters collectively elect two to six representatives. As a result, to obtain a majority in the House, a party like the LDP must elect several representatives each from many of the districts. To accomplish this, it necessarily must pit its own candidates against each other, but must also try to ensure that none of them dramatically overpowers the others. For if any one candidate does capture significantly more LDP votes than the others, the weaker ones may trail opposition candidates they would otherwise have beaten. As a consequence, the LDP will have elected one representative from a district that could have supported two or more if the party had but distributed its supporters more evenly.

To even out its votes, the LDP uses its control over government to build its candidates' personal support networks. LDP candidates foster these networks through a combination of government-dispensed "pork," cash, and in-kind gifts, as well as bureaucratic intervention services. In each case, the party's control over government matters crucially. Precisely because the party controls the government, LDP legislators can target pork-barrel items (such as highways, bridges, or profitable contracts) to their supporters. For the same reason, they can extract financial contributions from the business community, which they can then redistribute to other supporters. And again for the same reason, they and their staffers can induce the bureaucrats to help their constituents. The resulting system may strike observers as "corrupt," but it is an institutionally driven corruption: multi-member districts force the LDP to spread the vote around; the party can do that most competitively if its candidates cultivate personal support networks; and those candidates can cultivate those networks most effectively if they manipulate the party's control over the government.[11]

Through this scheme, the LDP potentially incurs two problems. First, by enacting pro-business policies, it moves away from policies desired by the median voter. It will generally find this move advantageous only if it generates business contributions large enough to enable it to regain as many voters as it loses through the policy shift. Such an outcome is possible, though hardly inevitable.

Second, its schemes may create significant welfare losses. Because its probusiness policies include anticompetitive regulatory programs, they potentially generate the usual dead-weight losses that accompany such programs. To be sure, voters will recapture some of the offsetting monopoly rents through LDP largesse. Given, though, that the losses to consumers from anticompetitive regulation usually exceed the monopoly rents to the regulated industry, the public will likely still incur a net loss. If the pork-barrel projects the LDP enacts constitute higher-than-optimal levels of public works, they again create a net welfare loss. And because rational voters will prefer programs that do not generate net inefficiencies to those that do, these stratagems could reduce LDP support (Becker, 1983).

For a couple of reasons, the LDP nonetheless finds its political formula advantageous. First, many voters do not notice widely dispersed welfare losses. Rational voters are seldom fully informed and seldom fully penalize representatives who enact inefficient policies.[12] Second, even when voters recognize their losses, the LDP can win by compensating only a majority of the voters. As a result, even if a redistribution scheme is itself inefficient, the LDP may find it advantageous to redistribute wealth from 49 percent of the population to the 51 percent that votes LDP. Although majority parties anywhere profit by doing this, the incentive is particularly strong in Japan, where the need to even out the vote in the multimember districts places a premium on organized blocks of voters. In a frictionless Coasian world, the 49 percent might bribe the 51 percent to forestall this scheme; in the real world transactions costs prevent such payoffs.[13] The result may be institutionalized corruption, but it is a corruption that satisfies a large percentage of the electorate. "Only a government for the people can buy the people," proclaimed one of Dick Tracy's nemeses. And so, to date, it has been in Japan.

Demographic changes have begun to change this. Urban voters in Japan have been more costly to identify and track and are generally less responsive than rural voters to pork-barrel policies. Because the personal network schemes split their votes less efficiently than they split rural votes, LDP leaders have increasingly sought to revise the electoral system. As Japanese continue to move to cities, therefore, those leaders may well adopt some single-member districts. As of the time this book went to press, that change had not yet been made. Meanwhile, however, LDP leaders had already begun to cultivate the party's following among the urban constituencies.

Backbenchers and Party Leaders

Like the Yangtze River coolies, LDP legislators structure their relations with each other through a hierarchical set of organizations. This makes it possible for them to commit themselves credibly to policies and also to mitigate several collective action problems they would otherwise face. We will consider, in turn, three related issues: how LDP legislators credibly commit themselves to programs; why they group themselves into factions; and what functions party and faction leaders serve.

Every legislator potentially plays an endgame, for each term in office could be his or her last. Consequently, every legislator potentially has an incentive to renege on any deals he or she makes (Selton, 1975). Even if individual legislators do not renege, their successors may. Because constituents are aware of this, legislators will lack credibility if they promise that the policies they enact will continue for any significant length of time. Unable to commit themselves, they will find it hard to extract significant payoffs from their constituents (Landes and Posner, 1975).

To mitigate this problem of promissory credibility, LDP legislators call on party leaders. LDP leaders have an incentive to keep any promises the party makes, and the authority and power to force party backbenchers to do the same. After all, the leaders control the distribution of large amounts of contributions. They have the longest tenures of any legislators and are among the least likely to lose an election. As leaders, they can look forward to a steady stream of large rents in cash and perquisites (Rasmusen, 1990). And should they choose to retire, they can transfer their electoral organization to their children.

LDP legislators organize themselves into factions to facilitate political entrepreneurship within the party. In effect, the competition among the factions functions much like the competition among the several divisions of a diversified firm. Most critically, it is through identifying with factions that LDP candidates compete among each other in the multi-member districts. Absent factions, they would have to compete as individuals. Although they could do so, they would find their fundraising hampered by economies of scale and by their inability credibly to disavow endgame strategies.

Instead, the faction leaders raise a significant percentage of the party's funds and then bankroll LDP candidates in the multi-member districts. The central party leadership intervenes only when the factions try to run more candidates than the LDP supporters in a district can safely elect. Effectively, the factions keep entrepreneurship alive within the LDP, and party leaders limit the entrepreneurship when it threatens overall party welfare. Although factions might otherwise destroy the LDP by competing among themselves for policy leadership and pork, party backbenchers mitigate this risk through two practices: they require the faction controlling the Prime Minister's office to distribute the benefits of office among the factions in proportion to their size; and they maintain factions that, by the most important indices, are microcosms of the party itself.

Party leaders mitigate three collective-action problems within the LDP: (1) they try to eliminate the excesive pork-barrel politics that control over government tends to create; (2) they make policy, which necessarily constitutes a public good to the party backbenchers; and (3) they serve as the designated monitors over the bureaucracy and judiciary.

First, because it controls the government, the LDP can divert enormous resources to its supporters. Were there no constraints, individual backbenchers would have an incentive to manipulate the government to maximize the pork they each extract. Should they do so, however, the ratio of private to public goods that the government dispenses would grow larger than optimal for the LDP. In the process, they would also increase the chance that voters would throw them out of office. At issue, therefore, is a classic "common-pool resource" problem (Ostrom, 1990): each individual legislator gains by extracting as much pork as he or she can, but the legislators as a group lose unless they can keep the amount in check. To limit the extraction to levels optimal for the party as a whole, they select and empower leaders who will restrain access to the pool.

Second, because party policy provides brand-name value to the party itself, the gains to policy accrue to all legislators. Party policy, in short, constitutes a public good—and in the absence of Mancur Olson's (1965) "selective incentives," the party will maintain a suboptimal level of policy. LDP legislators overcome this problem by giving their leaders the power to enforce such selective incentives.

Third, although as majority party the LDP potentially has complete control over the bureaucracy and substantial control over the judiciary, well-monitored bureaucracies and judiciaries are also public goods: the LDP gains by requiring bureaucrats and judges to enforce its policy preferences, yet those gains accrue to the party as a whole. Again, absent selective incentives, each legislator will have little incentive to monitor and constrain the bureaucrats and judges. LDP legislators solve this problem too by assigning the job to the party leaders.

Leaders and Bureaucrats

To date, most students of the Japanese bureaucracy merely note that bureaucrats conceive and draft most programs and exercise wide discretion in implementing them. This, they argue, shows bureaucratic supremacy. In fact, it shows nothing of the sort. The phenomenon is equally consistent with bureaucrats who faithfully implement LDP policy preferences—who conceive, draft, and implement programs in the shadow of the Diet.

Political leaders use bureaucrats to conceive and to draft programs because they have only small staffs of their own, and they keep legislative staffs small for political reasons. Because they head the long-term majority party, they can effectively use the large and elite national bureaucracy as their own private staff. Consequently, they have less of a need for personal staffers than American legislators have. Indeed, were large staffs authorized for LPD legislators, they would also have to be allowed to opposition legislators and LDP backbenchers. This would at once diminish the LDP's political competitive advantage and give backbenchers more resources to use in second-guessing the party's leadership.

LDP leaders have several ways to ensure that bureaucrats remain responsive. First, they retain a veto over anything bureaucrats do. They can refuse to pass any bills bureaucrats draft, and can overturn by statute any regulatory measures bureaucrats adopt. Second, they control bureaucratic careers. Acting as the ministers, they can promote and refuse promotions. Knowing this, prospective bureaucrats sharing LDP policy preferences disproportionately self-select into bureaucratic careers. In turn, these conservative bureaucrats have a natural self-interest in keeping the LDP in power. Third, party leaders require all elite bureaucrats to post large portions of their lifetime earnings as bonds. The bureaucrats then receive these amounts only if they perform satisfactorily during their tenure at the ministry.

LDP leaders also take a variety of steps to make sure they have the information they need to constrain their bureaucrats. First, constituents dissatisfied with bureaucratic performance regularly complain to LDP legislators. After all, LDP candidates build their personal support networks in part by offering bureaucratic intervention services. Second, party leaders maintain within the bureaucracy people who intend to become LDP politicians. These would-be politicians will rely on the leaders later for support, and thus have an incentive now to report any cases of agency slack they see. Third, the leaders encourage the ministries to compete for political support for their programs. In the course of these tournaments, each ministry has an incentive to provide information both about its own and about its competitors' political performance.

By all indications, LDP leaders find that their elite bureaucrats perform well. For example, the bureaucrats enforce a political agenda even at the Ministry of Finance (MOF) and the Ministry of International Trade and Industry (MITI): even at the ministries traditionally thought to be most independent, a political logic structures the administration of government. When by the exigencies of politics legislators need to change the programs they promote, they rely on bureaucrats to conceive and draft the alternative programs. At the same time, they also rely on these bureaucrats to implement the newer programs and do not try to replace them. Were bureaucrats acting upon a distinct, not electorally driven set of policy preferences, LDP leaders would be unable to rely on them in times of politically dictated policy change. The leaders show no sign that such might be the case.

Leaders and Judges

LDP leaders also keep as small as they can the agency slack (known traditionally as judicial independence) between themselves and judges. In the United States, some scholars argue, this slack helps legislators to make their commitments credible and to monitor bureaucratic performance. In Japan neither claim applies, for LDP legislators have largely solved these problems through the devices described above. Lacking a compelling reason to tolerate slack in the judiciary, the leaders rather try to ensure that judges follow LDP preferences.

Political leaders maintain their control over the judiciary through their influence on job assignments. Most Japanese judges approach the judiciary as a career. They take the job in their late twenties, and keep it for much of their working lives. During that time, whether they obtain advantageous job assignments depends on whether they can please the judges at the Supreme Court Secretariat (the court's administrative offices). The judges at the Secretariat are monitored by the Supreme Court justices, and the latter are appointed late in life for short terms by the LDP leaders. In effect, LDP leaders appoint to the apex of the judiciary only those who are politically reliable, and then designate those justices the monitors for the rest of the judiciary.

According to court records, the judges at the Secretariat do manipulate job assignments to strengthen LDP control over politically sensitive cases. To be sure, they do not punish judges merely for *holding* other party preferences. But they do sometimes punish them if they decide sensitive cases in ways contrary to LDP interests, particularly when Supreme Court justices have already made their views on the issues clear. In essence, the Japanese courts *are* part of the bureaucracy. Although the Constitution guarantees judges some agency slack (some independence), that slack does not serve LDP interests; hence one would not expect LDP leaders to promote it. By all odds, they do not. Instead, they try to reduce the slack in their relationships with all their agents, whether administrative or judicial. By all odds, they largely succeed.

Conclusion

It is our purpose to demonstrate that standard choice-theoretic principles explain the dominant patterns of Japanese political life. The principles are not those anyone invented to explain Japan. Indeed, they were not invented to explain any particular society. But that is our point. For we argue below that the essence of Japanese politics closely resembles the *essence* of politics in *most* other societies. We will not claim our model explains "all" aspects of Japanese politics. Regressions are not useless because some points lie off the line. Neither will we claim our model applies to "all" societies. University cocktail parties are full of academics who insist rational-choice models could not possibly apply to "their" tribe—and it is much too much trouble to disprove them.

We wish to deal only with Japan, and only with the basic contours of politics and regulation. That we consider challenge enough. And that is where we locate the importance of rationality. "Everyone has his reasons," bemoans Octave in Jean Renoir's *The Rules of the Game*—after an aristocratic Parisian retreat that left several marriages broken and at least one guest dead. The results were socially inefficient, but the players remained individually rational to the bitter end. One could say much the same thing about many aspects of Japanese politics: in this book, we do.

2

Electoral Rules and Party Strategy

Periodically, particularly after political scandals on the order of the Recruit affair,[1] one hears Japanese mutter that they "have a first-rate economy and third-rate politics." But it is the voters, after all, who refuse to "throw the rascals out." The Liberal Democratic Party has controlled the cabinet since its formation in 1955 as the result of the merger of two conservative parties. Except in 1976, when it needed coalitional help from a few renegade LDP members who had formed the New Liberal Club, it has constituted a Diet majority. Obviously, the LDP is still the party of choice for a plurality of Japanese voters. To understand why that is so we need to explain what voters want, and why, given Japan's electoral system, they have sustained an LDP majority.

A country's political institutions, and its electoral rules in particular, establish a distinct set of incentives for politicians and political parties competing for votes.[2] In Japan, the electoral system forces majority-seeking parties to undertake the daunting task of apportioning the vote evenly among multiple candidates in most districts. This feature of Japan's political institutional context, we will argue, has led the LDP to adopt a more particularistic set of policies than would be likely under a number of conceivable alternative electoral schemes. Understandably, its continued electoral success has made the LDP reluctant to change the rules of the game, though the costs associated with this set of rules have risen as well.[3]

Japan's two-to-six-member districts pit LDP candidates against each other, reducing the extent to which they can rely on a party label. A single label provides voters with no cues as to how to vote among candidates, and gives the party no assurance that one or two especially charismatic politicians will not garner a disproportionate share of the votes from LDP supporters. Candidates, for their part, put a great deal of energy into building up individual bases of support rather than pinning their chances solely on charisma.

The LDP's electoral strategy has at times lagged behind demographic changes. The party's share of the popular vote in its first election in 1958 was its largest ever, and after years of LDP slippage with each successive election, by the mid-1970s the LDP held a Diet majority only by a razor-thin margin. Political commentators began to announce the imminent demise of the LDP and the arrival of a leftist government. But this prognosis was premature. The LDP managed to turn the tide with a landslide victory in 1980, and the pundits began looking for reasons for the "new conservative momentum."

The LDP owes its success to two factors. First, the party has adapted—even if with some lag—to the changing composition of the Japanese electorate. Since the 1970s the party has gradually shifted the targets of its concern, reducing somewhat the amount of particularistic favors that were firmly linked to special interest groups and providing more public goods instead. The second reason is historical and path-dependent (North, 1990). The LDP had the good fortune to have been the first party in the post–World War II period to capture a Diet majority. It has used the government resources that come with that majority to help its members win reelection. Once the LDP gained control of these government resources, other parties were severely disadvantaged under Japan's electoral rules. Given the LDP's combination of savvy and luck, arguments stressing the "stupidity" of opposition parties appear to be superfluous.

The LDP, upon its formation as a majority party in 1955, could have changed the electoral rules. The rules are specified by statute rather than by the Constitution and would require a simple majority vote to overturn.[4] But, so far, the party has chosen to compete within the existing system. The LDP has used its control of budgetary and regulatory policymaking to nurture its candidates' individual support groups that sustain the party's Diet majority and, when necessary, to appeal to broader swaths of the electorate.

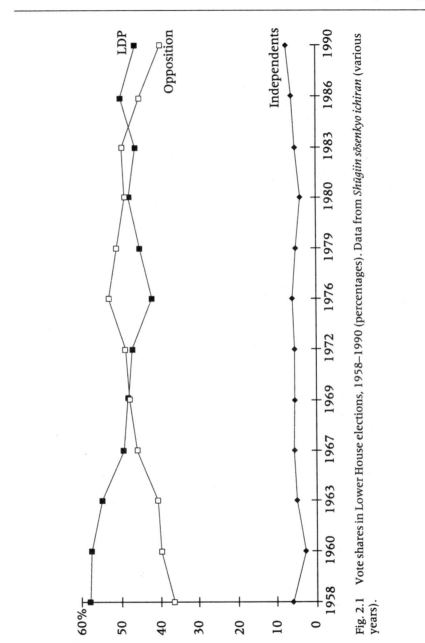

Fig. 2.1   Vote shares in Lower House elections, 1958–1990 (percentages). Data from *Shūgiin sōsenkyo ichiran* (various years).

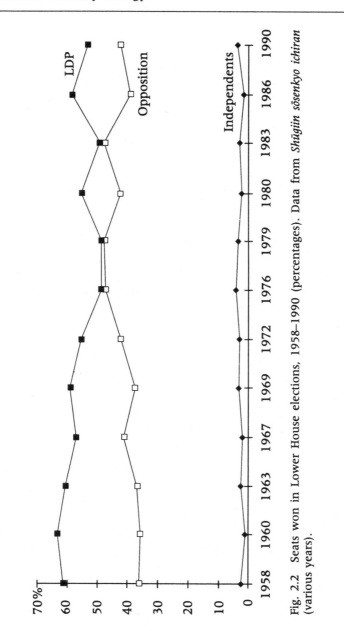

Fig. 2.2 Seats won in Lower House elections, 1958–1990 (percentages). Data from *Shūgiin sōsenkyo ichiran* (various years).

The Personal Vote

It has become customary to assume that politicians will, when able, provide their constituents with private goods as a way of enhancing their own electoral chances.[5] It is a simple logical observation that giving people private goods is a better way to get them to do something for you than giving them public goods. People would rather benefit from a private good that everyone else pays for than to pay for a public good from which everyone else benefits.

A number of scholars have argued that the private-goods electoral strategy is responsible for the apparent increase in the incumbency advantage in U.S. Congressional elections.[6] Fiorina (1977), and Cain, Ferejohn, and Fiorina (1987) documented how politicians provide constituency services in efforts to develop a core of loyal voters who are unlikely to be swayed by promises of intangible, less appropriable policies. By developing a "personal vote" through the provision of private favors, the argument goes, politicians insulate themselves from challenges on the basis of issues and public goods.[7]

The policy implications of the sort of personal-vote electoral strategy Cain, Ferejohn, and Fiorina describe are clear. The strategy should lead to more reliance on the provision of private goods and less on the provision of public goods than a strict spatial model would predict. From the standpoint of the median voter, there should be an underprovision of public goods.

As it happens, this personal-vote model fits Japan well. The LDP has beaten the political competition for over thirty-five years, and for this unparalleled success we credit the LDP's electoral strategy of using financial resources to provide favors. A lavish use of this strategy, however, is not cheap. Because resources have to be raised either through taxes or from contributors, we might expect politicians actually to prefer to campaign on the basis of broad party platforms rather than pork to the extent it is electorally safe to do so.

Not all countries illustrate the personal-vote model so well. Gary Cox (1989) outlined the rise in Britain of inter-party electoral contests on the basis of party platforms and the concurrent decline in the use of public policy for pork between the 1830s and the 1880s. As the British Parliament enlarged districts and gradually eliminated multi-member districts over the course of those decades, political parties found they had greater success appealing to the median voter with policy programs than in trying to buy off blocs of voters with particularistic favors. Larger districts made particular- *[handwritten: After this book was written, Japan went to 3/4 of seats from one large, nation-wide district, and the rest from single-member districts]* ism a more costly strategy for individual politicians, because they had more ground to cover and more individuals to woo for support. At the same time, the adoption of single-member districts made particularism less *necessary,* because parties needed to field only a single candidate in each district. This eliminated the politicians' need to build a personal following as a way of competing with candidates from their own party.

Although the personal-vote strategy does characterize LDP politics, Cain, Ferejohn, and Fiorina, do not fully explain why it should. They do not address either the inevitable costs of a heavy reliance on particularism or—given their American focus—the variation in the extent of particularism in other countries. The more policies are at the service of small groups of voters, the less able is a party in power to provide public goods, and the more vulnerable is the party to charges of neglecting the majority.[8] We need more information about the nature of political competition within a given country to judge how an optimal electoral strategy balances the provision of private and public goods.

Electoral Rules and LDP Strategy[9]

Japanese electoral rules differ markedly from the single-member district system of post-1880s Britain. Here we will briefly outline the pressure these rules bring to bear on any majority-seeking party essentially to "buy" votes. We give the most attention to Lower House election rules, because the postwar Constitution vests in the Lower House the highest degree of decision-making authority of any governmental body.[10]

In Japanese Lower House elections voters have a single vote, despite a district magnitude ranging from two to six members. Votes are not transferable to other candidates of the same party in the event that a voter's first choice has already made it past the post, as is the case in the single transferable-vote systems in Ireland and Finland. Under Japan's single nontransferable vote (SNTV) electoral rules, any majority-seeking party—or for that matter any party fielding more than a single candidate in any district—confronts the problem of distributing the vote among its candidates in order to win as many seats as possible.

Vote Division

In principle, apportioning votes should be very simple. A party need only to provide voters with cues on how they should cast their ballots to the party's best advantage. In a district where a party is fielding two candidates, for example, a party could send a preelection announcement telling all supporters with telephone numbers ending in an odd number to vote for candidate A, and those with telephone numbers ending in an even number to vote for candidate B. These cues would help party supporters elect as many members of their chosen party as possible.[11]

The obvious problem with such cue-giving is that party identification would have to be strong and predictable for this to work. Voters may, for a variety of reasons, have individual preferences and be unwilling to follow the party's cue. Parties therefore have to give voters a *reason* along with the cue.

A party could allow individual candidates to distinguish themselves from each other ideologically. This might seem a natural way for a large party to appeal to a wide swath of the electorate without losing the advantage of party size. But this strategy has some problems. For instance, a party could end up jeopardizing both its party label *and* the personal vote. If candidates of the same party attacked each other's platforms, voters would get little sense of the party's goals and intentions. If party members are at least adjacent in their policy formulation, they are their own fiercest competitors, leading to intra-party strain. Sufficiently negative campaigns could even lose rather than gain votes for the party, as American parties often discover during primaries (Bernstein, 1977).

If it allowed ideological diversification, the party would have difficulty predicting the electoral results of competition among party members on the basis of alternative platforms. Even with the help of sophisticated polling techniques, the party would be hard-pressed to predict precisely who would vote for whom over time, and to adjust for changes at the margin. Moreover, ideological distinctions alone give a majority party no advantage over the other parties without control of government resources. It is certainly conceivable that a nonmajority party could find an ideological point close enough to an ideologically "neighboring" candidate of the majority party to steal votes. There are benefits to competing on the basis of public goods, as we saw in the case of Britain, but there are also costs to not using private goods at all.[12]

Alternatively, a party could offer the prospect of pork to induce voters to follow party cues. This, in fact, is the strategy on which the LDP capitalizes. The party allows its candidates access to government resources with which to compete for votes. In addition to touting the party label, which all LDP Dietmembers share, LDP politicians differentiate themselves from one another by specializing in particular types of constituency services. Each politician's choice as to what types of services to provide is a niche-market decision, but it is the membership in the LDP that gives the legislator goods to deliver. In other words, the LDP's single most important advantage is control of the government resources that comes with a Diet majority.

By giving its candidates resources with which to target specific groups within the electorate, the LDP solves, or at least mitigates, most of the problems that ideological cues would present. Although particularism does not strengthen the party label, it at least does not weaken it with competing platforms. The party label remains broad but unchallenged. The niche strategy tempers intra-party competition and enhances the predictability of how the vote will divide. And finally, the LDP uses its clearest advantage over other parties—its control of government resources—to shore up its electoral prospects.

Personal Support Organizations

LDP members spend enormous sums of money organizing and maintaining the extensive personal-support networks *(kōenkai)* that form the core of their electoral constituencies. Take a typical LDP politician beginning a career, a young man in his thirties or forties. If fortunate, he has inherited an electoral support base from his father or mentor. Otherwise, he begins by organizing his relatives, friends, and local politicians. He links up with locally prominent figures—mayors, town leaders, local politicians—who are not already committed to another LDP candidate or who are dissatisfied with the other candidate. It is said to take often sizable sums of money to elicit their cooperation or at least their willingness not to cause trouble, though this stage of the process is typically facilitated by an LDP faction leader who is the neophyte's sponsor. The LDP candidate must then enlist the help of local political organizers, including local politicians, businessmen, and leaders in the agricultural cooperatives in establishing branches of his support network throughout the electoral district.

In many respects, the personal-support organizations of competing LDP candidates resemble each other. A typical LDP Dietmember has fifty to eighty constituency organizations, ranging from current-events discussion groups to hobby and sports clubs, women's activity circles, and social groups for the elderly.[13] Operating on subsidies from the Dietmember, these organizations sponsor baseball games, sumō contests, marathons, Japanese chess matches, fishing tournaments, golf competitions, cooking classes, volleyball games, chorus groups, kimono classes, tea ceremony classes, and keyboard lessons. These groups meet periodically to eat and drink, to go on occasional outings to hot springs or on other sight-seeing trips, and to convene for New Year's Eve parties with the Dietmember. In election years, group leaders ask the members to mobilize their friends to vote for their sponsoring Dietmember, but in other years they add little or no political content to the meetings.[14]

LDP Dietmembers are constantly searching for opportunities to woo more voters. One group of young LDP Dietmembers disclosed that they attend twenty-five to thirty funerals a month, about ten weddings a month, and numerous sports events and graduations (Iwai, 1990, p. 125). Former Prime Minister Kakuei Tanaka is said to have read the obituary column in his local newspaper before anything else (Komaki, 1983, p. 32–33). Japanese always bring large gifts of money to funerals and weddings, and so do Dietmembers.[15] They are also expected to provide a large number of constituency services free of charge. They help children of supporters get into private schools or find jobs. They assist supporters in securing loans and business connections, mediate in disputes, and help people get out of minor trouble with the law.[16]

According to one estimate, the average LDP Dietmember spends over 120 million yen a year in his or her district in support of all these activities (Iwai, 1990, p. 127). About a third of this amount goes to personnel and other overhead costs. While the government pays for two staff members for each Dietmember, LDP members pay for additional staff out of money they raise themselves.[17] Young LDP Dietmembers employ an average staff of five to six: two or three in their Diet office and the rest in offices in their districts.[18] More senior LDP members typically have more staff, some as many as forty (Hirose, 1989, p. 28). Direct subsidies of support group activities account for another 15 to 20 percent of LDP members' expenditures, and the money contributed at weddings, funerals, and other events amounts to about 15 to 20 percent as well. The rest of their spending covers their transportation around the district and other miscellaneous costs. These figures do not even include the money LDP members pass along to local politicians in exchange for their electoral support, or funds raised for the faction to boost their stakes within factional ranks.

In addition to the small favors the politicians render out of party, factional, or individual funds, LDP members use government re-sources to woo particular groups of voters. They use their influence over specific areas of regulatory, budget, and tax policy to differ-entiate themselves from other LDP candidates whose influence is in other areas. In a district where one LDP candidate has influence over small business policy and has close ties to small retailers, for example, other candidates will focus on agriculture, transportation, telecommunications, or construction. This niche-market strategy is a natural by-product of the competition among LDP candidates for reelection.

Building personal loyalty is the key to the LDP electoral strategy. The personal bonds that develop between support group members and their Dietmember aid the LDP in apportioning the vote effi-ciently among competing LDP candidates. Given the importance of constituency-specific investments that LDP members make in building up their support bases, it is no wonder that over 40 per-cent of LDP Dietmembers are "second generation" (see Table 2.1). Inheriting a well-developed set of support organizations from a father, father-in-law, or mentor gives these members a huge advan-tage over their competitors beginning from scratch. In turn, the prospect of being able to bequeath the organization gives an incen-tive to the politician to make the optimal investment in the orga-

Table 2.1 Second-generation Dietmembers (percentages in parentheses)

Year	LDP	JSP	Kōmeitō	DSP	JCP	Other	Independent	Total second generation
1980	118	10	6	1	0	0	5	140
% party	(39.9)	(9.3)	(18.2)	(3.1)	(0.0)	(0.0)	(45.5)	(27.4)
1986	132	8	2	4	0	1	1	148
% party	(43.1)	(9.4)	(3.6)	(15.4)	(0.0)	(25.0)	(11.1)	(28.9)
1990	122	12	3	2	0	1	5	145
% party	(44.4)	(8.8)	(6.7)	(14.3)	(0.0)	(20.0)	(23.8)	(28.3)

Sources: Ichikawa (1990, p. 14); *Asahi senkyo taikan* (1986, p. 18).

Note: "Percent party" refers to the percentage of Lower House members who were that party's second generation; under "Total," the percentage is of second-generation members in relation to all Dietmembers. LDP figures for all years include New Liberal Club members (they rejoined the LDP in 1986).

nization, and also mitigates some of the endgame commitment problems that might otherwise plague him or her late in life.

The personal-vote electoral strategy is obviously expensive (Table 2.2). Just the amount of money LDP candidates collect from campaign contributors in election years, apart from the government resources they take credit for distributing, is mind-boggling. Campaign contributors reported gifts of ¥170 billion (nearly $1.3 billion at ¥125 to the dollar) in 1986, a year in which both the Upper and Lower House held elections.[19] But the numerous loopholes through the reporting requirements are well known, and actual campaign contributions are widely thought to be four or five times the reported figures (Sasago, 1989, p. 39). For example, corporations purchase tickets to political fundraisers, which they are permitted to count in their books as "business expenses" (Fujita, 1980, p. 117). Political commentators estimated that Japan's five major political parties together spent about $5 billion on the election of February 1990, over half of which was spent by the LDP alone (*Economist*, Feb. 24, 1990).

Where does the LDP get this money and how is the party able to raise so much of it? Corporate contributors are willing to bankroll the LDP because of what they get in return: policies that favor them

Table 2.2 Reported political party revenues (in billions of yen)

Year	JCP	LDP	Kōmeitō	JSP	DSP	NLC
1979	16.9	14.3	7.6	4.4	1.7	0.5
1980	19.5	18.7	8.4	5.1	2.5	0.7
1981	20.0	12.3	8.9	4.9	1.3	0.5
1982	21.7	12.7	8.9	5.0	1.6	0.4
1983	22.9	21.9	10.1	6.5	3.5	0.6
1984	21.7	13.2	9.3	6.3	1.7	0.4
1985	21.7	19.0	9.8	6.6	1.8	0.4
1986	23.7	20.6	12.8	8.5	3.6	0.5
1987	26.2	15.0	17.2	6.8	1.7	—
1988	26.3	22.3	10.6	4.7	2.0	—
1989	29.9	24.6	14.9	5.6	4.2	—

Source: Asahi shimbun, various years. The Ministry of Internal Affairs releases reported party revenues and expenditures once a year, usually in September.

Note: The Japan Communist Party (JCP) owes its sizable revenues to its profitable publication, *Akahata* (The Red Flag). While the LDP's reported revenues are lower, particularly in nonelection years, far larger sums go unreported. No figures appear for the New Liberal Club (NLC) after 1986 because the splinter party merged back into the LDP in that year.

at the expense of the median voter. Producers pay the LDP for favorable budgetary, tax, and regulatory treatment. Voters continue to vote for LDP candidates, despite getting short shrift in many policies, because LDP candidates win their loyalty through small favors paid for by these corporate contributions. At least in Lower House elections, loyalty in exchange for personal favors makes many voters less inclined to vote for members of other parties even if they are not entirely satisfied with the broader policies the LDP espouses.

This huge cycle of money has curious features. Because corporations are unable to maintain a contributors' cartel, their bidding for favors from the LDP should reduce their net return on contributions to the party to near zero. And because LDP candidates compete against each other for electoral support through expensive services, many voters end up getting much of the money back that they unwittingly contributed through higher taxes or policy-induced higher prices. Were LDP candidates forced to compete on the basis of issues instead, the competition for votes would probably drive policies closer to consumers' and taxpayers' interests. While there would be fewer contributions from producers and less money to pass along to voters in the form of constituency services, voters would be giving up less money to producers at the outset.

In short, Japan's electoral system drives a redistribution of income from the general public to LDP voters, but with a couple of glitches. First, the system generates the welfare losses inherent in all in-kind redistributive schemes. LDP voters are not given a choice between, say, cheaper rice from agricultural liberalization and free *sake* at neighborhood festivals. Second, the amount coming back to the districts is short various efficiency losses: the dead-weight losses from the regulatory schemes the businesses demand, the chunks corporations take out to pay for their political lobbying expenses at geisha houses and golf courses, and the amounts politicians need as overhead to oil their electoral machines. The biggest gainers appear to be the LDP Dietmembers who greatly enhance their chances of political survival.

LDP Policymaking

As happens in other parliamentary systems, the Japanese legislature delegates a considerable amount of policymaking authority to the cabinet and the bureaucracy under the cabinet. Unlike presidential systems, where the executive branch is frequently under the control of a different political party than is the legislature, parliamentary systems have the cabinet at the mercy of the legislature. A no-confidence measure passed by a simple majority of the legislature forces the cabinet to resign and call for new elections. More important, the cabinet is formed by the legislative leadership, making such no-confidence measures rarely necessary. The legislature can therefore safely entrust the cabinet and its ministries with most of the policymaking burden, such as drafting legislation and implementing vaguely worded laws through more concrete ministerial ordinances.

Diet Deliberations

This depiction of how the Japanese democracy works is accurate in its broad strokes. The Diet does have a full complement of standing committees, thanks to the U.S. position (under the Occupation) that legislative activism was the best insurance against oligarchy. The Diet Act provides for eighteen standing committees in the Lower House and sixteen in the Upper House. Fourteen of the Lower House committees and twelve of the Upper House ones parallel ministries and agencies under the cabinet (only the Lower House has committees overseeing the Environment Agency and the Agency for Science and Technology). The other four standing committees are the Budget, Audit, House Management, and Discipline committees.[20] Nonetheless, in any given year 75 to 95 percent of all legislation passed originates in the bureaucracy (see Table 7.2); party discipline is virtually perfect; and substantive changes made in committee or on the legislative floor are minimal.

In what justifiably has become one of the most widely admired studies of the Japanese Diet, Mike Mochizuki (1982) argues that Diet deliberation is "viscous." By this Mochizuki means that the LDP must make a variety of concessions to the opposition members in order to get its preferred legislation passed. To support this counterintuitive claim, he cites two reasons. First, the law allots only a short time for deliberation. Hence, argues Mochizuki, opposition parties can use delaying tactics to extract policy concessions.[21] Second, the LDP is hamstrung by a "unanimity norm" that governs Japanese society in general and the legislature in particular.

Interesting as they are, these considerations may explain less than Mochizuki claims. First, the length of Diet sessions, hours of Diet deliberations, and filibuster rules are governed by legislation rather than the Constitution; the LDP could rid itself of the delay problem without much difficulty. In fact, a short debating time would seem to make sense for the LDP, since it can iron out all intra-party problems *before* it takes a bill to the floor. Second, the LDP violates the "unanimity norm" frequently, particularly when it has a large majority. Even with a thin majority the LDP maneuvers around opposition parties' objections fairly easily, and Mochizuki himself admits that concessions to the opposition are typically minimal.

Mochizuki is right that minority parties have some influence over policymaking, but for reasons different from those he stressed. Minority party opposition to the sales tax proposal, for example, delayed the passage of the general account budget in the Diet for fiscal years 1988, 1989, and 1990. The support the opposition generates for its proposals sometimes forces the LDP to modify its programs or at least delay their implementation. Although the LDP's personal-vote electoral strategy reduces the salience of issues at election time, it does not obliterate it. LDP voters have been known to swing their votes to opposition parties when they became angered (Kobayashi, 1991). The LDP therefore gauges the level of public sympathy the opposition parties receive for their programs and sometimes alters its policies accordingly. In making its electoral calculation the LDP may find it cheaper to change its policy program, even if that displeases some supporters, than to outrage a large portion of the voting public.

So far, our characterization of the Japanese legislative process makes it resemble that of Britain, the classic parliamentary system. In both countries, because the majority party controls the executive and maintains strict party discipline, the legislature is not an important deliberating body. The majority party prefers to delegate extensively to the bureaucratic specialists, secure in the knowledge of its ultimate ability to bring down the cabinet if electorally necessary.

However, policymaking in Japan is in fact profoundly different from that in Britain. We attribute the difference primarily to the electoral rules that underpin the two systems. In Britain, candidates compete in single-member districts largely on the basis of party platforms. By contrast, LDP candidates must compete against each other and find the party platform considerably less useful. To facilitate the necessary vote division among these candidates, the LDP allows its members to use the policymaking process to secure private benefits for their constituents to a greater degree than is customary in Britain. This is not to say that the LDP abandons all central control over policymaking; even under SNTV rules the LDP must provide voters with some public goods, and therefore must impose some constraints on the scramble for private resources. But to divide the vote efficiently, the LDP has no choice but to allow more "cheating at the margins" by individual LDP members than is the case for British parties.[22]

The LDP's Policymaking Apparatus

The locus of "permissible cheating" in Japan is within the LDP policymaking apparatus, its Policy Affairs Research Council (*Seimu chōsakai*, hereafter PARC).[23] Through their participation in the PARC's policymaking deliberations, LDP backbenchers press for policies and budget allocations that benefit their constituents. Although the LDP leadership keeps a ceiling on the total amount spent and balances policy benefits against the costs for the party as a whole, it allows individual Dietmembers substantial leeway in using policy as a device for winning electoral support. The party leaders, after all, cannot retain their own leadership positions without the election of a majority of backbenchers.

According to Article 43 of the LDP Constitution, all policy measures adopted by the party and submitted to the legislature must first acquire approval from the PARC.[24] The PARC has, roughly paralleling the cabinet ministries and Diet committees, seventeen divisions *(bukai)*. In addition to the divisions, the PARC comprises scores of other special research committees *(chōsakai)* and Dietmembers' leagues *(giin renmei)* that formed over the years around particular issues or that concern areas in which divisions have overlapping jurisdiction.

LDP members may belong to no more than four divisions, two of which must parallel the two Diet committee assignments made by party leadership. LDP members also may join up to sixteen other special committees and leagues, for a total of twenty memberships.

LDP Dietmembers tend to specialize in one or two areas of expertise during the early part of their careers, joining committees and leagues that relate in some way to the jurisdiction of their division. Members of the Commerce and Industry Division, for example, often also join the Small- and Medium-Sized Enterprise Research Committee, the Petroleum Affairs Research Committee, or the Raw Materials and Energy Research Committee. Similarly, many members of the Agriculture and Forestry Division join the Comprehensive Agricultural Policy Research Committee, the Dietmembers' Council on the Promotion of Agricultural Villages, and the League on the Improvement of Agriculture (Sasago, Abe, and Muraoka, 1990, p. 16–17).

Although the bureaucracy has primary responsibility for drafting legislation, bills must clear the relevant PARC committee before the cabinet adopts the bills for submission to the Diet. The bureaucracy receives its mandate from the cabinet and is, by design, most responsive to the party leadership. But PARC members use their committee positions to induce the bureaucracy to modify policy to promote their individual electoral needs.[25]

While division and committee membership is self-selective in principle, party leadership retains effective control. As noted, two of the division assignments follow automatically from the selection by the leadership to the Diet committees. Furthermore, promotion to leadership positions within the divisions and committees, which is critical for building policymaking influence, is controlled by LDP leaders. These checks give the party the ability to limit the otherwise inevitable tendency toward profligacy.

The party leadership seems to allow LDP members to exercise some choice in the selection of their division membership, however. The most popular committees, and hence the largest, are in areas associated with the greatest amount of budgetary and regulatory largesse available for distribution to constituents (Table 2.3). Agriculture and Forestry, Construction, and Commerce and Industry have been the top three committees for over a decade. Not surprisingly, the least popular committees, Science and Technology, Environment, and Justice, are concerned more with public goods. A disproportionate number of members in these committees are senior party members and members of the Upper House, both groups

Table 2.3 PARC division membership and pork-barrel legislating

PARC division	Members	Budget share (%)	Ministerial orders	Ministerial licenses
Agriculture	209	7.2	1,859.0	1,446
Construction	132	10.6	2,330.0	620
Commerce	114	1.9	653.0	2,080
Health and Welfare	80	30.6	261.3	874
Transportation	68	2.3	694.3	2,203
Posts and Telecommunications	64	0.1	897.7	147
Finance	61	5.5	350.0	971
Education	61	13.1	158.0	246
Defense	43	1.5	281.3	NA
Internal Affairs	42	38.1	197.3	84
Labor	42	1.4	94.7	530
Cabinet	38	NA	130.3	NA
Foreign Affairs	37	1.3	269.7	46
Justice	33	0.7	954.7	151
Environment	30	0.8	84.0	115
Science and Technology	29	0.7	25.7	155

Sources: Satō and Matsuzaki (1986, p. 259); Ōkura shō, *Kuni no yosan* (1990); Ōkura shō, *Hōrei zensho* (1987–89); Aiba, Iyasu, and Takashima (1987, p. 98).

Note: NA = Not applicable. Number of members data were taken from the 1985 PARC division membership rosters. "Budget share" refers to a ministry's net percentage share of the 1989 general account budget, minus interest payments on the government debt. "Ministerial orders" measures the mean number of orders issued within the ministry's area of jurisdiction in 1987–1989. "Ministerial licenses" measures the number of licenses issued by the ministry or agency in 1981. For simplicity, we have combined the memberships of the Agriculture Division (149 members) and the Fisheries Division (60).

of which have a less pressing electoral need for access to private goods (Fukui, 1987).

A second criterion for LDP members choosing their divisions and committees, next to the opportunity for private-goods distribution, is the avoidance of intra-party competition from their district. That is, LDP members from the same district typically distribute themselves across different division and committee affiliations so as to prevent needless competition for the same constituents. Every Diet-member from an agricultural district might want to be on the Agricultural Division, for example, but Dietmembers also seek access to a unique set of policy favors that their LDP competitors do not have. A by-product of this niche-market strategy has been the incorporation of an extremely wide array of interest groups into the LDP's fold (Muramatsu, Ito, and Tsujinaka, 1986; Yuasa, 1986).

The Personal Vote and Inter-Party Competition

The LDP's use of particularism to divide votes profoundly affects inter-party competition. The LDP's effective monopoly of government resources and the use of those resources to woo voters give it an enormous competitive advantage over other parties. Of course, hypothetically, a challenging party could try to convince voters that *it* would do a better job distributing the spoils than the LDP. But voters must first be convinced that the challenging party has a chance of winning a majority. For voters, the worst of all worlds is a minority representative who is incapable of influencing policies. Without a reliable way of apportioning votes evenly, an opposition party finds it hard to assure voters that their support is not in vain.

In the United States both the Republican and Democratic parties have reasonably good chances of controlling one or even both houses of Congress. It makes sense under these circumstances for legislators of either party to await their opportunity to gain a disproportionate share of the legislative output, once their party controls a majority. In years when they find themselves in the minority party, their party loyalty can be viewed as an insurance premium to ensure their share during the majority years. Members of the minority party also, of course, continue to enjoy use of their party label, which advertises to their constituents what types of services they *would* provide were they to regain a majority.

One might ask why Japanese opposition legislators, with so little hope of gaining a legislative majority, maintain their party affiliation. A cursory look at the prelegislative careers of opposition politicians is instructive. Politicians who have spent much of their lives working as labor unionists, as have many Socialists, for example, would be of little value to the LDP. Incorporating labor into the LDP coalition would be too costly to other LDP supporters. Quite apart from any ideological proclivities, then, such politicians would be unlikely to get LDP endorsement even if they sought it. They are better off gaining control of the smaller stream of benefits from minority status if they can use their opposition label to get elected with some certainty.[26]

The LDP would relinquish the advantage of being the only credible majority party if it were to abandon the current electoral rules in favor of a single-member district system. A single-member district system, as Maurice Duverger (1963) noted, tends to force all but two parties out of existence. This is because voters, not wanting to waste their votes for a party that has no chance of winning a plurality even if that party more closely matches their preferences, will vote strategically for the closest party with a chance. Politicians, knowing this, will affiliate with parties large enough to survive.[27] In Japan, the opposition parties would probably either merge or face extinction, leaving a single large party to contend with the LDP. Under those circumstances, the LDP undoubtedly still would use government resources to protect its majority. But it is also more likely that the opposition could forge an alternative majority coalition around a different—even if only slightly different—division of the spoils, because then its claims of being able to gain a parliamentary majority would be more credible.

A comparison of the LDP's performance in the Lower House and the Upper House gives us something close to a controlled experiment for electoral rules, since we can hold election timing and demographics more or less constant.[28] The 252 members of the Upper House have fixed terms of six years and are elected by a significantly different set of rules from those applying to Lower House members. One hundred Upper House representatives are elected by proportional representation on party lists in a single, nationwide district; fifty of them are up for reelection every three years. The remaining 152 are elected from prefectural districts, ranging in magnitude from two to eight candidates each. Here, too, the terms are staggered so half of the Upper House members face reelection every three years and only one to four candidates compete in each district in any given election.

The complexity of the Upper House electoral rules makes it difficult to draw clear conclusions from the entire election picture, but it is possible to examine how the parties perform in various parts of the election. In the party list portion of the Upper House ballot, in which party labels and nationwide issues are important in voters' choices, the LDP has scored consistently 10 and 11 percent lower than in the Lower House.[29] In the effectively single-member prefectural districts, the LDP has performed extremely well in all but

the 1989 election, when for the first time the opposition parties
managed to unite behind a single candidate in a number of districts.
So long as the rest of the electoral system gives other parties a
reason to survive, it will continue to be hard for the opposition
parties to cooperate among themselves in Upper House races, and
the 1989 election will be viewed as an aberration. The rest of the
prefectural district contests more closely resemble Lower House
races because of the LDP's need to divide the vote, though the
large size of the prefectural districts makes a highly particularistic
electoral strategy more difficult.

Conclusion

Political institutions matter in Japan. In particular, electoral rules
have broader consequences than most analyses of Japanese politics
to date have suggested. In order to divide the vote among several
of its own candidates in most districts, the LDP uses particularistic
favors lavishly. Relying on the personal loyalty that comes of these
favors, it buys itself room to implement business-oriented policies
at some distance away from the median voter's preference point.

Although the current Lower House electoral rules create large
advantages to the LDP, the resulting particularistic electoral strategy
is not without problems. Cultivating personalized Dietmember followings is an expensive strategy for party survival. It requires a
large amount of campaign funding, the allocation of government
budgetary resources, and the distribution of regulatory favors. Because these force the LDP to dedicate public resources to private
use, they necessarily reduce the party's ability to provide public
goods to voters at large.

The personal-vote strategy holds other dangers as well. Because
each candidate makes large, constituent-specific investments of
money and effort in building personal support networks, each candidate's support base is slow to adapt to broader demographic shifts
occurring across the country. As Japan's population urbanized over
the postwar decades, many of these support groups failed to include
the new groups of voters as rapidly as the older ones passed
from the scene. For various reasons, as we shall see, the LDP's
traditional array of pork-barrel favors was less successful in wooing
young, educated, white-collar workers than it had been in winning
the loyalty of farmers and small business proprietors.

The LDP is fortunate to have an internal organization that permits the party to make choices in the party members' collective best interests. Over time, the LDP has changed its mix of private favors and public goods to match better the shifting preferences of the Japanese electorate. Of course, the LDP has not been completely successful, as witnessed by the loss of its Upper House majority in July 1989. The LDP's pace of change is indeed impeded by its need to divide votes among competing candidates, and hence to provide private favors to several groups of constituents in each district. But it was the party members who have delegated to a group of leaders the task of imposing the chosen policy mix of public and private goods on party backbenchers.

3

Demographics and Policy

"Japan has chafed under the monopoly grip of the LDP long enough. Without a change in administrations, Japan cannot respond innovatively or appropriately to changing circumstances." This was one of the campaign slogans of the then-Socialist Party leader, Takako Doi, for the February 1990 election. Although the Socialist Party did relatively well in the 1990 election, winning 18 percent of the vote and 141 seats in the Diet, the LDP did far better, securing a solid majority of 308 seats. Over three and a half decades of a Diet majority have not dulled the party's competitiveness. We will examine how the LDP adapted its electoral strategy, its policymaking process, and its policies to its constituents' changing preferences.

Although a personal-vote strategy has given the LDP some latitude with which to favor the interests of organized blocs of voters and financial contributors, the party has been unable to compete with particularistic favors alone. Japan's steady urbanization has forced it to reach beyond the individual candidates' personal support networks to the unattached voter. Competing with a party platform or general public policies is awkward for the LDP because, as we have suggested, this form of electoral competition leaves the LDP with the thorny problem of how to divide the vote among its candidates. Rather than abandon the personal-vote strategy altogether, the LDP has adapted it to different demographics, both by targeting different voters with particularistic favors and by expanding the distribution of public goods.

Shifts in Japan's population contribute to changes in inter-party competition. In our view, the recent prominence of politicians in policymaking in Japan represents a response to changing demographics rather than a shift in the balance of authority between politicians and bureaucrats. We will outline the policy changes the LDP has undertaken and the electoral pressures that prompted them. A few concrete examples of policymaking—budget, tax, and regulation—will serve to illustrate how the party balances the competing needs for public and private goods. We conclude by noting the pressures on Japan, from within as well as from abroad, to reduce the LDP's electoral dependence on particularism.

Urbanization and the Political Landscape

Japan's rapid economic growth after World War II enticed record numbers of people to cities. In 1960, 80 percent of all electoral districts were basically rural. By 1975, according to government census data, only 35 percent of electoral districts were still categorized as rural (Kobayashi, 1990, pp. 13–14).

As Japanese voters increasingly moved to urban districts, party survival dictated a shift, albeit subtle, in electoral strategy. For several reasons, many urban voters are more difficult to catch in the net of traditional LDP personal support organizations.[1] For example, because of such factors as high land prices, urban voters are less likely to own their own homes; hence they move more frequently. As a result, winning personal votes is more continuous and therefore more costly for politicians.

The urban areas were the first to show the negative consequences of Japan's pro-producer policies. Air and noise pollution, congestion, and inadequate urban infrastructure were the public bad side of the private goods doled out to producer groups. Moreover, many urban dwellers are white-collar workers at large firms. Unlike farmers or small firm owners who are residual claimants on their output, office workers' income is less strictly tied to the income of the firm. White-collar employees typically have more diffuse interests—many of which are tied up in their role as consumers—than do farmers and proprietors, who are dominated by their interests as producers (Bates, 1985, p. 129).

It was a mark of the ingenuity of the LDP leadership that the party successfully adapted to these major demographic shifts and did not lose control over the Lower House of the Diet. Although it did lose ground to opposition parties, primarily in local elections, by the mid-1980s it had once again begun to win even those races.

The Socialist Stagnation

As Figure 3.1 shows, the LDP lost a share of the vote for much of the 1960s and 1970s, but not to its largest rival, the Japan Socialist Party (JSP).[2] Why the Socialists were unable to capitalize on urbanization remains something of a puzzle in the literature. Most scholars attribute the party's declining vote share to the party's ideological rigidity and the failure of its leadership to adapt to voters' changing preferences. But this still begs the question of why the Socialists did not, through trial and error, replace a party program that did not win votes with one that did.

Our answer begins with the Socialist's bad luck in 1955. The LDP, not the JSP, was the first party to form a stable Diet majority and hence to control government resources. Once cut out of access to these resources, the Socialists were left without the means to divide the vote in each district as effectively as the LDP. Socialist candidates were only able to make promises about the distribution of private goods and to pledge an array of public goods, if elected. But without

Table 3.1 The changing composition of LDP support (in percent)

	1955	1962	1965	1975	1980
Salaried workers	14 (36)	18 (42)	16 (41)	19 (34)	21 (43)
Managers	a	a	4 (56)	7 (48)	8 (54)
Laborers in manufacturing	16 (32)	18 (31)	8 (27)	11 (32)	14 (40)
Laborers in retail	b	b	12 (40)	14 (38)	14 (45)
Small business owners	25 (59)	27 (62)	28 (61)	25 (59)	23 (62)
Farmers	43 (52)	34 (53)	29 (64)	19 (62)	15 (70)
Other	3 (37)	3 (46)	3 (51)	5 (49)	5 (49)
Total LDP support	45%	46%	49%	44%	50%

Source: Murayama (1990, p. 58).

Note: Numbers on the left for each year indicate the percentage share of each social group in the LDP's total support base of 100%. The figures in parentheses indicate the percentage within each social group that supported the LDP. "Total LDP support" refers to the percentage of the vote the LDP received in nationwide elections.

a. "Managers" are included with "Salaried Workers" for 1955 and 1962.

b. "Laborers in retail" are included with "Laborers in manufacturing" for 1955 and 1962.

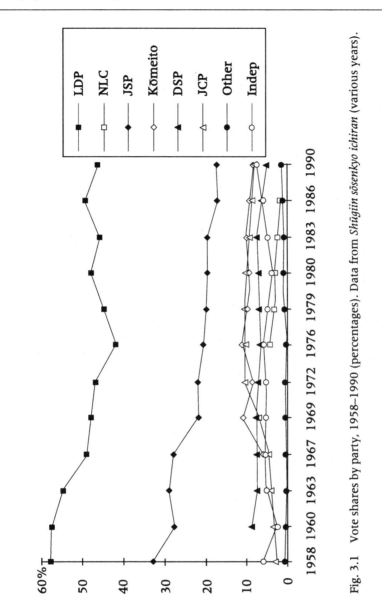

Fig. 3.1   Vote shares by party, 1958–1990 (percentages). Data from *Shūgiin sōsenkyo ichiran* (various years).

the means to build up effective personal support networks for individual candidates, the party's chances of winning a majority in the Diet became slim.

This still does not explain why the Socialists retained an ideological platform on defense and labor issues so far to the left of the median voter. Unlike Germany's Social Democratic Party, which adopted a more centrist platform in 1959, the Japanese Socialists clung to a rigidly Marxist party doctrine that began to appear more and more antiquated (Edinger, 1986, p. 168n). In a 1986 public opinion poll, even respondents who said they voted for the Socialists that year placed themselves, on average, to the right of the JSP (Miyake, 1989).

The simple answer for the dominance of the left wing within the Socialist Party is the importance of unionized labor in its electoral base. As Gerald Curtis (1979) noted, the JSP sometimes "is disparagingly referred to as 'the political section of Sōhyō [the General Council of Japanese Trade Unions].' " But again, why did the Socialists not move beyond their labor base? There seem to be at least three possibilities. One is that the Socialist leadership was simply misinformed and never realized the unpopularity of its ideological bias. But we reject this possible line of argument on grounds that so many people are unlikely to have been self-defeating over such a long period of time.

Another possible explanation is that the Socialists never established cabinet control as their first priority and were satisfied instead to champion Marxism from the sidelines. While more plausible than simple ineptitude, this reasoning also has its difficulties. We would need to know why any politician, whose basis for having a voice in government is premised on first winning a legislative seat, would willingly relinquish his or her election chances for the sake of "ideological purity."

A third possibility, and the one we find most compelling, is that a niche strategy of relying on the organizational backing of unionized labor was the logical option for Socialist politicians in Japan's particular electoral system. In a single, nontransferable vote (SNTV), multi-member district system, the equilibrium outcome in spatial terms is for multiple parties to array themselves across the ideological spectrum (Cox, 1991). A number of parties appealing to particular sectors of the electorate should be able to stake out stable, if minority, shares of the voting public. This seems to have been General Aritomo Yamagata's logic in choosing the SNTV system in the first place in 1900. The anomaly in Japan's case is not the Socialists for failing to become an alternating majority party, but the LDP for defying the centrifugal logic of an SNTV rule in a multi-member district system. The explanation for the anomaly, we have argued, is the LDP's "first-mover" advantage in controlling government resources with which to build up personal support networks.

The Socialist Party thrived in the early postwar years when organized labor had its heyday. But as Figure 3.2 shows, the JSP lost electoral support in tandem with the decline in the membership in the party's main support base, public-sector unions. The LDP has pursued a deliberate strategy of privatizing public corporations, including the Japan National Railways and the NTT telecommunications empire, to undermine the Socialists' bases of support.

The JSP did not find it easy to muster other groups of supporters to make up for the loss of public-sector union members. The challenge was to incorporate groups whose interests do not directly clash with those of its remaining core of labor support. The Socialist Party was slow in championing the citizens' movements that sprang up in reaction to serious pollution during the 1960s and 1970s, for example. The party's first concern was for the plight of the labor unions and the likely job and salary cuts in the event that corporations were forced to pay for expensive antipollution devices (Krauss and Simcock, 1980, p. 220). In the rice price issue in the 1980s and 1990s, the Socialists have taken the side of the farmers over the interest of consumers in lower food prices (Honzawa, 1989, pp. 68–77; *Mainichi shimbunsha*, 1991, pp. 89–90).

The Democratic Socialist Party and the Kōmeitō

The first parties to capture some of the urban vote were smaller parties that emerged in the 1960s. Aiming at voters to the left of the LDP but not as far left as either the Socialists or the Communists, the Democratic Socialist Party (DSP) split off from the Socialist Party in 1960 (Masumi, 1985, pp. 511–515). The party has relied primarily on support from the nation's largest federation of private-sector unions as well as part of the small business sector. But the

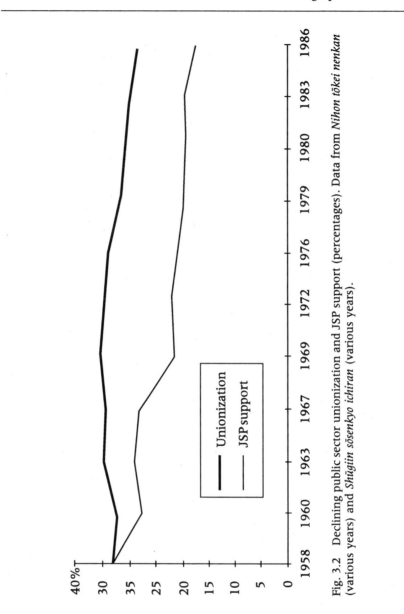

Fig. 3.2 Declining public sector unionization and JSP support (percentages). Data from *Nihon tōkei nenkan* (various years) and *Shūgiin sōsenkyo ichiran* (various years).

DSP's 8.77 percent of the popular vote in the November 1960 election was its highest share ever. Since then, its vote share has hovered in the 6 to 7 percent range and dipped as low as 4.84 percent in the 1990 election, when some voters apparently shifted to the Socialists in hopes of voting the LDP out of office for the first time (*Mainichi shimbunsha*, 1991, pp. 13–14).

A second "middle-of-the-road" party is the Kōmeitō, the political arm of the Sōkagakkai Buddhist organization.[3] Because its roots in this fundamentalist religious group give the Kōmeitō a ready-made organizational base for mobilizing the vote among its supporters, the party typically does well in election years with generally low turnout (Uchida, 1980, pp. 57–64). But the religious connection also limits the party's appeal to non-Sōkagakkai members. Since its formation in 1965, the Kōmeitō's share of the vote has ranged between 8.5 and 10 percent. In 1990 it dropped below 8 percent for the same reason the DSP lost votes to the Socialists.

An LDP Break-off: The New Liberal Club

In June 1976, a group of six exasperated LDP Dietmembers, primarily from urban districts, broke off from the LDP, cutting across factional lines to form their own party, the New Liberal Club (NLC). The LDP, they argued, had lost touch with the electorate's preferences and would lose its Diet majority if it continued on its course. The implication of former Prime Minister Kakuei Tanaka in the Lockheed bribery scandal seemed an opportune time to cast off from the LDP. Better to form a new party with a more popular platform than to be tied to a lost cause (Masumi, 1985, p. 655; Nishioka and Tanaka, 1979, p. 61).

At first, the gamble seemed to pay off. In the December 1976 election the party membership swelled to seventeen, twelve of the seventeen coming in first in their districts. The "reformist" NLC was the media's darling. By the summer of 1977, a Kyōdo News Agency public opinion poll named the New Liberal Club the third most popular party in Japan (Hrebenar, 1986, pp. 213–14).

Although the New Liberal Club had a solid base in several cities, the party was unable to build a nationwide following. It soon became clear to voters that the NLC would remain a "mini-party," unable to deliver on its promises of reform because it would never have a chance to control the cabinet. In the 1979 election, only four NLC members were returned to their seats, presaging the beginning of the end of a brief experiment. In 1986, all but one of the former NLC members rejoined the LDP, recognizing that their best chance for retaining their seats was still with the dominant party.

Opposition Success in Local Politics

Only at the level of local politics did the opposition parties have much success. For a few years, these parties made rapid inroads into the LDP's support base in mayoral and gubernatorial elections. Organizing themselves into coalitions, the opposition parties supported "progressive" candidates who emphasized that the LDP, in its quest for blocs of votes and campaign contributions, had sacrificed redistributive programs such as health care and pensions, and public goods such as environmental policy.[4] Although the LDP managed to retain its Diet majority, its margin had shrunk, and the loss of local government control in many cities and towns weakened the support bases of many urban LDP Diet incumbents. Tables 3.2 and 3.3 illustrate the LDP's tenuous hold on local governments in the mid-1970s. They also, however, show how the LDP began to retake local control—particularly urban control—by the next decade.

The Alleged Rise of LDP Policymaking

Japan's urbanization did not end LDP dominance, but it changed the way the LDP went about making policy. Much has been made in the popular press, and even in some academic writing, of the seemingly new influence of politicians over Japanese policymaking since the early 1970s.[5] Some observers credit Kakuei Tanaka with being the first LDP politician clever enough to outwit the bureaucrats who had long managed to fight off political meddling (for example, Johnson, 1986). It is implied in this analysis that PARC members seldom interfered in the bureaucrats' policymaking in the first two decades of LDP rule, largely because they were unable to do so. These authors speak of numerous handicaps LDP members faced in competing with bureaucrats for policymaking control, such

Table 3.2 Prefectural legislature seats by party, 1963–1987.

	LDP	JSP	DSP	Kōmeitō	JCP	Other
1963	1,689 (67.9)	491 (19.8)	79 (3.2)	41 (1.6)	21 (0.8)	165 (6.7)
1967	1,645 (60.3)	594 (21.8)	103 (3.8)	107 (3.9)	46 (1.7)	231 (8.5)
1971	1,656 (60.6)	504 (18.5)	95 (3.5)	120 (4.4)	123 (4.5)	233 (8.5)
1975	1,396 (53.4)	422 (16.1)	103 (3.9)	167 (6.4)	95 (3.6)	431 (16.7)
1979	1,407 (53.1)	379 (14.3)	106 (4.0)	166 (6.8)	122 (4.6)	466 (17.6)
1983	1,488 (55.9)	372 (14.0)	100 (3.8)	182 (6.8)	85 (3.2)	434 (16.3)
1987	1,382 (51.8)	443 (16.6)	104 (3.9)	186 (7.0)	118 (4.4)	437 (16.4)

Source: Chihō jichi nenkan (Local Government Annual) (Tokyo: Jichi kenshū kyōkai, various years).
Notes: Percentages in parentheses. The "Other" category comprises independent candidates, many of whom were loosely affiliated with one or more of the large parties. The Chihō jichi nenkan breaks the independents into "conservatives" and "progressives" in 1968 but not in subsequent volumes, presumably because a growing number of candidates began to forge ties with both the LDP and the opposition parties.

Table 3.3   Party success in mayoral elections, 1975–1983 (percentages in parentheses)

Candidate's party endorsement	1975	1979	1983
LDP, with or without coalition partners	31 (14.3)	120 (41.1)	261 (65.7)
(Of the above, LDP endorsement alone)	27 (12.5)	49 (16.8)	37 (19.3)
Other than LDP	185 (85.6)	172 (58.9)	136 (34.3)
Total number of mayoral candidates up for election	216 (100)	292 (100)	397 (100)

Source: Wataru Ōmori and Seizaburō Satō, eds., *Nihon no chihō seifu* (Japan's Local Government) (Tokyo: Tokyo daigaku shuppan kai, 1986), p. 225.

as inferior information, expertise, and prestige. We view events differently. Overt intervention in the policymaking process by LDP backbenchers was indeed less extensive before the mid-1970s. But we attribute this to satisfaction with cabinet-led policy rather than to party ineptitude. LDP incumbents began to lose that satisfaction, however, as their leaders began to respond to political exigencies by courting urban voters through a new mix of programs.

In its effort to win back its lost electoral ground, the LDP began shifting a growing percentage of budgetary resources in the 1970s to the redistributive policies and public goods successfully championed by opposition local governments. In 1970 the Diet was dubbed the Pollution Diet because it established the Environmental Agency and passed nationwide antipollution laws similar to those the Socialist government of Tokyo had enacted locally. In 1973 it passed so much legislation enhancing the national pension system that the year became known as the Inaugural Year of Social Welfare. And in 1975 it underwrote an expensive national health insurance system, again copying the model of Socialist-controlled Tokyo.[6]

While this shift away from more traditional private goods may have been politically necessary, it left in its wake scores of disgruntled LDP backbenchers. Incumbents had already made large, constituency-specific investments in their personal bases of support, and relied on the continual flow of private goods to protect those investments. The LDP leadership now calculated that a more generous outflow of these newer redistributive policies and public goods would stave off the electoral desertion of the party as a whole.

Nonetheless, the provision of traditional private goods remained the most effective means individual members had of dividing the vote and thereby securing their own reelection.

The apparent rise of LDP involvement in policymaking, then, is nothing of the sort. Kakuei Tanaka may have exemplified the greater activism of individual politicians in support of their constituents, but he cannot be credited with introducing genuine political representation to Japan: LDP legislators had been in control all along. In earlier years, they had delegated control over party policy to the party leaders, who in turn had assigned considerable discretion to bureaucrats. But these leaders had worked for the collective good of the party, where as individual legislators maximized their individual reelection chances. When political necessity drove party leaders to adjust the relative proportion of traditional LDP private and public goods and to increase opposition-championed redistributive programs, their actions clashed with those of individual Diet-members worried about their own political skins. Increasingly, these backbenchers asserted themselves in the policymaking process. They used the PARC mechanism to ensure adequate flows of traditional private perquisites to their constituents in a way that previously had been unnecessary because it had been part of cabinet policy. What *appears* as greater LDP control over policy, therefore, is merely greater backbench effort to get around party policy to further their political needs.

In the mid-1970s, the party leaders apparently saw the increased backbench involvement in policymaking as a necessary evil. The scramble for budgetary favors, even as sizable resources were committed to the new redistributive programs and public goods, put strong upward pressure on the government budget. Indeed, the LDP's addition of new expenditures without cutting old ones was an important factor contributing to the large government budget deficits beginning in 1975.

So long as Japan's electoral rules require large parties to field several candidates in many districts, the distribution of private benefits to groups of constituents remains the most effective way for the LDP to divide the vote and hence to retain its Diet majority. To be sure, not all private goods cost money. One urban LDP politician we know claims to get many votes from members of a new sect of Buddhism by attending their services. While his chauffeur negotiates the Tokyo traffic, he memorizes sutras in order to appear sincere and authentic. Yet most private goods do cost money, and the LDP leadership continues to give most backbenchers enough access to government resources to ensure their electoral success. At the same time, it has fought steadily to regain control over government deficits in order to be able to continue to provide electorally important public goods, such as reasonably low taxes.

Public and Private Goods: Budget, Tax, and Regulatory Policy

Our outline of the Japanese policymaking process begins to explain how the LDP uses it to provide voters with a combination of public goods, redistributive policies, and more traditional private favors. The following three examples of LDP policymaking—budget allocation, tax policy, and economic regulation—will disclose more concretely how the LDP manages the public/private balance. In all of these cases the shift toward policies aimed at the median voter is only incremental. A more fundamental reorientation of LDP policies would require a restructuring of the electoral rules that shape the LDP's policy incentives.

Budget Allocation and Fiscal Retrenchment

Kent Calder (1988) and Mathew McCubbins and Gregory Noble (1991) elegantly show that the LDP uses the government budget for electoral purposes. In exchange for votes and campaign contributions, the LDP has given subsidies to farmers and small businesses, and public works contracts to construction firms. Every PARC committee swings into full gear for the budgeting process, fighting for allocations to one special group or another. Because every LDP Dietmember incurs high fixed costs in maintaining a personal support base, all things being equal, the party leadership allows budgetary allocations to rise with the number of LDP members (McCubbins and Noble, 1991).

At the same time, the LDP fears the electoral consequences of runaway spending. The LDP's constituents—general voters and especially its business contributors—would not take kindly to higher inflation or higher taxes.[7] The annual budgetary process illustrates how the LDP balances immediate demands for pork against its need to limit the government budget deficit.

Every spring, the Ministry of Finance (MOF) Budget Bureau and the MOF's Fiscal System Advisory Council *(Zaisei seido shingikai)* work closely with the LDP leadership in setting broad guidelines for the following fiscal year's budget (April-March). Meanwhile, each ministry and agency compiles its own budget requests for submission to the cabinet Legislation Bureau *(Naikaku hōsei kyoku)* by August 31.

When submitting a copy of its budget requests to the cabinet, each ministry simultaneously provides a copy to its parallel PARC division. Over the successive few weeks, divisions hold biweekly meetings to discuss the ministries' budget proposals, typically from 8:30 in the morning until the Diet committees convene at 10:00 A.M. Divisions call in deputy directors of the ministerial sections to explain the budget, line by line. It is at this stage of deliberations that the PARC divisions have a formal opportunity to make sure their constituents receive adequate pork. But in fact, amendments of the budget proposals by the divisions are rare because the ministries are careful to clear their requests with the divisions in advance.[8]

If this were the full extent of the budgeting process, the LDP would be at the mercy of its greediest members. PARC committees could conceivably load up the budget with large allocations to favored constituents, at great cost to taxpayers. That this does not happen is attributable to a couple of checks built into the institutions of LDP decision making. First, LDP leaders have appointment power over all party and cabinet positions. This gives PARC division chairmen and vice-chairmen a strong incentive to work with the party leadership in reviewing the parts of the budget that their divisions oversee. Indeed, one of the jobs of the division chairman is to soften the demands of the division's junior members before party elders even have to deal with them.

The second institutional feature that tempers the size and particularistic orientation of the budget is that the entire patchwork must clear the Executive Council *(Sōmukai)* of the LDP before it is submitted to the cabinet and, ultimately, to the Diet. The Executive Council is an organ of the party leadership whose job is to weigh competing claims on scarce resources in the party's overall best electoral interests (Hirose and Ishikawa, 1989, p. 221).

Once a budget bill clears the LDP policymaking apparatus, the cabinet adopts the bill and submits it to the Diet for passage. Because the LDP has had a continual Diet majority, the ensuing haggling between the LDP and the opposition parties is largely a rhetorical charade for public consumption. Everyone knows the LDP can force any bill through with its majority, but the opposition parties use their allotted air time to the hilt to express moral outrage and disgust at the LDP's benighted policies. Meanwhile, most of the opposition parties happily accept payoffs from the LDP in exchange for not embarrassing it by boycotting the Diet session in which the LDP passes the bill. There is a famous safe in the Secretary General's office with money for this purpose and—gambling being a lesser sin than bribery—LDP members often pass this money along by deliberately losing to opposition representatives at majong.[9]

We have already noted that the LDP increased the proportion of public goods in the Japanese budget in the mid-1970s. Allocations to less targetable programs such as national health insurance, welfare pensions, and educational programs increased from about a fourth of the combined total of the general account and supplementary budgets in 1970 to about a third by 1975.[10] Meanwhile, spending easily identifiable as pork—allocations for public works (including those paid through transfers to local governments), small business, and agriculture—declined from 41 percent in 1975 to 26 percent in 1987 (*Kuni no yosan*, various years). Subsidized government lending through the Fiscal Investment Loan Program followed a similar pattern.

Along with changing the budget's composition, the LDP reduced the rate of the budget's growth in the early 1980s, in some years to a negative real rate, to get the government deficit under control. The government budget deficit shrank from its peak in 1979, when it accounted for 35.4 percent of the general account budget, to 10.5 percent in 1990. This is more surprising than just a relative decline in private benefits; we would expect LDP backbenchers to fight strenuously against an *absolute* reduction in government resources available for distribution.

Insofar as fiscal responsibility reduced fears of inflation, this too resembled a public good. But the strongest pressure on the LDP to control government spending came from the LDP's business contributors. A large portion of the Japanese corporate sector began expressing concerns about the size of the government deficit in the late 1970s and early 1980s (Kumon, 1984, pp. 143–165). The party's collective welfare required the fiscal restraint. Fight as they did for their individual constituents, the backbenchers were unable to buck the party discipline that the leaders imposed.

Tax Policy and the Sales Tax of 1989

Tax policy, like budget policy, can be used to give special breaks to particular groups of constituents, or it can be distributed "fairly" across society to raise funds for public goods. In keeping with our expectations, the LDP often uses tax policy to reward its supporters. But recently it also seemed to jettison some of its traditional support groups, including the small business sector.

The LDP coordinates tax policy through the LDP Tax Policy Research Committee (*Jimintō zeisei chōsakai,* hereafter LDP Tax Committee) in the PARC. Though it had been in existence since the party's formation in 1955, the committee has openly preempted policymaking leadership only since the 1970s, taking over from the MOF Budget Bureau and the Government Tax Policy Research Committee *(Seifu zeisei chōsakai)* attached to the Budget Bureau. The reason for the greater party tax committee activism in recent decades is the same as that for the increased involvement of backbenchers in general policymaking: the party leadership's shift of priorities (at the margin) to urban salaried voters has forced incumbent LDP Dietmembers to work harder to deliver favors—in this case, tax breaks—to their constituents.

Over half of the LDP's Lower House caucus is on the LDP Tax Committee. Its popularity is matched only by the PARC's Agriculture Division, which speaks of the committee's importance in delivering private favors. Indeed, after a recent breakfast with one of us, a ranking LDP politician explained that he was off to meet with a newspaper employee from his district. "An interview?" "No," he answered, "I'm on the Party Tax Committee and they want a tax break." It is the job of the Tax Committee's executive committee—composed of one chair and 24 vice-chairs, including all eight PARC vice-chairs—to balance the backbench requests for tax breaks against the need for revenues (Yuasa, 1986).

In December of each year, after the budget process has yielded

an estimate of planned expenditures, interest groups approach
members of the LDP Tax Committee for exemptions. The committee
compiles the requests, so numerous in recent years that the list is
referred to as The Telephone Book. Following a plenary meeting
of the Tax Committee to decide on a general target, subcommittees hold hearings on the tax-exemption requests. Private-sector
groups, as well as their allies in various PARC divisions, plead
their cases. The committee works its way through the hundreds
of requests, often accepting the subcommittees' initial yea-or-nay
recommendation.

The upshot of this process is that the LDP permits—sometimes
explicitly, sometimes implicitly—sizable tax exemptions to an array
of electoral supporters. Japanese often remark cynically that their
taxes are assessed according to a 9-6-4 system. Urban salaried workers pay taxes on 90 percent of their income; small business proprietors pay taxes on 60 percent of their income; and farmers pay
taxes on 40 percent. Note the politics of this: farmers and small
business proprietors have been ardent LDP supporters for decades
while the urban salaried workers have been more apt to vote for
opposition candidates. More recently, the LDP leadership has begun
to woo them.

Although the 9-6-4 quip is an exaggeration, there is also some
truth to it. Salaried workers have little opportunity to underreport
because most of their taxes are withheld from their pay at source.
Inevitably, small business owners have more of a chance to shave
receipts and pad expenses. According to 1985 MOF statistics, tax
revenues from small business proprietors increased during the first
years of the decade at a consistently lower rate than revenues from
white-collar workers, despite good business conditions for small
firms (Kishiro, 1985, p. 126). And according to a 1985 LDP report,
only 20.3 percent of farmers and 49.6 percent of nonagricultural
small business owners paid *any* taxes in 1983.[11]

The introduction of the sales tax, effective April 1989, was the
revenue side of the budget retrenchment story (Mizuno, 1989). It
was a move by the LDP to take some of the tax burden from its
corporate contributors and urban voters, even if that meant reducing tax advantages to small businesses. The MOF and the LDP
leadership had discussed since the 1950s the possibility of shifting
Japan's tax base away from its (American-imposed) overwhelming

dependence on income tax to a more broadly based value-added tax (Mabuchi, 1987; Kaneko, 1988, pp. 57–69). But it was not until the government budget reached enormous proportions in the mid- and late 1970s that the corporate sector, fearful of inflation or higher income taxes, pushed for an indirect tax.[12]

The LDP undertook but then abandoned attempts to introduce an indirect tax in 1978 and again in 1986.[13] Finally, after a great deal more pressure from the corporate sector and despite continued backbench grumbling, the LDP forced the sales tax bill through the Diet on December 21, 1988, over the opposition of all other par- ties.[14] The final version of the law bought small firm proprietors some time. Rather than a value-added tax, which could have gener- ated records of costs and sales at each stage of production and distribution, the sales tax was a simple final-goods levy.[15] Initially, small firms did remain relatively free to under-report their profits. But since the passage of the bill, the LDP has begun to tighten the reporting requirements on these firms.[16]

As with budgetary retrenchment, the sales tax answered the behest of the large corporate sector. But both responses also suggest the LDP is edging away, if ever so slightly, from electoral depen- dence on the traditional support bases of agriculture and small business. A third case, of financial regulation, underscores the same point.

Regulation: The Case of Credit Cards

Economic regulation in Japan has, in general, favored producers over small consumers. Although cartels can be unstable even in Japan, the Ministry of International Trade and Industry (MITI) has used various sanctions to help manufacturing firms maintain cartels longer than the firms would have been able to on their own.[17] In the financial sector, the MOF has restricted competition for decades under the guise of "depositor and investor protection." Under pres- sure from the LDP, the MOF did not allow the competition among financial institutions to outpace the capabilities of small, less effi- cient banks and securities firms. Competition from the Euromarket eroded the effectiveness of financial sector coddling, at least in the wholesale market. But deregulation in the retail market has been much slower in coming (Ueno, 1989).

Banks in Japan historically have been prevented from issuing credit cards that give customers the option of rolling over their balance. They were free to issue debit cards, with which customers drew down their own bank accounts with every purchase, or charge cards on which customers paid the full balance every settlement period. But it was the credit card market that banks have been increasingly eager to tap.

The ban on bank credit cards favored small shopkeepers who do not want to pay credit card fees, shopkeepers who profit from their own credit facilities, and small credit card companies *(shin'yō hambai)*. Banks had first expressed an interest in entering the revolving credit card market in the early 1970s. But two nationwide federations of small shops, the Japan Federation of Shopping Alley Stores *(Nippon shōtengai rengōkai)* and the Japan Federation of Specialty Stores *(Nippon senmonten rengōkai)*, together with small credit card companies then lobbied LDP members successfully, particularly members of the Commerce and Industry Division.[18] In 1984, the Diet passed a resolution stating that banks should not be permitted to issue instruments that would hurt small stores or small credit card companies.[19]

By 1989 the LDP had changed its policy, despite strong objections from the small shopkeepers and small credit card companies. As in the case of the sales tax, the LDP judged that the marginal costs of protecting this traditional group of LDP supporters were beginning to overtake the electoral benefits. Several things contributed to this calculation. First, the United States and other trading partners were growing impatient with Japan's regulated retail financial industry, even threatening to retaliate if Japan refused to open its highly segmented markets to greater competition. Second, as banks' profit margins shrank in the more competitive wholesale markets, banks eyed the consumer loan market with greater interest. Third, deregulating consumer finance was a way for the LDP to appeal to urban salaried workers.

In 1989 and 1990 the PARC's Commerce and Industry Division and the Finance Division hammered out an agreement, to be implemented by MOF and MITI.[20] Banks would be given freedom in the credit card business in exchange for which small credit organizations would be able to link up with bank ATMs. The life of consumers would probably be somewhat cheaper and more convenient, but it was no secret that the entry of powerful banks into this market would spell the end for the shopkeepers' credit federations and many of the smaller credit card companies, and would generate a paper trail that would inevitably raise effective tax rates. Once again, the LDP had decided to jettison a long-time constituent in order to adapt more effectively to demographic change.

Conclusion

Our purpose has been to show how organizations—in this case, the LDP—evolve to make the best use of the institutional framework in which they find themselves. So far, the LDP has chosen to adapt rather than to alter that framework substantially. During the LDP's early years, when its majority was large and stable, the party delegated extensive decision-making powers to bureaucrats, who in turn duly rewarded LDP supporters. Later the LDP's traditional bases of electoral support weakened, and the leadership began to direct more resources to urban voters. As the polls began to show, there is little gratitude for government construction projects in cities, where the problems are likely to be congestion, pollution, and high land prices. But LDP backbenchers, through the LDP's PARC divisions, fought for continued use of the budget, tax policy, and regulation to reward the constituents whom they had already spent large sums organizing.

In addition to demographic trends, a second pressure for change on the LDP is the increasing divergence of interests between the LDP's large corporate supporters and the LDP's traditional support base of farmers and small firm proprietors. Corporations have been willing to pay considerable sums in campaign contributions to support the LDP's personal-vote electoral strategy as long as they receive, in return, policies that benefit them. The LDP has accommodated many of the corporate sector's requests, even at some cost to its traditional supporters, because farmers and small firm proprietors are demographically less essential for reelection than they were even two decades ago.

Pressure from the United States and Japan's other trading partners to open Japan's markets tends to reinforce the divide, because large corporations are more dependent on exports than are most small firms. Exporters, eager to avoid a punishing trade war with the United States or any other country, are increasingly impatient with government measures that protect the agricultural and small business sectors from foreign competition. It is the exporters, after all, that would bear the brunt of any trade retaliation aimed at Japan.

In summary, the LDP continues to play a balancing act to maintain a majority coalition among divergent constituency interests. The combination of demographic change and corporate demands has forced the LDP to move, if slowly, away from agricultural and small business interests. But urban voters and corporate contributors do not necessarily make easy bedfellows either. The LDP, as in the past, will continue to look for ways to satisfy voters with small favors so as to reduce the salience of big issues at election time. To the extent this personal-vote strategy works in urban and urbanizing districts, the LDP will have room to favor the corporate sector with policies. The electoral evidence is that the LDP's room for maneuver has shrunk, but has not disappeared.

4

Party Factions

"In Japanese politics, parties divide themselves into factions, even though the inter-factional squabbling interferes with the party's goals. . . . Factions are but one instance of the general Japanese tendency to structure organizations into vertically competitive groups."[1] Or so the popular wisdom goes. Here we suggest an alternative explanation for at least the continuation of LDP factions, based on the electoral needs of LDP members. In our view, David Mayhew's observation about Congress applies equally well to the organization of the LDP: it "meets remarkably well the electoral needs of its members" (1974, p. 81).

Our argument, in brief, is that factions help the LDP with its vote division problem described in Chapter 2. The electoral system alone is sufficient to explain the survival of LDP factions. The distinctive *type* of faction that exists in the LDP—a faction that is a nonideological conduit of particularism—we attribute to the combination of Japan's electoral rules and parliamentary system of government, which places the selection of the chief executive in the hands of the legislative majority.

The LDP's factional organization reflects a typical principal-agent relationship: groups of backbenchers (as principals) delegate certain functions to their particular faction leader (as agent). Party members are not forced to pay allegiance, whether by tyrannical leaders or by dint of some cultural predisposition. Rather, LDP party members join factions out of self-interest. Faction leaders help members win party endorsement, rise through party ranks, and gain access to funding—in short, to improve their reelection chances. To promote their faction leaders' ability to perform these services for them, faction members support their leaders in the prime ministerial races.

An examination of Japanese political history will show how factions have evolved into their current election-enhancing function in the LDP. Factions in Japanese politics date back as far as political parties themselves, to the 1890s and early 1900s. Their form and function shifted in conjunction with changes in Japan's electoral rules. We will examine the evolution of factions within the LDP since the party's formation in 1955 and the proposals for their reform. Even if factions emerged for historical reasons, we argue, they survive because they help the LDP divide the vote under existing electoral rules. We conclude by explaining why factions have grown in size since World War II and assess the role they play in policymaking.

Although factions play an important electoral function, they also create possibilities for destructive fighting within the party. The LDP's tinkering with party rules to limit the fallout from un-tempered prime ministerial races has met with only a modicum of success. But the LDP's adoption of an internal proportional-representation rule for party and cabinet posts has ameliorated the negative effects of inter-factional competition. Furthermore, the most debilitating kind of competition—issue-based competition among factions—remains minimal. Factions, in competing for size, have adopted memberships that are more or less complete cross-sections of the party as a whole.

The History of Factions in Japanese Politics

Party factions in Japan predate the introduction of multi-member electoral districts. Between 1890 and 1900, when Dietmembers were elected from single-member districts, factions emerged within the two largest parties, the Jiyūtō and the Kenseikai.[2] But members of contemporary LDP factions would have difficulty recognizing them as the sort of factions to which they belong. Most Dietmembers from the Yamaguchi area, for example, joined the Seiyūkai party in 1900, when Yamaguchi oligarch Hirobumi Itō became party president. Within the party they then formed a distinctly regional faction—the Yamaguchi faction, composed of Itō and the other politicians from the same area.[3]

In 1900 the electoral system was changed to a single nontransfer-able vote, large (five- to thirteen-member) district system, allegedly because oligarch Aritomo Yamagata wished to prevent parties from becoming too strong. The Meiji Constitution seriously circumscribed the powers of the Diet in any case, but legislative parties were at least capable of making life difficult for the unelected oligarchs—governing in the name of the emperor—in the cabinet, Privy Council, and military. Yamagata's logic was presumably that if parties were forced to compete within themselves in district elections, party leadership would be impaired (Osadake, 1943, pp. 45–49).

If that was in fact Yamagata's reasoning, it was shrewd. Parties struggled to divide the vote without themselves splintering into smaller parties. While the electorate was still a small fraction of the population, parties were somewhat successful in carving up their districts geographically among their candidates (Satō and Matsuzaki, 1986, pp. 56–59). But the parties' efforts at operating a centralized electoral machine were only partially successful, and candidates began to compete among themselves with expensive electoral campaigns. The regional character of factions began to fade because of intra-party competition in each district, and elections became, we are told, extremely expensive.[4] The personal-vote strategy was obviously at work.

Factions began to evolve into organizations that funneled money to members in exchange for support of a faction boss as party leader. But at least until the brief period of party cabinets between 1918 and 1932, party leaders had relatively few resources with which to reward support, and membership in factions was small and erratic.

The largest and most rurally based party, the Seiyūkai, made no secret of preferring a single-member district system. One of the party leaders, Takashi Hara, drafted a proposal for single-member district electoral rules in 1911, when he was Minister of Home Affairs in Prince Kinmochi Saionji's cabinet. But Yamagata and the other oligarchs, eager to avoid the development of strong political parties, squelched the plan (Soma, 1986, pp. 23–25).

When Hara became Prime Minister in 1918, he finally convinced Yamagata that grassroots pressure for universal suffrage would bring with it a rise of Communist representation in the Diet unless new electoral rules squeezed out small parties altogether. Only his revulsion against communism, it seems, exceeded Yamagata's well-known distaste for political parties. Yamagata agreed to the introduction of a "small member district system" in 1919, with 295 single-member districts, 63 two-member districts, and 11 three-member districts (Soma, 1986, pp. 42–44).

From the standpoint of the Seiyūkai, the small districts worked like a charm. In the first election under the new system, the Seiyūkai won a Diet majority with 278 out of 464 seats. The party leadership also enjoyed unprecedented strength and unity within the party since, for backbenchers, receiving party endorsement was now the single most important factor in electoral success.

The experiment with single-member districts was too brief to be a good basis for extensive comparison. Yamagata, and the Privy Council which shared his distrust of political parties, decided that a strong party system fostered by single-member district rules was too risky. Intra-party competition, factional bickering, and a multitude of small parties with which to forge coalitions against the large parties seemed closer to the Privy Council's vision of manageable politics (Mitarai, 1958, pp. 201–202). In May 1925, the Diet passed a bill reestablishing a three- to five-member district system. Given the need, once again, to divide the vote, intra-party factions reasserted themselves (Kiseki, 1965, pp. 50–53; Hayashi, 1975, pp. 120–125).

Since 1925, the only deviation from the multi-member district electoral rules was the 1946 election under the American Occupation. As part of the "democratization" campaign of the early years of the Occupation, American officials in conjunction with the Home Ministry devised a large (four to fourteen seats) electoral district system with plural-entry ballots. In districts with four to ten members, voters were allowed to vote for two candidates. In districts with eleven or more representatives voters had the right to three votes (Fukunaga, 1986, p. 418).

The large-district, plural-vote system was very nearly the worst system imaginable for the large established parties. All things equal, larger parties lose some advantage over small parties as district magnitude increases. The plural vote was an additional problem for the large parties. Many voters selected a candidate from one of the large parties for their first choice, and then chose a member of a small party or an independent—many of them women—for their second and third choices. Of the 464 representatives elected in 1946, 38 were members of small parties while 80 were not affiliated with any party at all.[5] Large parties were saddled with all the vote division problems of multi-member districts, without the benefit of smaller district magnitude or of a single-ballot rule.

The large parties lost no time in pressing for a different set of electoral rules. At least hypothetically, the parties could have chosen a single-member district rule instead. But at the time it was not at all clear which two of the three largest parties would prevail under those conditions. The Liberal Party, which had a plurality but not a majority, convinced the Progressive Party to join forces in urging the occupation to accept a return to the 1925 multi-member district system.

The Liberal and Progressive (soon to be Democratic) parties chose a system which left them with the problem of intra-party factions. But given the multi-party configuration of the early postwar period, alternative electoral systems harbored other problems. One can only speculate what the choice would have been had the two conservative parties already merged by 1946. They may have chosen a single-member district system, though they would still have had to weigh the benefits of small-district magnitude and the absence of factions against the costs of a unified opposition. Under the circumstances, they were delighted when MacArthur relented (Fukunaga, 1986, p. 421).

The Prime Ministerial Race and Attempts to Obliterate Factions

While factions owe their existence to the electoral system, it is in the race for the prime ministership that factional competition is at its rawest and most intense. The contest has brought the LDP to the brink of party rupture at least once, and has led businesses to decry the faction system as evil incarnate. The trail of amendments and revisions in the LDP constitution over the past three and a half decades testifies to the party's frustration with the fallout of factionalism. But so long as the LDP needs factional competition to assist in spreading out the vote during national elections, a messy, factionalized prime ministerial race seems inevitable.

The president of the LDP is elected by a majority of the LDP caucuses of the Lower and Upper Houses, and one representative from each of the forty seven prefectural chapters of the LDP. In their bid for the party presidency, faction leaders try to strike deals with leaders of opposing factions as to which cabinet and party posts they are willing to trade for support. They maneuver behind each other's backs, trying to outbid one another. In the party's early years, this maneuvering often produced minimum winning coalitions in which only the Prime Minister's faction and a few factional allies enjoyed a disproportionate share of the party positions and cabinet seats.

Proportional Representation

Over time, the party moved toward a proportional representation system for all factions regardless of which factions voted for which candidate. The winner-take-all practice generated threats of defection by the "outsider" factions; these threats, though not acted upon, attracted negative public attention. By the mid-1960s all factions were allocated party and cabinet slots in rough proportion to their Diet membership. In this way all factions had a stake in the performance and public image of each cabinet.

While a proportional representation system lowers the stakes for prime ministership, since all factions share in the spoils accruing to the majority party, the Prime Minister retains some discretion over how the *best* posts are apportioned. He is likely to save a number of the most desirable cabinet positions—the Minister of Finance position or Minister of Posts and Telecommunications, for example—for his faction or an allied faction (Leiserson, 1968). And while a Prime Minister's policymaking role is circumscribed by his party organization, he retains some agenda-setting power. The stakes are still high enough, in other words, to whet ambitions.[6]

The popular press has blamed much of the LDP's famed plutocratic tendencies on factions and the factionalized prime ministerial race. The LDP has obliged the press only with rhetoric and a succession of well publicized but wholly ineffectual "public hangings" of the faction system. Soon after the LDP was formed in 1955, the new party president Tanzan Ishibashi and his party secretary Takeo Miki called for an immediate end to factions and the "senseless use of money to fight each other when we should be concentrating on defeating the other parties" (Fukui, 1978; Tanaka, 1986, pp. 66–67). Nothing came of this call, or of any of the other LDP

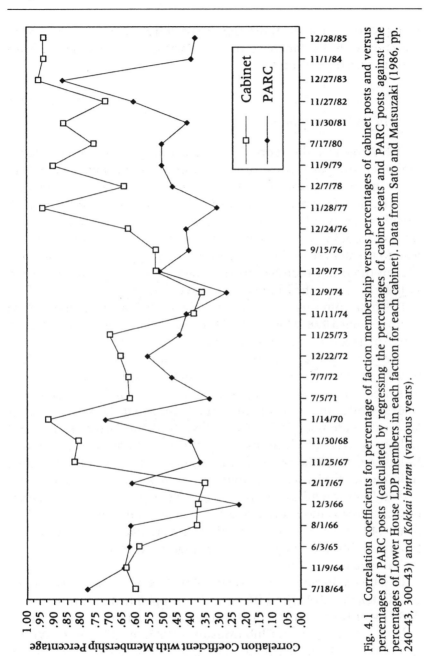

Fig. 4.1 Correlation coefficients for percentage of faction membership versus percentages of cabinet posts and versus percentages of PARC posts (calculated by regressing the percentages of cabinet seats and PARC posts against the percentages of Lower House LDP members in each faction for each cabinet). Data from Satō and Matsuzaki (1986, pp. 240–43, 300–43) and *Kokkai binran* (various years).

pledges to abolish factions that have followed with a regularity matched only by Japanese trains.[7] Factions survived, as did rancorous presidential races.

The 1977 Amendments

In 1977 the LDP did more than rhetorically denounce factions; it amended the party constitution to introduce a primary system to elect the party president. The stated rationale was that placing the decision for party president in the hands of the broader LDP membership would destroy the faction leaders' ability to use factions as stepping stones to the party presidency, and would thereby lead to the demise of these cliques. Nonetheless, given the role they play in the multi-member districts, factions—and the messy prime ministerial races they engender—have continued.

The first primary race under the new party constitution occurred in November 1978. Masayoshi Ōhira and Takeo Fukuda spent huge sums of factional funds rounding up local votes for themselves in the primary (Tanaka, 1986, p. 112; Satō and Matsuzaki, 1986, p. 75). Ōhira won the primary for the party presidency, but the intended impact on factions was entirely missing.[8] The rivalry between Ōhira and Fukuda continued unabated. Less than a year later, in September 1979, Ōhira dissolved the Lower House and called for general elections, over the objections of the Fukuda, Nakasone, and Miki factions. Ōhira's goal was to lead the LDP to a solid electoral victory and thereby to put his administration on a firmer footing within the party. The Keidanren, Japan's premier business association, predicted the LDP would win 278 seats, up from 249. It was not that the other faction leaders had a different prognosis, but that they did not want Ōhira to be able to take credit for an electoral victory.

To Ōhira's dismay, the October 1979 election went unexpectedly poorly for the LDP. The LDP actually dropped to an all-time low of 248 Lower House seats, which constituted a majority only with the help of the New Liberal Club (Masumi, 1985, pp. 308–309). Within the party, Fukuda began to hint that Ōhira should step down, charging the president with violating his pledge to relinquish the position to Fukuda after one year; the political climate turned stormy. In November, when Ōhira convened a session of the party caucus for prime ministerial selection, some young members of the "outsider" factions set up a barricade of tables and chairs outside the meeting hall to forestall his election. Following a brief scuffle in the halls among some backbenchers, the meeting was held, and Ōhira was once again voted the party's candidate for Prime Minister (Masumi, 1986, p. 312).[9]

The Fukuda faction's boldest move was yet to come. In May 1980 the Fukuda faction led a four-faction boycott (Fukuda, Miki, Nakagawa, and part of the Nakasone faction) of a no-confidence motion brought against the Ōhira cabinet by the Socialists.[10] The boycott was crucial, for it gave the Socialists a totally unexpected victory.[11] Ōhira decided to call general elections rather than resign, even though not a year had lapsed since the last elections.[12]

Ōhira and the other party leaders considered imposing sanctions on the errant members, as party rules dictated. While they could have withheld party endorsements from all LDP members who took part in the boycott, they decided instead to leave the endorsement decisions to the local party organizations. The value of maintaining a Diet majority drew the warring factions back from the brink of party dissolution.

In another shocking turn of events, Prime Minister Ōhira died suddenly of heart failure during the arduous campaigning that this unplanned election required. Fortunately for the LDP, his death elicited a large "sympathy vote." The LDP recaptured a comfortable Lower House majority of 284 seats. But the factional maneuver that precipitated the events could just as easily have had negative electoral implications for the LDP. Such are the potential costs of a factionalized party. If it were not for the benefits in facilitating the LDP's vote-division in multiple-candidate districts, it might well be thrown out as a form of organization.

In an attempt to fix up the previous tinkering, the party amended the LDP constitution once again in 1981 to reduce the probability for having to run primaries. Candidates would henceforth need fifty endorsements (up from twenty) by LDP Dietmembers to qualify for the prime ministerial race. Furthermore, if three or fewer candidates qualified, the primary process would be bypassed altogether. As before, the presidential post would go to the winner of a majority of the Party Conference, composed of the LDP Diet caucus and one representative from each prefectural party organization (Miyake, 1982, pp. 9–11).

Contemporary LDP Factions

To argue that a party organization based on factions contributes to the electoral prospects of party members may appear paradoxical. Factions have an incentive to commandeer party resources for factional rather than party goals and to squabble openly about personnel matters. Witnessing factional maneuvering for the prime ministership, commentators on Japanese politics speak of the LDP being "beset" by factionalism. While not denying that factions complicate leadership decision making, we argue that these are small and manageable problems compared to the large electoral competition problem that they solve.

Our argument, in brief, is that LDP members utilize interfactional competition to enhance their chances of maintaining a legislative majority in Japan's multi-member district electoral system. Although the party could channel services to constituents from centralized election headquarters, competition for votes results in a more efficient provision of services. Large corporations often encourage a similar phenomenon, when they allow their own divisions to produce close-substitute products for the same market. General Motors, for example, allows Chevrolet and Pontiac to compete for the same customers, and Oldsmobile and Buick to do likewise.

Such intra-firm competition not only allows firms to use more focused incentive structures internally, but also ameliorates some of the information problems endemic to large hierarchical organizations. This type of competition should be particularly useful in markets—such as electoral markets—that are heavily regulated.[13] To be sure, factional organization will have to trade some gains resulting from coordination for some gains resulting from competition. In the case of the LDP, factions may depreciate the party's label and hamper its fundraising. In compensation, factions ameliorate the vote division problem described in Chapter 2. That the party steadfastly retains its factional organization suggests that those gains may be large.[14]

Recruitment

One of the most important roles factions play in the LDP is in
recruiting political talent. Faction leaders, in building up their own
bases of support within the party, have an incentive to find members who are likely to win elections with the least possible support
and effort. Hence leaders scour the ranks of the Upper House members, local politicians, bureaucrats, and, increasingly, retiring members' children or secretaries for people who show political promise.

For politician-hopefuls seeking LDP endorsement, factional backing is virtually indispensable. Faction members get first priority
when the party leadership hammers out its endorsement list. Only
a handful of LDP members have managed to get elected and stay
in office without factional affiliation, though endorsement is more
or less guaranteed to incumbents, even if they first ran as independents and joined the LDP upon election.

Because faction leaders generally promise—implicitly at least—to
fund the candidates they recruit, they often prefer second-generation politicians to those without any legacy to inherit. Over the
course of their careers politicians make substantial constituency-
specific investments. As a result, those who inherit support bases
are likely to require less funding and other support than candidates
starting from scratch. This makes them particularly appealing to
faction leaders, who want to stretch their resources as far as possible.[15]

Consider the four politicians who competed for the Takeshita
faction in 1992: Ryūtarō Hashimoto, Keizō Obuchi, Ichirō Ozawa,
and Tsutomu Hata. Hashimoto and Obuchi were both 26 years old
when faction leader Eisaku Satō urged them to run from their
fathers' districts for the first time in 1963 (Shiota, 1991, p. 192).
At the time, Hashimoto was on the management track at a textile company, and Obuchi was studying comparative literature in
graduate school. Both inherited their fathers' organizations, were
elected handily, and have never lost an election since.

Kakuei Tanaka recruited Tsutomu Hata and Ichirō Ozawa into
the Satō faction in 1968 when their fathers retired. Hata, by his
own account, was not at all sure about wanting to become a politician, having seen more than he cared to of the difficulties of a

political career. But Tanaka's charisma, savvy advice, and funds won Hata over. Ichirō Ozawa required less coaxing, but also claims to have been inspired by Tanaka's energy and enthusiasm (Shiota, 1991, p. 200). Again, both have had successful careers. All four men—Hashimoto, Obuchi, Hata, and Ozawa—benefited from their political inheritance, and it was because the faction leaders knew the four would so benefit that they coaxed them into political careers.

Promotions and Demotions

Discipline is imposed on nonconformist LDP members primarily through factions. Once elected to office, new recruits of the LDP rely on factions for continued financial and organizational support. Without factional backing, an LDP member has little chance of advancing up the rungs of the party ladder. The few LDP Lower House members who, for whatever reasons, prefer not to join factions almost never get a cabinet position and certainly have no hope of ever attaining a leadership post.

As in many organizations, LDP factions use a seniority rule to induce junior members to work hard for expected future benefits. To the extent that responsibilities increase with seniority, the system may also take advantage of the greater productivity of more experienced members (Ferejohn, 1990). Moving up the ladder on a normal schedule is a signal to the electorate that this politician is taken seriously by the party leadership, will be given a share of the private goods to be disbursed, and deserves future election. This signaling mechanism, as Shepsle and Nalebuff (1990) and Katz and Sala (1991) point out in the American context, also creates a barrier to entry for would-be competitors. Since politicians' policymaking influence—and hence their ability to deliver favors—rises in tandem with their time in office, one would expect voters to be reluctant to replace them with challengers.

It should be noted that the custom of advancing LDP members regularly up the ranks is somewhat costly to the party. People in cabinet and party positions learn a considerable amount on the job, over time. Cycling them out before capturing the full return on their learning is apparently a cost the party is willing to bear.[16]

Beyond the first cabinet position or a mid-level party position, however—that is, after about six terms in office—seniority is displaced by "contribution to the faction." Only faction members who have demonstrated loyalty, superior vote-getting potential, and fund-raising talents continue to move up into the party's upper reaches. It is these people who are considered players in the "tournament" for executive LDP positions, faction heads, and the prime ministership.[17] The criterion for winning the competition at each step along the ladder is the level of contribution—electoral, managerial, and financial—to the faction of which one is a member.

Losing an election in mid-career seriously damages a would-be contender in the competition for advancement. Even if a politician returns to office after electoral defeat, contributors may search for lower-risk candidates. Building factional support is clearly impossible without enthusiastic funding. No politician with a mid-career electoral defeat has ever made it as a faction leader or Prime Minister.

Refusing to go along with the faction's voting instructions is also a career-bender, though probably more reparable. Once the LDP decides on a policy position, factions share with the party secretary the job of "whipping" party members for a Diet vote. Few politicians dare to disregard these instructions. But in 1987, for example, Kunio Hatoyama (Tokyo 4th) voted his district against the unpopular sales tax bill. As punishment, his faction leader Noboru Takeshita held him back from his expected advancement to a political vice-ministerial position for one year (Fujimoto, 1990, p. 81; Ishikawa and Hirose, 1989, p. 208). This sort of punishment only works because factions agree implicitly to party-wide rules about party discipline. Otherwise factions would cry foul if members of one faction were treated more leniently than those of another.

The Size of Factions

Both Liberals and Democrats brought a number of factions to the 1955 merger. By all accounts, in the early years of the party factions were rather fluid in their membership; they joined with other factions and sometimes split off again. But the trend over time has been a monotonic decline in the number of factions, from about eleven or twelve in 1955 to about five since the early 1980s.[18] We will explore this trend by looking at the arguments for economies of scale in faction activities, in the supposition that factions have grown large through maximizing their representativeness within the LDP. To corroborate this point, we review the empirical record of failed attempts at faction building.

Size of Factions: The Argument

One might adduce several reasons for the tendency of factions to grow larger and hence become fewer in number over the past 45 years. An important floor on faction size is the ability to destroy the LDP's majority upon defection. Being too small to hurt the LDP is clearly to be consigned to insignificance. But this floor has dropped, rather than risen, as the LDP's margin of seats in the Diet has shrunk over time.

Seizaburō Satō and Tetsuhisa Matsuzaki (1986) suggest that the LDP created economies of scale for factions by limiting the number of important party posts. Because there are only a few top party positions, factions that cannot muster enough members to claim title to one of these top leadership positions lose power over time. But this argument seems a bit contrived, since it would be easy enough for the LDP to create enough leadership positions for each of the factions. As we have noted, the lines between the layers of party leadership are sufficiently blurred that this could be done easily. In fact, the number of positions that are considered top posts seems to depend on the number of factions rather than the other way around.

Zen'ichirō Tanaka (1986) imputes the strongest impetus for faction growth to the faction leaders, who want to line up as many votes as possible behind their candidacy for party president and prime minister. As long as the LDP holds a Lower House majority, its party president will be elected as Prime Minister by that House. But even the largest factions still have to get the votes of other factions to get a majority in the LDP's Lower House caucus. There has never been a faction large enough to command a caucus majority on its own. Tanaka would have to argue that larger factions have a significant advantage over smaller factions in attracting new members, though he does not suggest reasons for why this should be so.[19]

We are left with evidence of, but not fully satisfactory reasons for, economies of scale to Lower House factions. Our alternative explanation arrives at economies of scale by way of economies of scope. Faction leaders striving for the top position want be supported by factions with functional and geographical diversity. This is because the faction controlling the prime ministership will have a disproportionate say in decisions affecting the distribution of government resources. If a faction is either functionally or geographically biased, the other factions would reasonably expect the disbursement of government resources similarly to be skewed. A faction whose members enjoy a wide range of expertise, connections with all important ministries and various levels of local government, and nationwide representation would give little ground for concern among the other factions and party members that it would distribute private benefits in a way unrepresentative of their interests.[20]

One might still wonder why small factions would not survive quite apart from the prime ministerial race. A small faction—any group just large enough to destroy the LDP's majority—should be able to hold out for huge returns in exchange for its crucial votes. If there were just one such group, the LDP would presumably be willing to give it anything short of the gains from an LDP majority in the Diet. But we do not observe this particular form of strategic behavior within the LDP. The reason for cooperation seems to be that the threat of collective sanctions from the main factions is credible. They could collectively block a hold-out strategy by calling immediate nationwide elections, withholding the party endorsement from all would-be cheaters, and fielding more cooperative candidates.[21] Only politicians with the wildest sense of adventure and negligible regard for their political lives would volunteer to play against those odds.

It is also interesting to speculate why factions do not grow even larger than they currently are. James Buchanan, in explaining why clubs often restrict membership, argues that the benefit of collective reputation diminishes beyond a certain size.[22] Presumably party factions would likewise diminish in quality if they recruited and advanced their members indiscriminately. The failure of the less talented politicians in getting reelected would naturally hold down the size of the faction despite its leader's intentions. A second argument, from the standpoint of internal factional discipline, is

Table 4.1   Membership of Prime Minister's faction before and after elections

Election date	PM	Faction			Party			Faction gain over party
		Before	After	% Gain	Before	After	% Gain	
Nov. 1963	Ikeda	53	50	-5.66	296	283	-4.39	-1.27
Jan. 1967	Satō	44	57	29.55	283	277	-2.12	31.67
Dec. 1969	Satō	57	59	3.51	277	300	8.30	-4.79
Dec. 1972	Tanaka		48		300	282	-6.00	
Dec. 1976	Miki	36	32	-11.11	282	257	-8.87	-2.25
Jan. 1979	Ōhira		50		249	257	3.21	
June 1980	Suzuki	49	55	12.24	257	287	11.67	0.57
Dec. 1983	Nakasone	43	49	13.95	287	250	-12.89	26.85
July 1986	Nakasone	49	63	28.57	250	304	21.60	6.97
Feb. 1990	Kaifu	24	26	8.33	295	286	-3.05	11.38

Sources: Kokkai benran (various years); Satō and Matsuzaki (1986, p. 243).

Note: In 1976 and 1980 the incumbent Prime Minister did not form the immediate postelection cabinet. Fukuda replaced Miki in December 1976, and Suzuki inherited Ōhira's faction and the prime ministership after Ōhira died during the 1980 campaign.

that a faction could not provide selective incentives to more than a certain number. At the margin, members of oversized factions would be tempted to conclude that their behavior would go undetected and thus would more often cut deals with other factions or otherwise cheat. Both arguments suggest that diminishing marginal returns to size should set in at some point, but neither tells us where that point might be.

The magnitude of Japan's electoral districts seems to provide the strongest clue. A faction cannot run more than one candidate in a single district without incurring the costs that factions were "invented" to reduce. So long as there are districts where the LDP can elect as many as five representatives, there will always be an incentive for at least five factions to compete for survival.[23] That, indeed, seems to be about the current equilibrium number of LDP factions.[24] A change in the electoral system, of course, would alter that.

Size of Factions: The Evidence

When the Liberal and Democratic parties merged in 1955, the Liberals were divided into three groups led by Shigeru Yoshida, Taketora Ogata, and Bamboku Ōno, respectively. The Democratic Party brought to the new party factions headed by Ichirō Hatoyama, Nobusuke Kishi, Bukichi Miki, and a fourth group of former Progressive Party members that was itself subdivided under five leaders. Altogether, the new LDP comprised eleven factions. In addition, about 80 LDP members did not belong to any faction at all, though some of them pledged loose alliance to unaffiliated member Tanzan Ishibashi.

Over two or so decades, the factions shook down into five as members of weaker factions defected to more successful factions. The typical pattern was for members of factions whose leaders failed to win the prime ministership after successive bids to pledge their loyalty elsewhere if possible. Corporate sponsors tended to cut their contributions to unpopular party leaders, hastening their demise.

The first intra-party group to disappear was the Ishibashi "nonfaction." Ishibashi was elected Prime Minister in December 1956 as a compromise candidate supported by the Matsumura/Miki, Ōno, Ishii, and Ikeda factions. The winning coalition claimed a disproportionate share of the cabinet posts as well as all of the top party posts. But Ishibashi was unable to convert his prime ministership into an ongoing stream of income and access for his group members. Less than two months after he came into power, Ishibashi fell ill and was replaced by Kishi, who was supported by a set of factions that excluded the Ishibashi group.[25] In the election of November 1960 Ishibashi's group was down to four members, and in 1963 Ishibashi himself lost his bid for reelection. His group never recovered.

The Ishii faction, once large, met with a similar fate. After two failed bids for the prime ministership in 1956 and 1960, and an unsuccessful nomination of Eisaku Satō in 1964, Ishii lost credibility as a serious contender and with it, his power as a fundraiser. By his retirement in 1972, members of Ishii's faction had taken refuge in more promising factions. Similarly, Aiichirō Fujiyama, who unsuccessfully ran for the office in 1960, twice in 1964, and again in 1966, finally lost most of his assets in trying and his members defected to Takeo Fukuda by 1967.

Being part of the winning coalition in the prime ministerial race seemed to buy factions some time, but did not guarantee survival. Prime ministers Ikeda, Satō, and Tanaka awarded a key party slot or two to the Shōjirō Kawashima faction, and its successor, the Etsusaburō Shiina faction, in exchange for its support. But the faction did not obtain enough positions to keep its members satisfied, and in 1978 the last members of the Shiina faction finally joined Fukuda's faction.

Other failed attempts to form factions include one by Kenzō Matsumura, who broke off with four members from the Takeo Miki faction in 1963 only to return to the fold in 1969 with three members. In another instance, Kiyoshi Mori challenged Yasuhiro Nakasone's inheritance of the Ichirō Kōno faction in 1963, taking with him 14 of the 46 and passing them along to Sonoda in 1968 before Sonoda's members joined the Takeo Fukuda and Kakuei Tanaka factions a few years later. Ichirō Nakagawa took ten members of the dwindling Mikio Mizuta faction (of the Ōno/Murakami lineage) in 1977, before killing himself in 1983. And Shintarō Ishihara, before becoming a celebrity writer, ran for Prime Minister in 1983. He had the support of the six remaining Nakagawa group members, but he lost his bid and joined the Fukuda faction (Naka, 1980, pp. 279–281; Kitaoka, 1990, pp. 199–207).

The factions that have become the "big five" were, by the early 1970s, already about twice the size of the next tier of factions. By 1978 the smaller factions had virtually disappeared. To be sure, the party's proportional representation rule for allocating party posts should have helped small factions; the rule should have reduced the gains to just winning the prime ministerial race. Nonetheless, large enough advantages still accrued to the faction controlling the prime ministership to make the race worth winning, and the economies of scope favored large factions in the race. Small factions were not representative enough to convince members of the other factions that their distribution of pork, in the event they won the prime ministership, would be sufficiently even and unbiased. The party's decision in 1978 to experiment with party primaries seemed to have an additional effect. Small factions simply could not muster the large sums of money needed to "buy" an adequate number of local votes to compete with the biggest players.

Assessing Factions

Policymaking

The LDP's policymaking process can be described with scarcely a mention of factions. Factions, in fact, have virtually no role outside of personnel matters. This is because each faction is more or less a microcosm of the entire party in terms of policy preference and expertise.[26] Factions are happy to delegate policymaking to the PARC, where the policy differences are as much within factions as among them.

Isomorphism across factions is, as we noted, an artifact of the prime ministerial race. Because faction leaders want to maximize their chances of becoming president of the LDP, and hence Prime Minister, they want to be in the strongest position possible, first, to attract talented politicians into their faction's fold and, second, to bargain with other factions for support. Bidding for high-quality politicians entails promising them financial help and securing for them policymaking influence in areas important to their constituents. The need to form coalitions with other factions to win a majority vote in the prime ministerial competition also creates an incentive to be a "median" faction. Both of these impulses have led factions, over time, to recruit politicians from all types of districts, to diversify their funding sources across all industries, and to expand their connections across all policy jurisdictions.

An Assessment

Although LDP factions generally receive bad press, both in Japan and abroad, much of the concern is unwarranted. Factions do help the LDP divide the vote, and many of the problems thought to be generated by factions are overstated. It is as true with the LDP's factional organization as it is generally that the solution to one problem often creates other problems. But the problems factions create are not insurmountable.

The LDP deals with the smaller inefficiencies that factions introduce in two ways. First, each faction in the LDP is large enough to destroy the party's majority if it chooses to defect. This effectively creates an inter-factional unanimity rule for all important party decisions.

Second, and more important, to mitigate the policy immobility that could result from a unanimity rule, the LDP has made policy-making supra-factional. Voters do not choose among alternative factional policy labels; 63.8 percent of the respondents in a nationwide poll of people who had voted for the LDP in the 1983 election said they did not know the factional affiliation of their candidate (Watanuki, Miyake, Inoguchi, and Kabashima, 1986, p. 160). Factions recruit the candidates and help fund the campaigns, but leave the candidates free to develop their own vote networks.

Conclusion

In this chapter we provide a conceptual map for the seeming labyrinth that is the LDP. Factional layers of organization that appear to be culturally or historically preordained, because they seem otherwise incomprehensible, are explicable in terms of electoral necessity. The argument, in sum, is that factions contribute critically to the electoral chances of rank-and-file LDP members.

Factions are an intermediate level of organization within the LDP, and the units of competition at the district level. In exchange for endorsement, financial support, and personnel management, all of which are key to electoral success, individual members back their faction leaders for Prime Minister. The party as a whole is able to tap the inter-factional competition so as to increase the likelihood of maintaining a Diet majority.

Counterintuitively, factions do not prevent the LDP from providing its electorate with public goods. The LDP's adoption of an implicit proportionality rule among factions for party and cabinet posts has reduced the stakes of being part of a "winning coalition" of factions. Regardless of which faction claims the prime ministerial seat, all factions get a cut of the spoils in rough proportion to their size.

A second reason for the absence of policy-based factional warfare lies in the logic of prime ministerial competition. In bidding for the support of a party majority, each faction leader needs to assure party members that he would not skew policies against the interests of their constituents. By dint of competition for party support, factions accept candidates specializing in any given area of private goods, and all of them end up looking more or less alike. It is therefore unusual for any single faction to try to subvert the policymaking process to serve factional goals.

Should a faction gain disproportionate influence in any particular area of policymaking, all other factions still possess the ultimate weapon to discourage factional opportunism: the defection of any faction would destroy the LDP's majority. Since the distribution of all goods and services, public let alone private, rests on the maintenance of a legislative majority, to date no faction has dared play the power game.

Clearly, factions produce some negative side effects. Business contributors complain that the LDP spends far more money on elections than would a nonfactionalized party. But because only a change in the electoral rules could eradicate factions, party contributors would have to be convinced that economizing would be worth risking a possible LDP defeat. LDP supporters have paid vast sums for the party's continued majority. It may be that some contributors have begun to feel they are no longer getting their money's worth. But until they are willing to face an administration under the control of one or more opposition parties, they will have to continue doling out the huge sums in LDP campaign contributions that the current system requires.

5

Party Organization

"The Liberal Democratic Party," Marxists were fond of saying, "is neither liberal, democratic, nor a party." We have argued that the LDP does in fact compete within a democratic system, though its policies may seem illiberal to the Left. In describing how the LDP functions as a *party*, we found that while factions weaken its ability to function as a unit, they do not destroy it. One question to be discussed is why LDP members delegate crucial party-management functions to a collective, transfactional leadership.

Japan's multi-member district electoral system, as we explained, gives individual LDP backbenchers a powerful incentive to provide constituency services so as to enhance their reelection. The LDP's extra-parliamentary policymaking apparatus is a device to facilitate the provision of these constituency services. While the inevitable intra-party competition for election is organized along factional lines, neither constituency service nor factional organization assures the election of LDP members. The LDP has an additional layer of organization that contributes importantly to the electoral success of party members. A central party leadership, drawn from factions but transcending factional leadership, coordinates policymaking among the PARC committees and brokers differences among factions.

LDP backbenchers entrust party leaders with a variety of powers for reasons similar to those motivating the coolies on the Yangtze to hire overseers to beat them. In cases of multiple principals, the principals need to constrain themselves and each other in order to provide themselves with collective goods. LDP backbenchers and factions, acting independently, would face classic prisoners' dilemmas in the provision of collective goods. Lacking a means to coordinate their actions, they would most likely act myopically and self-destructively.

This chapter outlines who the LDP leaders are and how they provide party backbenchers with collective goods. For members of the LDP, the collective goods are the party's reputation for delivering promised services, the party's policy platform, and limits on the dishing out of pork. To provide these collective goods, LDP leaders establish the basic policy direction of the party and restrain wayward LDP backbenchers.

Any principal-agent relationship also harbors the danger of agent opportunism. We will thus examine the means by which LDP backbenchers keep their leaders—and agents—constrained. If LDP backbenchers have put their leaders on a long leash, it is not because they lack the means to rein them in.

Why Party Leadership?

We have already established that Japanese politics is highly particularistic; in that sense factional organization helps individual LDP Dietmembers provide particular favors to their constituents. Many people vote on the basis of personal favors they receive from politicians. But even the provision of private goods requires the collective action of party members. Legislators must decide which favors to fund, at what levels, and with what resources. The party also must maintain a credible party reputation that attracts campaign contributions, and it must monitor bureaucratic behavior. But each legislator or each faction is inclined only to take credit for the provision of favors, not to be associated with the costs of the favors. The single nontransferable vote electoral system with its large built-in bias toward particularism thus creates major collective-action obstacles to any group of legislators who must cooperate in order to maintain a legislative majority.

The problems LDP members face are compounded by their need to provide some public goods to the general voting public in order to get elected. The LDP cannot reach all voters with private favors: a large group of "floating voters"—typically urban, educated, white-collar workers—is harder to incorporate into the LDP's traditional support networks. There is some evidence that these voters make their electoral choices on the basis of, among other things, general economic indicators that provide clues about their expected earnings (Miyake, 1989; Arai, 1990). Lavish favors at the expense of inflation or large government budget deficits might tilt the electoral balance away from the LDP. The LDP must therefore calculate and maintain a balance among the private goods it provides to groups of supporters, the public goods with which it woos harder-to-catch floating voters, and the tax cost of both kinds of benefits. Even if the balance between private and public goods is, say, 65 or 70 percent in favor of private goods, the LDP has to make tough choices in setting spending ceilings and distributing the tax burden.

The Electoral Imperative and LDP Organization

Despite the broad similarities among democratic systems, what politicians must do to get elected varies by electoral system. In a single-member-district, parliamentary system such as Britain's, a politician's electoral fate is determined largely by the popularity of his or her party's platform in the district. It comes as no surprise to learn that in such a system the party's backbenchers delegate considerable powers to party leaders.[1]

In Japan, as we have seen, politicians need to deliver a far higher level of particular services. But even in Japan's LDP, where politicians compete for election with members of their own party and therefore work assiduously to build a personal following with factional help, party members recognize advantages in delegating certain tasks to a collective party leadership. The delegation is not as complete as in Britain, to be sure. LDP Dietmembers insist on more involvement in policymaking, and we have seen that factions undertake most personnel matters for the LDP.

Nonetheless, the strong party organization helps Japanese legislators avoid potentially suboptimal behavior. While unaffiliated politicians would have difficulty raising campaign contributions because the contributor has little reason to believe the politician's pledge to provide policy favors in return, parties are inter-generational, ongoing concerns with a long-term reputation to protect. Parties can therefore more readily make credible promises about favors in exchange for contributions.

Political parties also institutionalize a particular portfolio of policy choices that allow legislators to diversify the product they offer.

Although each legislator can specialize in only a few types of policy areas, party affiliation gives voters cues about what range of favors the legislator can deliver with the help of his or her party. Without a party label, it would be impossible for individual legislators to take credit, with any degree of credibility, for favors other than those in their own areas of jurisdiction.

Furthermore, a party label may include a commitment to provide certain public goods. An unaffiliated politician cannot make credible promises regarding public goods, since the provision of these requires the agreement of a legislative majority. Finally, parties reduce the transactions costs of forging minimum winning coalitions on every issue. All political parties cannot, by definition, win a majority every time. But they are the primary unit of competition for forming majorities. The costs to legislators in terms of reduced flexibility of partners may be more than offset by reduced bargaining costs.

Factions in the LDP only incompletely solve these problems. Although they do help members with fundraising, factions do not represent alternative portfolios of policy choices for either private or public goods. As we have discussed, policy differentiation along factional lines would cause more problems than it would solve. Nor do factions eliminate the transactions costs for members of forming permanent coalitions. No faction has ever been close to forming a Diet majority on its own. LDP members overcome these prisoners' dilemmas and coordination problems by delegating powers to a transfactional party leadership.[2]

Who the Party Leaders Are

Our discussion so far has suggested a sharp line between party leaders and backbenchers. The distinction is in fact more blurred, because many Dietmembers are on their way up the LDP organizational ladder. It is probably best to think of LDP leadership in terms of concentric circles. The smallest circle of LDP leaders includes only the heads of the five or so LDP factions. The Prime Minister is often, though not always, one of this inner group. It is not uncommon, in fact, for heads of factions not to hold any formal position within the party organization, though it is well understood that all important personnel decisions must meet with their approval.

It is the second tier of LDP leadership that is most responsible for the routine management of the party. This group includes the party president (who is also Prime Minister), in the event that he is not the head of a faction. Also in this group are the party secretary *(Kanjichō)*, chairman of the PARC *(Seichō kaichō)*, and chairman of the Executive Council *(Sōmu kaichō)*, who together make up the party's Committee of Three *(Tōsanyaku)*. The Committee of Three is effectively an executive committee of the party that is consulted when there are disagreements within the party that neither the PARC nor the Executive Council can iron out. They often bring into their executive meetings lower-ranking LDP leaders, depending on the nature of the problem. During their tenure as party leaders, they refrain from holding factional posts or even from attending their respective faction's business meetings.

The broader leadership circle—senior party members awaiting further advancement—holds many positions, including chairmanships of PARC committees, administrative posts at the LDP's headquarters, and cabinet jobs. As we will discuss later, seniority is the first criterion for advancement up the ladder. Political savvy is also rewarded.[3] But a willingness to work with the top leadership is essential to promotion beyond a certain point.

Party Management

LDP leaders contribute to their members' electoral prospects in several ways. First of all, they protect the party's brand-name capital by formulating the party's stance on public goods and maintaining a ceiling on the private goods that backbenchers dispense; and they broker the interests of factions when they impinge on the party's overall electoral performance and policy choices. They play a smaller role in two areas one might expect to place within their jurisdiction: fundraising and party discipline.

The Party Label

To the extent that a significant percentage of voters do not respond to facilitation services, creating and maintaining an identifiable party brand name is critical. There is no good empirical measure of the electoral value of the LDP's supply of public goods. But one way to get a clue is to look at public opinion surveys. In an NHK

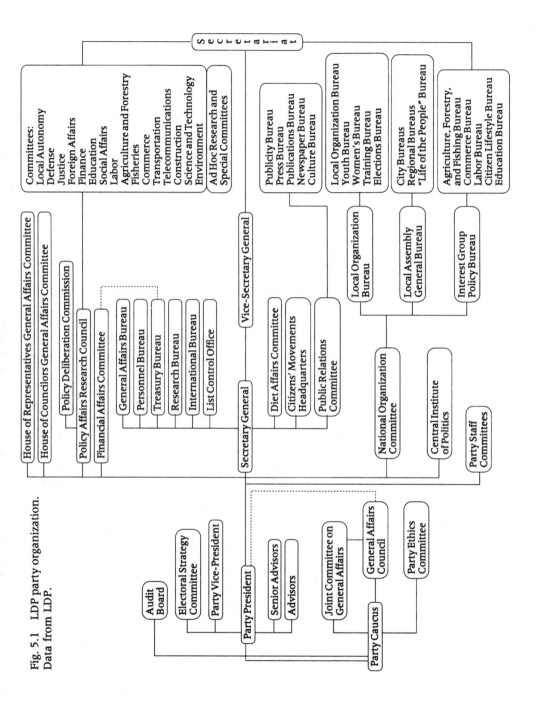

Fig. 5.1 LDP party organization. Data from LDP.

Table 5.1 A typical career path for an LDP member

Term in office	Party or government post
1st term	PARC committee member
2nd term	Diet committee secretary Political vice-minister Vice-Chairman of a PARC committee
3rd term	PARC committee chair
4th term or 5th term	Party vice-secretary Director of an LDP bureau Faction management position
5th term or 6th term	Cabinet position

Source: Satō and Matsuzaki (1986, p. 39).

Note: This table indicates the stage at which a Dietmember typically *first* rises to a particular level in the LDP ladder. Because LDP members may hold two or three of these positions simultaneously, they could continue to hold a particular job or level of job—such as PARC Committee Chair—for several terms.

poll conducted two weeks after the 1986 Lower House election, 59 percent of the respondents in cities of over 500,000 stated that the government's macroeconomic policies factored importantly in their decision.[4]

A second clue lies in a comparison of Upper and Lower House election results. The LDP has consistently won five to ten percent fewer votes in elections for the Upper House than in Lower House. The LDP's performance on the party list portion of the Upper House ballot contrasts poorly even with the votes LDP candidates get in the Upper House prefectural districts. In 1983, the basis of selecting the Upper House nationwide representatives was changed from a SNTV for a particular candidate to a vote for a party list. The LDP as a party has tended to win four to eight percent fewer votes in the proportional representation nationwide district than what individual LDP candidates have won in the Upper House prefectural districts. Nonetheless, the point is that the LDP *does* compete largely on the basis of its party label in the Upper House nationwide district, and until 1989 had won nearly twice as many votes as its nearest competitor, the Socialist Party.

The LDP leadership is pivotal in the provision of private goods as well. Choosing among competing spending programs and ensuring faithful bureaucratic implementation of party decisions entail coordination among party members. Finding the electorally optimal balance between public and private goods is a task party members delegate to the leadership.

Within the LDP, the leadership retains ultimate control of major policy decisions—that is, decisions with electoral significance—including tax and budgetary policy. The LDP Tax Committee hammers out party positions for all tax legislation. While over half the party's members are typically members of the Tax Committee at any given time, the committee's chairman and vice-chairman are handpicked by the party leadership and work in close consultation with the cabinet. Budgetary policy is similarly guided by the leadership. The cabinet acts with the help of the experts in the MOF's Budget Bureau and takes into consideration electoral necessity in setting an overall budgetary ceiling. Deliberations within and among the PARC committees ensue as to budgetary allocation. But as with all legislation, the leadership retains two checks: the party's Committee of Three takes up controversial matters that the PARC cannot resolve, and the cabinet has to approve all party-sponsored legislation.

Shifts in the LDP's fiscal policy reflect the party's broadest electoral concerns. This is true regardless of the personal proclivities of the Prime Minister or Finance Minister in any given year. Takeo Fukuda, an ex-MOF bureaucrat and a known fiscal conservative, was Finance Minister during the 1965 recession, when the LDP abandoned its balanced budget policy and began issuing deficit bonds for the first time. As Prime Minister in inflationary 1977, Fukuda informed MOF bureaucrats that introducing a sales tax was premature from the standpoint of the LDP's electoral calculations.[5] In the early and mid-1980s Prime Ministers Zenkō Suzuki, Yasuhiro Nakasone, and Noboru Takeshita, none of whom was known for his financial expertise or fiscal conservatism, presided over consecutive years of low or negative growth rates in the government budget and the imposition of a nationwide sales tax (Yanagisawa, 1985, pp. 26–63). These are decisions made not by one or two political figures, but by the LDP's collective leadership.

As another example of how LDP leaders successfully constrain their backbenchers, consider the 1978 program to aid firms and workers in "structurally depressed regions."[6] Institutionally, the program presented backbenchers with enormous opportunities for redistributive rent-seeking: in 1978 alone, the government allocated ¥500 billion for areas designated as structurally depressed (*Chūshō kigyō chō*, 1979, p. 345). Legislators able to have their district so designated thus potentially stood to divert considerable sums to their constituents.

Despite this redistributive opportunity, Table 5.2 suggests that LDP leaders successfully prevented party backbenchers from transforming the program into a pork barrel. To be sure, we have not been able to compare directly the amounts of money distributed to LDP and opposition districts. At least at the level of area designations, however, the government seems not to have indulged any bias for areas represented by LDP legislators.

Factional Endorsements

The primary role of factions in the LDP is personnel management. But the party shares some of this function. The LDP headquarters sets a ceiling on the number of party endorsements, not to let them exceed what the party's Election Planning Office deems electorally feasible. A second party rule regarding endorsements is that incumbents are given preference over newcomers. This is a property rights

Table 5.2 Districts designated as structurally depressed compared with all districts, 1978 (percentages in parentheses)

LDP Representation	Structurally depressed districts ($N = 24$)	All districts ($N = 130$)
Districts with majority LDP representatives	12 (50.0)	68 (52.3)
Districts with at least half LDP representatives	15 (62.5)	84 (64.6)
Districts with at least two LDP representatives	20 (83.3)	104 (80.0)
Districts with no LDP representatives	0	0

Sources: Chūshō kigyō shō, ed. (1979, p. 344); *Kokkai binran* (1978).
Note: Districts and representatives refer to Diet electoral districts and Diet legislators.

arrangement that reduces the incentive of weak incumbents to play an endgame strategy. However, the party reserves the right to withhold endorsement in the event of egregious violation of party rules.

As sensible as these rules are for the party, they pose a problem for factions trying to expand their numbers. There is also a latent danger for the party in the incumbent-preference rule: under some circumstances a newcomer could win a seat for the LDP where an incumbent could do so no longer. Factions do, in fact, flout both rules to some extent. On the basis of a revised ceiling they set among themselves, factions support an additional 30 to 60 candidates, depending on their electoral calculations, without the party's endorsement. Many of these factionally supported "independents" run in districts against weak incumbents, giving the party an effective way around the incumbent-preference rule in selected cases.

There is a danger, of course, that too many LDP candidates fighting in any given district would actually lose seats for the party. If we count faction-backed "independents" as LDP candidates, the LDP typically loses 10 to 20 seats to over-endorsement. But it

Table 5.3   Overendorsement

Election date	Total seats	Candidates		Failures		Cases of over-endorsement		% of failures due to over-endorsement	
		LDP	JSP	LDP	JSP	LDP	JSP	LDP	JSP
May 1958	467	413	246	126	80	35	8	55.6	20.0
Nov. 1960	467	399	186	103	41	23	3	44.7	14.6
Nov. 1963	467	359	198	76	54	16	3	42.1	11.1
Jan. 1967	486	342	209	65	69	13	5	40.0	14.5
Dec. 1969	486	328	183	40	93	5	16	25.0	34.4
Dec. 1972	491	339	161	68	43	8	4	23.5	18.6
Dec. 1976	511	320	162	71	39	7	3	19.7	15.4
Jan. 1979	511	322	157	74	50	10	5	28.4	20.0
June 1980	511	310	149	26	42	0	15	0.0	71.4
Dec. 1983	511	339	144	89	32	15	0	33.7	0.0
July 1986	512	322	138	22	58	5	3	45.5	10.3
Feb. 1990	512	338	149	63	13	22	2	69.8	30.8

Source: Asahi nenkan (Asahi Annual) (Tokyo: Asahi shimbunsha, various years).
Note: In 1958 LDP actually endorsed more candidates in a single district than there were seats available.

is also clear, as Matsubara and Kabashima (1984) and Satō and Matsuzaki (1986) have pointed out, that a strict incumbents-only rule when there are no open seats would also generate losses. Weak incumbents would lose and no stronger newcomers would have been permitted to contest the seats on behalf of the LDP. It is hard to test Matsubara and his coauthors' point that "shadow endorsements" have resulted in net gains for the LDP, because one cannot surmise what voters would have done in the absence of a new contender. But the LDP's longevity suggests that its preference for incumbents has at least not been a major detriment to the party's electoral fortunes.[7]

Fundraising

Raising campaign contributions is another area where a party might have a comparative advantage over unaffiliated legislators. Contributors may rightly fear that a particular individual is at the end of his political career, whereas a party has a longer time horizon by virtue of its inter-generational structure. It is far less likely that a party will suddenly disband than that an individual politician would retire with little prior warning. Promises from parties, because of their visibly longer orientation, are more credible. A party should therefore be able to command a higher price for a policy favor than could an unaffiliated politician for the same favor.

If parties have adequate means of disciplining errant members, parties may also be able to raise funds more efficiently for another reason. Individual politicians competing against each other for contributions will bid down the price of favors (Rasmusen and Ramseyer, 1992). If a party can control the flow of funds centrally and punish party members who try to raise money on their own, the party may be able to charge monopoly rents for favors.

Because of these considerations, one might expect the LDP to collect most of its money centrally. In fact, it does nothing of the sort. About ten percent of the reported contributions to LDP members comes by way of the party. Another fifteen percent or so is channeled through faction leaders, and the remainder makes its way directly to rank and file politicians. But the unreliability of publicly reported contributions gives us at best a murky picture of political finances. According to "Utopia," a group of reform-minded first- and second-term LDP representatives, the amount of money required for an election campaign far exceeds the reported figures. Most of the money apparently is raised by the candidates themselves, though party and faction leaders doubtless provide LDP members with important introductions to contributors.

A party that wished to centralize its fundraising could, at least hypothetically, punish individual fundraisers. By eliminating the competition for funds among individual members or groups within the party, the party could charge a higher "price" for the policy favors it dispenses and everyone in the party would benefit potentially. But the factional organization of the LDP makes this extremely difficult, if not impossible. Because the party's leaders are also heads of competing factions, they have a strong incentive to divert funds for the factions' purposes. Party leaders also have an incentive to encourage individual politicians within their factions in any given district to raise as much money as possible relative to members of the other factions in that district.

The LDP has adopted an implicit party rule to reduce the likelihood of the Prime Minister's faction siphoning off contributions intended for the party. Since the early 1970s the party secretary, who supervises the party's coffers, has belonged to a different faction from that of the Prime Minister's (Mori, 1982, p. 179).[8] Despite these precautions, however, competition among factions for funds is inevitable, and the LDP could maximize campaign contributions to the party only by eliminating factions. But because factions are the units of *electoral* competition and entrepreneurship at the district level, eliminating factions would endanger the party itself. The

Table 5.4 Sources of campaign funds for ten "Utopia" Dietmembers (in yen)

Source	Average	(%)	Low	High
Public financing	18,800,000	(15)	18,800,000	18,800,000
Party, faction, and senior members	10,376,000	(8)	7,000,000	17,000,000
Kōenkai, sponsors	54,342,000	(43)	6,160,000	90,000,000
Fund-raising parties	20,407,000	(16)	0	45,000,000
Loans	15,143,000	(12)	0	33,060,000
Other	7,468,000	(6)	4,000,000	17,780,000
Total	126,536,000	(100)		

Sources: Hirose (1989, p. 64); and Iwai (1990, p. 126).

organization of the LDP, then, would appear better suited for max-imizing votes than for maximizing revenues.[9]

On the supply side, much of the LDP's financial support comes from the business sector and hinges on the LDP's commitment to fiscal conservatism and basic business-oriented policies. The LDP uses these contributions, as well as government resources, to pro-vide private favors to voters for whom such policies are insufficient. Businesses would be better off if they could maintain a contribution cartel to eliminate bidding among firms for policy favors. They could all, hypothetically, get more for less. Japan's leading corpora-tions have indeed attempted to do this through the Keidanren. Since the LDP's formation in 1955, the role of this business federa-tion in allocating contribution shares among industries and firms has been legendary. Nihachirō Hanamura, for many years the vice-chairman and managing director of the Keidanren, annually sent what came to be known as the Hanamura Memos to member firms with their expected contribution, based on firms' capital base and profitability (Honsho, 1985, pp. 119–127; Hirose and Ishikawa, 1989, p. 178).

Firms have been no more successful than the LDP in maintaining a contribution-related cartel. The competitive stakes are far too high, and risk of detection and reprisal far too low, to sustain such a level of cooperation. What has emerged instead is a three-tier pattern of contributions. The Keidanren continues to coordinate contributions to the party, but industries and firms give even more generously to faction leaders, and more still to individual politicians.

One might ask why firms give money to the party at all, rather than bid down the price of favors by giving to factions and individu-als. Our argument is that there are favors—of the public goods category—that only the central party leadership can supply. Given the importance to the business community of certain broad policies such as low inflation, moderate corporate taxes, and a generally favorable business environment, it is not at all surprising that firms funnel a substantial amount of money to the LDP headquarters—to the people who ensure that the party will enforce those policies even when the factions would not. The Keidanren is not cohesive enough to maintain an absolute cartel, but it is capable of reducing the impulse to free-ride among member firms. For this reason, large corporations give relatively more to the party than do small firms which are not as well organized on a national level.

Contributions to factions and to individual Dietmembers, by contrast, are likely to be in pursuit of particular favors. Industries and firms want not only low corporate tax rates, but also loan subsidies or special tax breaks that would break the budget if everyone else received them. Even though the LDP leadership ultimately controls these decisions as well, the leadership has to allow, for the sake of dividing the vote among competitors within a given district, considerable "cheating at the margin" in the provision of private goods.

Party Discipline

As with endorsements, most party discipline is left to the factions. Under the SNTV electoral rules, access to particular favors is indispensable for reelection; thus promotion to pork-dispensing positions within the party and cabinet is of great importance to backbenchers. While a proportional-representation rule divides these party and cabinet positions among the factions, it is the factions that allocate the positions within their respective membership according to criteria of seniority and "contribution to the faction." Factions have the means to make or break the careers of backbenchers, and are therefore the logical units for enforcing party discipline.

Some anecdotal evidence, however, suggests the party leadership can collectively protect party members who act outside a faction's narrow interests. In 1978 the Nakasone faction cut off from its membership roster a rising leader, Michio Watanabe, when Watanabe supported Masayoshi Ōhira as Prime Minister in defiance of the agreement among the Fukuda, Miki, and Nakasone factions. Watanabe still managed to land the coveted Minister of Finance position in the Zenkō Suzuki cabinet despite the lack of factional backing at that time in his career. His gamble paid off: Watanabe returned to the Nakasone faction several years later with no loss of seniority in the faction's rankings (Shiota, 1991, pp. 172–183).

In another instance, Takeo Nishioka was cut off from the Miyazawa faction in 1990 when he refused to give up his position as chairman of the party's Executive Council in favor of another Miyazawa protégé, Kōichi Katō. Nishioka was a personal friend of Prime Minister Toshiki Kaifu, and retained his chairmanship as an "independent" within the party.

Nishioka was backed by the other party leaders in July 1991, when the Miyazawa faction again pressed for his resignation from that leadership position. The Miyazawa faction's displeasure with Nishioka was compounded by its frustration over Prime Minister Kaifu's attempt to use the electoral reform plans to stay in office for a second term. At the beginning of July, the Miyazawa faction and an assortment of other LDP members spearheaded an unprecedented mutiny in the Executive Council over Nishioka's handling of the electoral reform bills. They forced him to reopen discussion of the bills, but the Committee of Three closed ranks behind Nishioka and stated flatly that party discipline would apply in the Diet vote for the electoral reform bills as for any other bill.[10] Delegation to a collective leadership allows the party to prevent factional squabbling over personnel matters from interfering with the party's policy choices.

Monitoring Party Leadership

Backbenchers entrust a group of party leaders with the task of calculating the party's collective electoral interests, and equip it with sufficient powers to enforce decisions made on the basis of these calculations. How much "cheating" is electorally optimal is a decision someone has to make for the party as a whole. As with any principal-agent relationship, the challenge is to give the agents (the party leaders) enough discretion to secure collective goals, but not so much as to create runaway agents in pursuit of their *own* private gain.

Backbenchers have to allow themselves to be constrained against their individual interests at times. The cost of not submitting to such constraints is the risk of massive free-riding by other backbenchers. Having an agent enforce collective interests, under these circumstances, may well be the best way of pursuing self-interest. But if backbenchers were to grant decision-making powers to the leadership without maintaining effective checks on leadership discretion, they would endanger their collective interests as well. Leaders would have an incentive to use collective resources to pay themselves more than fair wages (whether money or perquisites) for their work.

The LDP members have assigned their leaders considerable power. Like the leaders in many other parliamentary parties, the

LDP top men require strict party-line voting on cabinet-sponsored bills that are submitted to the Diet for passage. To enforce this discipline, they can rely on their control of candidate endorsement, advancement up the party ladder, and indirectly, the disbursement of government resources. The political life of a maverick in the LDP would be poor, nasty, brutish, and short. But through a variety of monitoring mechanisms, backbenchers ultimately do hold their leaders accountable.

One way to align leaders' preferences with those of backbenchers is to pay leaders a high salary. Giving them prospects of a large future steady income increases their costs of getting caught with their hands in the party's till[11] (Rasmusen, 1990; Shapiro and Stiglitz, 1984). LDP salaries are not in fact extraordinarily generous. But the higher the rank within the LDP, and hence the greater the influence over policymaking, the greater the ability to attract campaign contributions.

As corporations have found, using stock option plans and the like to give managers residual claims on their productivity in addition to a salary can raise their effort level (Rasmusen, 1989, ch. 6). Similarly, the LDP might be able to motivate party leaders to raise more funds for the party by allowing them to keep funds they raise beyond a certain level as a bonus. But better-than-average fundraising ability may contribute more to a politician's private estate than to the party's interests, unless there are other means of tying his or her personal fate to that of the party.

High-ranking LDP members do indeed show signs of earning larger commissions on the funds they raise from the private sector. Faction leaders use up some of these commissions in trying to increase the size and cohesiveness of their factions, and senior faction officers do the same in jockeying their way up the factional ladder. But they also are conspicuous consumers of some of this money. Leaders typically do conduct more meetings at expensive Akasaka restaurants and pay for more geishas to attend them at these evening meetings than do backbenchers.

Although this conspicuous consumption could represent agency slack, it need not. Given the competitive nature of internal LDP organization, for example, it could well represent market wages. Klein and Leffler (1981) suggest why it may be in all LDP members' interests for party leaders to consume conspicuously. Through the overt displays of financial means, leaders can sometimes signal that they are highly respected within the party.[12] This may allow them to raise funds for the party from private contributors at a rate commensurate with their greater effectiveness in influencing policy decisions.

A second way, other than ample remuneration, to keep leaders at the service of the party might be to select leaders only from safe districts. The LDP has, in fact, used this monitoring device (Matsubara and Kabashima, 1983, pp. 76–77). Secure politicians are more likely to plan for the longer run, and there is thus less risk to the party that these people will be opportunists playing an endgame strategy. In addition, representatives from safe districts are more apt to pass on their seats to their sons. This transferability further mitigates the likelihood of a leader's abusing his influence. Moreover, politicians who have higher probabilities of reelection than the average party member are also better able to raise campaign contributions for the party.[13]

The basic problem with relying excessively on "safety" as a criterion for leadership is that a safe seat merely gives a politician the *capability* but not necessarily the *incentive* to work on behalf of the party. For example, many safe districts are rural districts with different interests from those of the party's broader electoral base. A leader from such a district may be loathe to shift away from the LDP's traditional rural protectionism even though a growing number of the LDP's coalition are urban voters. The fact that rurally based LDP leaders have been on the forefront of the gradual move in the party toward agricultural liberalization suggests that the party has other incentives to align leaders' interests with those of the party as a whole.

A third way the LDP might constrain the independence of its leaders is to cycle leadership posts often, but this is less likely to be effective than the preceding two methods. One intuitive assumption is that keeping leaders involved in a wide variety of party activities would minimize their temptation to build empires in any particular area at the expense of any other. This, however, would be a costly monitoring device, since effectiveness in many party jobs is built over time.[14] Cycling would also probably be relatively ineffective in reducing piracy. Rapid job rotation could even encourage leaders to take *more* advantage of their position if the shortness of tenure made it difficult to trace the results of irresponsible behavior to any particular leader.

The LDP does in fact rotate certain jobs rather frequently, including most cabinet positions. The rationale for doing so, however, seems to have little to do with keeping leaders in check, since top leadership posts rotate less frequently than do positions in the second and third tiers. Faction heads, the most powerful party leaders, give up their faction leadership only upon retirement or death. But as we explained in the previous chapter, the strongest single constraint on the independence of faction heads seems to be their desire to become Prime Minister. Egregious cheating would be likely to dissuade other party members from entrusting the cheater with the party's top leadership position.

Conclusion

In the course of our argument we have disputed the notion that party backbenchers could just as well ensure their reelection by providing private goods through specialized legislative committees or even through factional affiliation alone. LDP members depend on their party (1) to provide a "stamp of approval" for raising campaign contributions; (2) to give voters cues about the range of private goods they would be able to provide; (3) to provide voters with valuable public goods that individual politicians would be unable to provide alone; and (4) to reduce the transactions costs of forging minimum winning coalitions on every issue. While specialized committee structures or factional organizations may be viable substitutes for some of these functions, party leadership is probably a lower-cost provider of most of them, and possibly the only provider of public goods.

Another central question we raised was, how does a party leadership composed of faction leaders act collectively? Even if LDP factions recognize the importance of maintaining a Diet majority, how do they escape the prisoner's dilemma of mutual cheating? The evidence is that the cheating is in fact minimal: overendorsements are typically not a problem, factions winning the prime ministerial race do not freeze out the other factions from the benefits of office, and policies generally promote the interests of the party as a whole rather than those of a particular faction or group of factions.

We find that this inter-factional cooperation occurs in part by design and in part by accident. The LDP's proportional representation rule for party and cabinet posts was a plan to foster cooperation that apparently worked. It has been more or less honored in subsequent cabinets, even if not enforced by any external constraint. The accidental, though equally important, device that promotes cooperation is a by-product of inter-factional competition rather than design: each faction resembles all the others. Because factions do not differ along important policy dimensions, they effectively delegate policymaking to party executives whose job it is to calculate the best interests of the party as a whole.

The greatest problem for the LDP is the expense of electoral campaigns. But to derive a causal relationship between factions and the use of money in elections would be a mistake. As we have tried to show, it is the multi-member district electoral system that causes both. Factions, as well as the lavish use of money in elections, are both symptoms of the need for a personal-vote strategy.

Had factions *not* evolved into nonideological units of electoral competition, the problems of factional organization would probably have been much greater for the LDP. Most likely, the party would have been forced to consider electoral reform much sooner. Our guess is that nothing short of that would have saved the party from rupture along factional lines.

6

Political Structure and Bureaucratic Incentives

Several years ago, one of us attended regularly a research group sponsored by MITI. During the meetings, the organizers customarily supplied tea. Most of the organizers were young fast-track bureaucrats who had joined MITI from the preeminent University of Tokyo (Tōdai). When the scheduled outside speaker brought his personal secretary to one of these meetings, she could not have been happier. Here, with a dash of sarcasm, she flavored the awe that Japanese routinely save for their bureaucrats: "Wow. I've never been poured tea by a Tōdai grad at MITI before."

It is an awe American scholars have shared, though it is not necessarily justly earned. Many observers routinely exaggerate the power and autonomy of Japanese bureaucrats. When most modern scholars describe the world of these men and women, they stress the control and independence they wield. In fact, however, that control and independence may be mere appearance. Basic principal-agent theory suggests that they are more likely just implementing LDP preferences.

Accordingly, we turn to the possibility that LDP leaders rationally delegate power to bureaucrats—and for good reasons. We then investigate the institutional constraints that the leaders have developed to monitor and police their bureaucratic agents.

How well does this monitoring system work? Monitoring is not free in the United States. Neither is it free in Japan—and given positive monitoring costs, one would expect positive agency slack. Nonetheless, modern theories of institutional change do suggest that political organizations should evolve in ways that enable them to exploit the tactical opportunities created by the institutional shape of government (North, 1990, ch. 1). More simply, through political evolution, political actors should come to structure their organizations and manipulate the institutional framework in ways that maximize their political returns. Unless agency slack increases those returns, therefore, they should come to develop ways to minimize it. LDP legislators have been doing just that.

Bureaucrats and Professors

In locating the source of Japanese policy, most observers point to bureaucrats rather than to legislators. Legislators do not much matter, they suggest, while bureaucrats largely do as they please. A few writers insist that Japanese legislators do have some power, and many speculate that legislators have more power now than they had twenty years ago (see Chapter 3). But most students of Japan locate policymaking in the bureaucracy. According to this orthodoxy, policy is less a function of a distinctly political logic than it is a projection of a peculiarly bureaucratic vision. As Bernard Silberman (1982, p. 231) elegantly put it, bureaucrats ran the country before World War II, and bureaucrats still do: in the prewar years, "the bureaucracy continued to enjoy the highest status and most powerful place in the formation of public policy, a place it continues to enjoy today under a quite different structure of authority." Apparently, that the institutional structure of politics changed radically after the War matters not at all.

More than any other American scholar, T. J. Pempel (1974, 1978) pioneered this analysis.[1] In this early work, Pempel first asked who drafted the bills that the Diet passed. He found that bills drafted by ministries passed overwhelmingly, while bills drafted by legislators almost never did. If bureaucrats are writing the statutes (a point confirmed by Table 7.3), Pempel reasoned, then politicians must not be making policy. Second, Pempel examined the use of ministerial regulations. He found that bureaucrats increasingly relied on regulatory measures to implement policy,[2] and concluded: "The emerging picture is of an increasing proportion of the serious political policymaking in Japan taking place outside the public arena of the Diet and under the increasing control of a democratically unresponsible bureaucracy" (1974, p. 656).

In what probably remains the finest study of any single Japanese government institution, Chalmers Johnson (1982) confirms Pempel's analysis. Johnson distinguishes between "reigning and ruling" in Japan (1990, p. 80; see 1985, p. 60), and argues that where politicians reign, bureaucrats rule. Although "influenced by pressure groups and political claimants," bureaucrats "make most major decisions, draft virtually all legislation, control the national budget, and [are] the source of all major policy innovations in the system" (1982, pp. 20–21; see 1985, p. 59). As a result, the Japanese Diet "is one of the weakest parliaments among all the advanced industrial democracies," while the bureaucracy remains "probably the most powerful of that in any contemporary capitalist democracy" (1985, pp. 60–61). Although Japanese legislators may recently have captured some power, at least "from the time of the Occupation and at least until Tanaka's prime ministership (1972–74), the official bureaucracy made all the policies and actually supervised the government" (1990, p. 79; see 1989, p. 182).

Pempel (1982, p. 311; 1992a, 1992b) himself has come to emphasize the ways politicians constrain bureaucrats, but others continue to echo his earlier work. In his elegant study of Japanese law, John Haley (1991, ch. 7) finds that the bureaucracy dominates the Japanese government. Ronald Dore (1986, p. 22) claims that "there is no question of the bureaucracy's intellectual dominance over the Diet." B. C. Koh (1989, p. 257) argues that bureaucrats "continue to play a pivotal role in policy formation, while virtually monopolizing the power of policy implementation." Bradley Richardson and Scott Flanagan (1984, p. 50) contend that "the most important policy decisions" are made outside the Diet. Edward Keehn (1990, p. 1036) claims that the LDP "has passed no reforms that would permit meaningful political management . . . of the bureaucracy's use of standard informal operating procedures." And James Q. Wilson (1989, p. 308) simply declares: "in Japan, the bureaucracy *is* the government."

There have been exceptions. Hans Baerwald has consistently stressed the centrality of politics to the Japanese government (for example, 1986, p. 150). Gerald Curtis (1988, p. 243) argues that Japanese political change has resulted not from "bureaucratic fiat" but from "the responsiveness of the political system to shifting public demands, a responsiveness that in turn has been produced by the LDP's determination to return electoral majorities and retain political power." Several other prominent scholars have begun to hint that bureaucrats may not be all that powerful.[3] And however important he finds the Ministry of Finance (MOF), even John Campbell (1977; see 1989, p. 133) concludes that the LDP participates in many of the most important stages of the budgetary process. Throughout, however, the emphasis on politics has been the exception. Most recent observers find that bureaucratic preferences, not political exigencies, determine Japanese policy. In his recent bestseller, Karel van Wolferen puts it all much more colorfully: legislators "merely rubber-stamp what the bureaucrats put under their noses."[4] In the end, Japanese politicians resemble no one so much as Mencken's Coolidge: "He had no ideas, and he was not a nuisance."

The Indeterminacy of Academic Data

Theory

Where the extant Japanological analysis went wrong is simple and obvious, but only in retrospect: "the process of policy administration by autonomous [ministries] is observationally equivalent to that under strict [legislative] control."[5] So write Randall Calvert, Mark Moran, and Barry Weingast in explaining how American bureaucracies work, and the logic applies equally to Japanese bureaucracies. If bureaucrats—whether Japanese or American—regulate as legislators want them to regulate, then legislators will leave them alone. Absent significant monitoring and policing costs (an issue to which we will return), if—but only if—bureaucrats ignore legislative preferences will legislators intervene. If bureaucrats flout legislative preferences, legislators may reverse those bureaucratic decisions and cut the bureaucrats' discretion and perquisites. Because bureaucrats prefer that these evils never happen, they will try to predict legislative desires and implement them on their own. So long as legislators can cheaply intervene in the bureaucratic process, bureaucrats will seldom ignore legislative preferences and legislatures will seldom interfere in bureaucratic work. Bureaucrats will do what legislators want, but only because legislators will punish them if they do anything else.

An easy analogy is to litigation and settlement. Parties to disputes in Japan (or anywhere else) seldom sue; they settle their quarrels out of court. Yet if either party can threaten to take the dispute into court, the disputants will generally reach out-of-court settlements that deviate from the expected litigated outcome at most by the marginal costs of litigation. Although the parties will not sue, they will settle their disputes according to legal rules (Ramseyer and Nakazato, 1989). In turn, the variance in the settlements they reach will correlate positively with their litigation costs.

The comparison extends to bureaucrats and legislators. Bureaucrats will not be perfect agents; some slack will necessarily inhere in the agency. Given that monitoring and constraining agents takes resources, one would not expect agency slack to be zero. "Because there are increasing marginal costs to measuring and policing performance," as Douglass C. North (1990, p. 32) put it, "the master will stop short of perfect policy." But bureaucrats know that if they deviate too far from legislative preferences, disgruntled legislators will intervene. The legislators will then impose their preferences by statute and, possibly, punish the deviant bureaucrats. Rather than risk that fate, rational bureaucrats will administer programs in ways that deviate from majority legislative preferences by—at most—the costs of legislative action. Bureaucrats will administer in the shadow of the legislators, in short, but with leeway. The amount of that leeway, in turn, will correlate positively with the costs of monitoring and constraining bureaucrats (Calvert, McCubbins, and Weingast, 1989).

Although orthodox Japanologists note how bureaucrats take initiative and exercise discretion, they miss the role initiative and discretion play within principal-agent relationships. Legislators need not shift the locus of power by letting bureaucrats take initiative or exercise discretion. For reasons we have seen, LDP leaders may rationally instruct bureaucrats to draft designated bills. They may even find it advantageous to instruct the bureaucrats (explicitly or implicitly) to draft any bills they think the LDP would find politically advantageous. The leaders do so because they can relatively cheaply police their bureaucratic agents. If the LDP leaders do so delegate, the power will appear to lie with the bureaucracy, for the legislators will appear to "rubber-stamp" the bureaucrats' bills. But the appearances will be deceptive. Legislators will be rubber-stamping them only because the bureaucrats wrote bills the leaders liked.

The Data to Date

Students of Japan have yet to test this hypothesis of relatively faithful bureaucratic agents. Take Pempel's pioneering early work described above. If Japanese bureaucrats will draft the statutes that LDP leaders want, the leaders may rationally delegate those drafting jobs to them. The Diet will then pass the statutes that the bureaucrats draft, but only because the bureaucrats drafted the statutes the LDP leaders wanted anyway. Similarly, suppose that regulations are cheaper than statutes in transactions and organizational costs. If bureaucrats can implement the desired policies through regulation, then LDP leaders may rationally relegate policymaking to the regulatory (rather than statutory) process. The Diet will let stand any regulations that the bureaucrats draft, but only because the bureaucrats draft the regulations the LDP leaders want in the first place. By themselves, neither the percentage of cabinet bills passed nor the ratio of regulations to statutes discloses the relative power of legislators and bureaucrats.

That Japanese bureaucrats draft and regulate in the shadow of the Diet also explains what Johnson and others saw at the ministries. At MITI, Johnson rightly found smart and hardworking bureaucrats discussing policy, drafting statutes and regulations, and doing all this with scarcely a wink from the Diet. But if the MITI bureaucrats were implementing LDP policy preferences, LDP leaders had no reason to interfere. Such bureaucrats would appear autonomous, but in effect they were doing what LDP leaders wanted them to do.

Much the same conclusion follows from Campbell's careful work on the budget. MOF, he nicely notes, "can maintain its power (or its reputation for power) only by refraining from using it; if Finance officials were to attempt, say, a major transfer of funds from one ministry or policy area to another . . . opposition sufficient to veto the move [would] quickly arise." But power one cannot exercise is not power, and all this is not a word game. By Campbell's own description, MOF bureaucrats do *not* independently make policy.

Rather, they operate in the shadow of the LDP. They work on their own, but according to a distinctly political logic.[6]

Rational Delegation

The extent to which Japanese bureaucrats implement legislative preferences remains an open question. Before considering the issue directly, we turn to two subsidiary issues: why LDP leaders might rationally delegate to bureaucrats the jobs of making and implementing policy; and how the leaders would monitor and police their bureaucratic agents.

In part, legislators delegate for some of the same reasons firms subcontract. Firms sell competitive goods or services to stay in business; legislators give their constituents a competitive mix of policies and programs to remain in office. Yet neither firms nor legislators can do this all themselves: they need help. To be sure, firms could hire the requisite employees and legislators could hire more staff. Alternatively, both firms and legislators could subcontract for those services. Even if a firm lacks sufficient employees to do a job, it need not hire more people *into* the firm to survive, but can contract for the services from workers *outside* the firm. So too can legislators purchase the necessary services externally. This is not to say that either in-house staffing or cross-market subcontracting necessarily saves more resources than the other.[7]

More specifically, consider each legislator a program-producing firm. Each firm's profitability (each legislator's payoff in votes and money) will depend on its productivity. In turn, that productivity will be measured by the firm's ability to supply desired programs. To produce those programs the legislative "firm" can either hire its own staff to write the necessary statutes internally, or it can subcontract (through explicit or implicit promises or threats) with someone outside the firm (like a bureaucrat) for those statutes. All else being equal, a legislator will not necessarily prefer one scheme over the other.

But all else is not equal, and the difference between firms and legislators lies in locating *that* difference. By subcontracting with a central bureaucracy for the requisite programmatic services, LDP leaders gain a distinctly *political* advantage. Essentially, the leaders face a threefold choice: (a) supply no staff to any legislator; (b) supply all legislators with the staff necessary to produce programs; or (c) maintain a central government bureaucracy that can write bills and devise programs.

If the LDP leaders picked either the first choice (no staff) or the second (many staffs), they would capture no competitive advantage. Anything LDP legislators obtain, opposition legislators obtain as well. By contrast, if the LDP leaders adopt the third strategy (few legislative staff members but a large central bureaucracy), they potentially provide themselves—but no one else—with an efficient, informed staff. Bureaucrats know that the LDP leaders control the Diet and (potentially) their own careers, while the Diet controls all legislation and their bureaucratic budget. As a result, bureaucrats have a great deal of incentive to please the leaders by acting as their private political staffs. With opposition party members, bureaucrats have no such incentives. As one bureaucrat at the Environmental Agency recently told us: "When an LDP politician asks for information, we give him a hundred pages. When an opposition politician asks, we give him two pages. Basically, we're here to be the LDP's secretariat."

If nothing else, this discussion solves a minor puzzle: why do Japanese legislators allow themselves only two state-funded staff members?[8] From time to time, scholars have noted the small staffs and added that fact to the evidence proving that Japanese legislators do not matter. Ezra Vogel (1979, pp. 60–61; see Fukui, 1987, p. 11), for example, reasons that the staff shortage forces legislators to depend on bureaucrats for expertise. Johnson (1989, p. 199) cites "the lack of staff support" as one of the "reasons for substantive Diet weakness." And Richardson and Flanagan (1984, p. 50) credit the "comparatively weaker staff resources of Japanese Dietmen" for part of the reason the Diet makes so few important policy decisions. If they hired additional staff, these scholars imply, the legislators could be more productive. If they were more productive, they could presumably wrest from the bureaucrats the control over policy.

Why, after all, are there so few state-funded staff members? Legislative staffing is a function of statute, and legislators pass statutes. Trebling the size of their staffs would hardly bankrupt the national budget. If legislators could increase their power by adding staff members, why have they not done so? The answer, we argue, is that they have no reason to do so. LDP leaders already have a responsive personal staff in the government ministries. By forcing others who want more staff members to pay for the staffers themselves from their political war chests, they gain a partisan advantage over the opposition.[9]

Monitoring and Policing Costs

To monitor and police their bureaucratic agents, LDP leaders (and, at times, backbenchers as well)[10] use several devices that, however different in form, resemble in substance many devices corporate firms use to constrain their managerial agents. The leaders face problems of agency slack, after all, and agency slack is common to large organizations of all sorts. More specifically, LDP leaders use the following four devices:

(1) They retain a veto over anything bureaucrats do. Much like corporate directors, they keep the power to refuse any bills the bureaucrats might draft and to overturn by statute any regulations the bureaucrats might promulgate. In the case of a "showdown" between LDP leaders and bureaucrats, the leaders will win—and the bureaucrats know this.

(2) They control promotions. In turn, knowing that the leaders control their professional future, bureaucrats are not likely to ignore LDP policy preferences. Knowing that bureaucrats cannot ignore LDP preferences, leftist college seniors, for example, disproportionately self-select out of bureaucratic jobs.

(3) To obtain the information they need to monitor bureaucrats, LDP leaders use three schemes. They encourage dissatisfied constituents to complain to their local LDP legislator, who can then intervene in the bureaucracy to increase his or her reelection probabilities. They maintain within the most important ministries bureaucrats who intend to join the Diet and who therefore have an incentive to prove their party loyalty by reporting cases of agency slack. They encourage tournaments among the ministries for policy influence, and these tournaments in turn generate information.

(4) Because they require all bureaucrats to retire in their forties

and fifties, LDP leaders force them to treat their anticipated postretirement earnings as a bond. Bureaucrats potentially earn a large fraction of their lifetime wages in postbureaucratic jobs. Because the LDP leaders often control access to those jobs, the leaders can hold those earnings hostage.

Vetoes

Legislators enact bureaucratic programs only at will. The point is obvious and common to most democratic societies, but crucial nonetheless: programs become law only if legislators choose to enact them. And Japanese legislators do not necessarily enact the programs bureaucrats draft. From time to time they do defeat bills that the bureaucrats want badly.[11] As a result, any discretion bureaucrats have in drafting bills is discretion they must exercise in ways legislators will not oppose.[12]

In the same line of argument, legislators decline to overrule programs that bureaucrats implement through regulation (rather than legislation) only if they want to do so. Bureaucrats may pass regulations, but statutes trump regulations and legislators are the ones who pass statutes.[13] Granted, overruling is not always simple. But comparative analysis is crucial here, for this legislative correction is significantly easier in Japan than in the United States. In effect, "structure-induced equilibria"[14] theory predicts that—all else being equal—Japanese legislators are better able to constrain their bureaucratic agents than are American legislators.

The key to this legislative control over regulatory (rather than statutory) measures is Japan's parliamentary structure, combined with the LDP's stable majority and centralized party control. Legislators in presidential systems with alternating majority parties can less readily correct bureaucrats who refuse to implement programs the legislators want. Figure 6.1, for example, shows the policy preferences of a president and unicameral legislature (the "ideal

Fig. 6.1   Bureaucratic implementation and legislative correction (I)

points" P and L) in two-dimensional policy space. The president and legislature delegate the job of implementing their programs to a bureaucracy with its own preferences (point B). A bill becomes law only if the legislature passes it and the president signs it.

Note first that all Pareto-optimal outcomes for the legislature and the president lie on the line segment between their ideal points (the contract curve $C(LP)$). The legislature and president will therefore enact only the programs on the segment. Should the bureaucracy implement the program at a point off the segment (like B), the legislature and president will enact a second statute "correcting" the bureaucracy's policy. Because both the legislature and the president will prefer the points between y and z (the points of intersection between $C[LP]$ and their indifference curves passing through B) to point B, both will agree to enact a statute moving the program from B to a point on $C(yz)$.

Suppose the legislature and president pass a statute locating the program at x (see Figure 6.2), but the bureaucracy implements it instead at b. If the legislature now passed a statute (with less than two-thirds support) to relocate the program to x, the president would veto it. Similarly, if the bureaucracy preferred a point to the left of x, the president would ask the legislature for a corrective statute and the legislature would refuse. Effectively, so long as the bureaucracy implements the legislative program on $C(LP)$, it may be able to insulate itself from statutory correction.

Problems similar to those that plague the legislature and president will also plague legislative coalitions. Suppose two or more political parties must collaborate to pass a statute, but the bureaucracy implements it at a Pareto-optimal point different from the one they specified. The two parties may not be able to correct it.[15] If two or more policy-based groups within a party must collaborate to pass a statute, the same dilemma ensues.

Many of these problems disappear in a parliamentary system with a stable and disciplined majority party. Because the chief

Fig. 6.2   Bureaucratic implementation and legislative correction (II)

executive (the Prime Minister) is also the legislative leader, the ideal points for the chief executive *(P)* and the legislature *(L)* will coincide. Hence the bureaucracy will be unable to exploit any policy space between the two. If one party commands a solid majority, the bureaucracy will also be unable to exploit any policy space between the two (or more) parties to a legislative coalition. And if party leaders can control their backbenchers, bureaucrats will be unable to exploit the policy space among intra-party groups.

These conditions largely describe Japan. It has a parliamentary system, a stable majority party, and strong LDP leaders. Although the party contains several factions, these factions do not reflect policy differences and thus will not create the problems described here. Consequently, the LDP's control over the Japanese bureaucracy should be stronger than that which Congress exercises over American agencies.

Promotions

Legislators can also determine bureaucratic careers. In the United States they appoint, promote, and fire senior bureaucrats. Knowing this, senior bureaucrats appoint, promote, and (where civil service rules do not intervene) fire subordinate bureaucrats in ways that advance legislative preferences since, by doing so, they also advance their own careers. By monitoring and disciplining bureaucrats at the apex, legislators monitor much of the entire bureaucracy.

LDP leaders have the same power over bureaucratic careers. They head the bureaucracy as ministers, ministers control promotions,[16] and the senior bureaucrats heed this. To be sure, it is far from clear how often LDP leaders actually punish renegade bureaucrats. Some scholars argue that "political leaders get involved only rarely in making personnel decisions within the bureaucracy."[17] Others disagree. Yung Chul Park (1986, pp. 61–77) explains in elaborate detail the way politicians, particularly those affiliated with a ministry's PARC, dominate personnel matters. Pempel (1974, p. 653) argues that bureaucrats who push policies contrary to LDP preferences seldom advance beyond bureau chief. B. C. Koh cites a recent study finding "that bureaucrats in . . . top-level positions could lose their jobs should they antagonize key politicians in the ruling political party."[18] Kent Calder (1982, p. 10) notes that Kakuei Tanaka self-consciously manipulated "intraministerial personnel selection policies in a systematic way." Muramatsu and Krauss (1984, p. 143) write that the LDP leaders may even contact private-sector employers to insure that deviant bureaucrats do not find good jobs when they leave the ministry. And one eight-term LDP politician categorically assured us: "People who are not popular with the LDP don't get promoted."

Whatever the case, the quarrel over how often LDP leaders punish bureaucrats bears less on bureaucratic control than one might think: in equilibrium, one would not observe many penalties anyway. LDP leaders can—potentially—punish bureaucrats. Indeed, one agriculture minister began his tenure with a speech to his subordinate bureaucrats (Park, 1986, p. 66): "It is said that art is long and life is short. You must think that 'agriculture lasts long and the minister's life is short.' You fellows don't last long either. My term is at most one year, but I can fire you through evaluations of your work performance. The truth is that 'agriculture is long and the bureaucrat's life is short.'" Bureaucrats know they serve at the pleasure of party leaders and will seldom ignore them. Some bureaucrats even help legislators raise political contributions from corporate constituents, while others threaten regional officials with reduced pork unless they raise votes for the LDP (Sone and Kanazashi, 1989, p. 136; Takeuchi, 1988, pp. 56–68).

Likewise, the bright seniors at the elite national universities who constitute the pool of potential bureaucrats also know that LDP leaders can make or break bureaucratic careers. Students hostile to LDP policies will therefore generally shun bureaucratic careers. Notwithstanding the Marxist domination of Japanese social science faculties, the young people who do join the ministries disproportionately share LDP policy preferences. According to one survey (Koh, 1989, p. 169), 73 percent of the students entering the University of Tokyo law faculty in 1977 identified themselves as "progressive" or "somewhat progressive," as did 40 percent of the freshmen six years later. The poll did not test whether liberal students joined ministries and became conservative, or conservative students chose ministerial jobs; neither did it compare Tokyo graduates in the ministries with other Tokyo graduates of the same age. But it did find that only 16 percent of the graduates of the Tokyo law faculty who worked as bureaucrats labeled themselves as at least "somewhat progressive."

With conservatives disproportionately staffing the bureaucracies, bureaucrats have a self-interest in seeing the LDP maintain its control over the Diet. For if the bureaucrats who staff the ministries largely share LDP policy preferences themselves, they would not enjoy working for a Socialist cabinet. In short, Japanese bureaucrats, like the LDP leaders for whom they work, have a *personal* interest in their party's electoral success.

Information

LDP leaders also manipulate the institutional structure of the Japanese government to acquire the information they need to constrain their bureaucratic agents. Some scholars argue to the contrary. Many years ago, for example, Johnson (1975, p. 8) argued that the LDP's failure to maintain "cabinet assistants" who would coordinate the various ministries explained the legislative weakness he found. Yet as he himself has more recently suggested (1990), many legislators have also worked in the bureaucracy (see Tables 6.1 and

Table 6.1 Former elite bureaucrats newly elected to the Lower House

Election Year	Bureau chief and above			Section chief and below		
	LDP[a]	JSP	Other	LDP[a]	JSP	Other
1946	4	1	0	6	3	0
1947	9	0	0	8	1	0
1949	18	0	0	15	0	0
1952	29	2	0	16	0	0
1953	7	0	0	4	1	0
1955	9	2	0	3	0	0
1958	3	1	0	0	0	0
1960	9	0	0	3	0	0
1963	5	0	0	2	1	1
1967	2	0	0	5	1	1
1969	6	0	0	4	0	0
1972	2	0	0	8	1	0
1976	8	0	0	6	1	1
1979	2	0	0	4	0	2
1980	0	0	0	3	0	0
1983	1	0	0	7	0	1

Source: Satō and Matsuzaki (1986, p. 223).
   a. The figures for the LDP include the New Liberal Club and the pre-1955 conservative parties. Only central national bureaucrats were counted.

6.2). They understand it well and know how to manipulate it. Other legislators acquire basic expertise through their years in PARC. Without ignoring these sources of expertise, we note three less obvious but at least equally basic ways the LDP leaders stay informed.

First, LDP leaders encourage constituents dissatisfied with bureaucratic service to complain to their local legislator. LDP Diet-members use these interventionist services to maximize their "personal support" networks; LDP leaders encourage these networks to maximize the party's strength under Japan's multi-member district system. In the process, the party acquires information about bureaucratic attempts to subvert LDP policy preferences (McCubbins and Schwartz, 1984).

Second, LDP leaders monitor the bureaucracy through *present* bureaucrats who intend *later* to join the Diet. Bureaucrats regularly abandon their jobs for LDP seats in the Diet. Table 6.1 details the extent of these lateral moves. On average, thirteen new bureaucrats join the LDP in the Diet at each election. Even excluding the aberrant elections of 1949 and 1952, nine new bureaucrats join at every election.

Whether bureaucrats successfully switch to explicitly political careers depends critically on the goodwill they have earned with senior LDP legislators. For civil servants who want to go into politics will generally succeed only with substantial financial and organizational help from the LDP. While they are still bureaucrats, therefore, these political hopefuls will seek to curry favor with senior legislators. If other bureaucrats try to flout LDP preferences, they will have an incentive to constrain them or to report them to the leadership. For their part, the party leaders scout the ministries for political talent, train these potential politicians in a preliminary way (often by arranging to have them seconded to a minister as secretary), and then require them to make their postretirement legislative jobs and earnings contingent upon their good behavior. Effectively, they use them as LDP "moles" within the ministries.

This bonding system does not work equally well everywhere. As Table 6.2 shows, it more effectively facilitates monitoring at some ministries than at others. For instance, bureaucrats apparently enter politics most regularly from the Ministries of Internal Affairs,[19] Finance, Foreign Affairs, Agriculture and Forestries, International

Table 6.2 Former elite bureaucrats in the Lower House

Former ministry	Year of election													Mean
	1949	1952	1953	1955	1958	1960	1963	1967	1969	1972	1976	1979	1980	
Internal Affairs[a]	4	6	15	15	15	15	19	16	18	16	11	13	8	13.15
MOF	1	4	10	8	10	11	11	12	11	12	15	16	14	10.38
Foreign Affairs	4	8	7	6	11	7	6	3	6	6	5	5	2	5.85
Agriculture and Forestry	2	4	5	2	5	4	5	8	7	7	6	3	3	5.00
MITI	1	4	5	8	5	6	7	7	4	5	4	1	3	4.62
Transportation	0	3	3	3	3	4	6	6	5	5	5	4	4	3.92
Justice	4	4	2	3	3	4	3	3	2	2	2	2	1	2.69
Labor	0	1	1	1	0	1	1	1	1	1	1	5	6	1.54
Health and Welfare	0	0	2	1	1	1	0	1	1	1	1	1	1	.85
Posts and Telecommunications	1	2	0	1	0	0	0	0	0	1	1	1	1	.62
Construction	0	0	1	0	0	0	0	0	0	1	1	1	2	.46
Education	0	0	0	0	0	0	0	0	0	0	0	0	0	.00
Other	1	1	1	2	5	2	3	3	2	3	2	1	0	2.00

Source: Naka (1980, pp. 486–88).

Note: The table lists only former bureaucrats who joined the LDP, had reached at least the level of section chief at the central national ministry, and ran for the Diet immediately after resigning from the ministry. Thus it covers a slightly different range of legislators from those in Table 6.1.

a. The Ministry of Internal Affairs includes both the prewar Naimu shō and the postwar Jichi shō.

Trade and Industry, and Transportation. At least at those ministries, the LDP may have the moles it needs.[20]

Third, political leaders generate information by encouraging competition among the ministries (Bagnoli and McKee, 1991). That Japanese bureaucrats fight over turf is commonplace, of course. MITI and MOF quarrel regularly over tax incentives. MITI and the Fair Trade Commission quarrel over cartel policy. MOF and Posts and Telecommunications quarrel over postal savings. And MOF and everyone else quarrel over the budget.

Through such bureaucratic turf battles, the LDP leaders acquire crucial information. To see their programs realized, bureaucrats must compete against each other for political support. After all, LDP leaders sponsor only programs they believe will boost the party's electoral success. To locate those programs, they effectively conduct policy tournaments among the ministries. Obviously, within these tournaments each ministry has an incentive to tout the virtues of its own programs. Less obviously perhaps, it also has an incentive to advertise the faults of everyone else's.

This process is much like that which occurs in most economic markets (see Milgrom and Roberts, 1986). To attract customers, sellers have an incentive to provide positive information about their own wares, and negative information about those of their competitors. Even without mandatory disclosure rules, therefore, most competitive markets will generate information. More precisely, except when the information is a public good, most competitive markets will generate the optimal amount of information. So too will this market for political programs. By fostering rivalry among ministries and a competitive market for policies, LDP leaders generate much of the information they need.

Bonds

Despite these arrangements, LDP leaders may still acquire less-than-optimal information, and may acquire it late. At the same time, by delegating important work to bureaucrats they inevitably create the risk that their bureaucratic agents will expropriate part or all of their constituents' interests (Williamson, 1990, p. 27). To mitigate this agency slack, they require even non-Diet-bound bureaucrats to post their late-career earnings as a bond (Lazear, 1979, 1981, 1991).

Without the bonding device to act as deterrent, the prestige that Japanese bureaucrats hold and the discretion they wield would likely attract all sorts of recruits, not only those committed to LDP preferences. Thus leftist bureaucrats would find it convenient to lie about their preferences and enlist in the ministries. They could then skew government administration leftward. When discovered, they would lose their jobs. But so long as they earned a market wage in the interim, many would find the jobs attractive.

LDP leaders mitigate this agency slack by requiring bureaucrats to post their postministerial salaries as bonds that they forfeit if they fail to implement LDP preferences. During their time at the ministry, the bureaucrats work for less than their spot-market wage. If they ignore LDP preferences, they then forfeit the shortfall; if they implement those preferences faithfully, they receive the shortfall as high salaries in the jobs they get after their mandatory retirement from government service.

During their tenure in office, Japanese bureaucrats earn far less than what they could command in other jobs (Matsui, 1984). Table 6.3 shows the salaries elite bureaucrats earn; Table 6.4 shows what they might earn elsewhere. These bureaucratic salaries are low compared even to general income levels: the monthly mean national wage is ¥357,000 (Rōdōshō, 1990, p. 369), while a rough

Table 6.3 Monthly salary ranges for elite national bureaucrats (in yen)

Pay grade	Salary range	Number of persons within range
3	146,600–279,900	1,865
4	177,800–329,100	628
5	193,900–345,300	912
6	212,200–378,000	863
7	230,100–387,400	767
8	249,500–410,000	2,315
9	280,000–444,100	1,192
10	315,100–466,500	982
11	359,200–529,700	1,207

Source: Jinji in (1990, pp. 71, 86–87, 190–91).

Note: Salary ranges effective April 1, 1989 ($1.00 equalled ¥132.5); personnel distribution as of March 31, 1989. Given the Japanese custom of biannual bonuses, government employees generally receive approximately 17 months' salary each year. "Elite national bureaucrats" are bureaucrats hired upon passing the National Public Servant Examination I.

Table 6.4   Comparative monthly salaries (in yen)

Political posts[a]	
Prime Minister	1,892,000
Cabinet member	1,319,000
Large firms—male college graduates (by age)[b]	
20–24	173,000
25–29	213,500
30–34	283,000
35–39	363,300
40–44	438,100
45–49	522,100
50–54	578,900
55–59	545,300
Large firms—senior positions[c]	
Chairman of the board	2,780,000
President	2,440,000
Vice-president	1,750,000
Medical personnel[d]	
Hospital director	1,312,252
Hospital assistant director	1,297,400
Hospital department chair	962,415
Physician	762,558

Sources: For *political posts;* Nihon minshu hōritsuka kyōkai (1990, p. 471). For *large firms, male college graduates:* Rōdōshō (1989, p. 114). For *large firms, senior positions:* Yakunin no hōshū, shōyo, nenshū (1990, p. 14). For *medical personnel:* Jinji in (1986, p. 74).

  a. As of April 1, 1989.

  b. Mean salaries for employees at firms with 1,000 or more employees, 1988.

  c. Mean salaries at firms with 3,000 or more employees, 1989.

  d. Mean salaries, 1986 data.

average of Table 6.3 (we do not know the distribution *within* each pay grade) gives a mean elite bureaucratic wage of ¥318,000. This comparison understates the sacrifice bureaucrats make, however. For the ministries hire as elite bureaucrats the brightest students at the preeminent national universities. These graduates would have commanded much more than the mean national wage.

    Bureaucrats collect a large part of their potential lifetime earnings only if they successfully "retire" with their reputations intact. Between the ages of 40 and 55, elite bureaucrats leave the ministries to take positions located for them by their ministry, either in private firms that deal with the ministry or in one of a variety of government-affiliated firms.[21] Effectively, they exit their ministries through a one-way, one-time revolving door and take high-paying senior jobs at public or private firms (a practice known as *amakudari*). Consider one sample of 108 bureaucrats who had retired from the bureaucracy into 51 government-affiliated firms. They later retired for good from those firms, between November 1989 and October 1990. Before quitting, the former bureaucrats had earned a mean monthly salary of 833,000 yen. When they did quit, they received additional benefits averaging 14,430,000 yen.[22] Essentially, they earned low wages for the bureaucratic one-half to two-thirds of their careers, and high wages for the corporate remainder.

Bureaucrats will find these lucrative postretirement jobs only if they perform in ways acceptable to LDP leaders. As Muramatsu and Krauss (1984, p. 143) note, the leaders can easily kill unresponsive bureaucrats' chances in the postbureaucratic job market. Just as American CPAs guard their reputations for honesty in the local community to protect their future incomes, so too Japanese bureaucrats guard their ties with the LDP to protect their back-end returns.

Consider a simplified two-period account of all this. During the first period, bureaucrats work at a ministry for infra-market wages. They know the ministry will give them no help in finding a second-period job if they perform poorly, but it promises them a high-paying job that compensates them for their low first-period earnings if they perform well. It keeps its word because it would radically raise its costs in the first-period market if it reneged.

Table 6.5   Final positions of former bureaucrats who attained level of bureau chief or higher, 1988

Ministry	Political posts	Private firms	Special firms[a]	Other	Total
Posts and Telecommunications	4	37	41	1	83
Health and Welfare	3	8	39	21	71
MITI	4	71	33	6	114
Transportation	13	44	67	4	128
MOF	11	59	62	7	139
Agriculture and Forestry	18	16	71	8	113
Education	1	12	17	13	43

Source: Seifu kankei tokushu hōjin rōdō kumiai kyōgikai (1989, p. 100).
    a. Includes *tokushu hōjin* (special firms) and *kōeki hōjin* (public interest corporations), which are likely to have particularly close ties to the government (Johnson, 1975, pp. 23–27).

If the ministry places a second-period bureaucrat in a government-funded firm, the recruit will be staying on the government payroll during his or her entire career. The government will simply pay his or her wages for the two periods from different lines in the national budget. If the bureaucrat moves to a financially independent firm, that private firm will be paying the second-period wage. The wage will have to be high enough to compensate the bureaucrat for his or her low first-period wages. Nonetheless, the firm willingly pays it since the bureaucrat will bring government connections that generate pork in compensation. Effectively, the government will still be paying the supra-market portion of the second-period wage.

Given the bad press this arrangement receives in Japan (see Murobushi, 1983, pp. 116–37; Seifu, 1981–91), one should stress that it need not *necessarily* be inefficient. Private firms may hire bureaucrats to help them feed at the public trough, but they hire them in a competitive market in which they command salaries that capture for themselves much of the pork they obtain. In turn, the ministries also hire first-period bureaucrats in a competitive market in which the employer agrees to pay only first-period wages that are low enough to offset the expected high second-period wages. Ultimately, the bureaucrats will receive market lifetime earnings, the government will pay market wages, and the firms will earn zero profits.

The arrangement *could* be inefficient, but the potential problems are not those listed above; they will most likely derive from two seldom mentioned sources. First, ex-bureaucrats will rarely be able to obtain pork through a simple phone call. Instead, the rent-seeking process itself will dissipate resources.[23] Second, the government may choose to compensate the ex-bureaucrat's employer through anticompetitive restraints rather than through simple financial grants (Stigler, 1971). If so, the usual dead-weight losses will also ensue. Unfortunately, the logic of Chapter 2 suggests that this may be the norm in Japan.[24]

Conclusion

Despite decades of Japanese studies arguing the contrary, the LDP does monitor and police its bureaucrats. The party leaders keep the power to veto any actions their bureaucrats take. They retain control over individual bureaucratic careers. They encourage disaf-

fected constituents to complain to their legislators about unresponsive bureaucrats. They maintain within the bureaucracy young
would-be politicians who have every incentive to report bureaucratic violations of LDP preferences. They force ministries to compete for policy implementation. And they require bureaucrats to
post large portions of their lifetime earnings as bonds contingent
on faithful performance.

The result ought to be a relatively responsive bureaucracy. There
is evidence that LDP leaders can and do entrust bureaucrats with
the job of furthering the party's distinctly political aims. The image
of a largely autonomous bureaucracy that promotes its own distinctive vision of the Japanese commonweal may be no more than a
mirage. Real Japanese bureaucrats, the evidence suggests, administer in the shadow of the LDP.

7

Bureaucratic Manipulation

The Japanese firms in the low-end textile market have been obsolete for decades. Not, however, that one could tell by looking at government policy. In 1956 MITI drafted and the Diet passed a statute to reduce competition. In 1964 the Diet passed another statute to let the firms collude. In 1967 it passed another, and again in 1972, 1974, and 1979.[1] Even though the firms had long since lost any comparative advantage,[2] MITI bureaucrats madly drafted statutes as if somehow, given just one more anticompetitive chance, the firms might yet survive. Those officials American academics and journalists so relentlessly praise as the architects of Japan's "plan-rational developmental state" were writing and rewriting laws to salvage terminally unsalvageable firms, in the process potentially transferring massive wealth from consumers to industry.

"So what?" a fast-track MITI bureaucrat asked one of us several years ago. "We know the industry won't last. We've known that for years. But in the meantime these textile firms use people who vote LDP. The party's got to be able to show them that it cares. So we do our part. We give the politicians a new statute to show the textile people every year."

The MITI bureaucrats were indeed giving the politicians politically convenient statutes, even if not quite one a year. The pattern is not peculiar to textiles, however, but basic to Japanese politics, for Japanese bureaucrats routinely draft, regulate, and implement in the shadow of politics. They write the bills that will best promote LDP electoral odds, and administer them in ways that will best lead to the same end. They do so because they have no choice. Should they try anything else, LDP leaders will not pass the statutes they write, will legislate against the regulations they promulgate, and may do what they can to see that their careers go nowhere.

Having explored the organizations and institutions that LDP leaders use to gain and retain bureaucratic control, we will outline evidence that suggests—however tentatively—that they largely succeed. We ask, first, how deeply voters care about a politician's ability to control the bureaucracy and, second, how extensively politicians delegate control over politically sensitive matters to the bureaucracy. Finally, we measure how successfully they rely on bureaucrats to craft their politically driven policy changes.

Bureaucratic Control and the Voting Market

All else being equal, voters prefer politicians who can manipulate the bureaucracy to those who cannot. Although the point applies to most modern democracies, it is basic to Japan. Given the combination of a single nontransferable vote with multi-member electoral districts, politicians have traditionally competed in part through personalized bureaucratic interventionist services. More than occasional mediation is at stake. Politicians affiliated with a party that controls the bureaucracy can redistribute extensive wealth from the national treasury to their home districts, and shift undesirable consequences of development from their home districts to areas under opposition control. LDP leaders work hard to keep such pork-barrel politics in check. Subject to the (often stringent) limits these leaders impose, however, politicians who dominate the bureaucracy can bring into their districts highways, schools, airports, and cash; out of their districts they can send toxic wastes and sewage plants.

As a result, politicians who can dominate the bureaucracy hold a major electoral advantage. At root, voters like representatives who can manipulate bureaucrats. Indeed, Japanese bookstores routinely stock books (for example, Inō, 1984) explaining how to use Diet-members to obtain commercial licenses, to place children in public schools outside one's school district, or to have streets repaired, trash collected, bicycle lanes created, and sewers installed.

The acknowledged master of bureaucratic manipulation was former Prime Minister Kakuei Tanaka. Tanaka represented a district Chalmers Johnson (1986, p. 3) once nicely described as a cross "between Mississippi and Vermont." Railroads to such an area were hardly a national priority. But Tanaka's was a face that launched a thousand trains. He promised his constituents he would double-track the local railroad, and by 1967 he did. Never satisfied, he promised them a bullet train as well. Thanks largely to his bureaucratic influence, the state-owned railroad authority then laid 300 kilometers of the wide-gauge track to take the bullet train into his district, dug 103 kilometers of tunnels, and built five special stations, all at a cost of ¥480 billion. As MOF Minister and senior LDP statesman, Tanaka increased the subsidies to his prefecture from ¥12.1 billion in 1962 to ¥24.1 billion in 1965 and ¥53.3 billion in 1970. By the time he became Prime Minister in 1972, he had raised the subsidies to ¥80.6 billion. In 1982, the residents of his prefecture paid an average $541 in taxes and received per capita public works of $1,644. By contrast, Tokyo residents paid $3,060 for public works of $815.[3] Local voters duly appreciated all this bureaucratic manipulation. They continued to reelect him by massive margins even after the Lockheed bribery scandal, and one local singer cut a record about him that seems sappy by any standard (Kobayashi, 1989, p. 157):

> Oh, I'd like to give [my daughter]
>   to a man like Tanaka,
> With a big heart and compassion.
>   Oh, I'd love to find a groom like him.

Although most politicians operate at more mundane levels—if only because of the limits party leaders impose—Japanese voters prize politicians who can control bureaucrats. By way of ethnographic example, consider the local electoral politics of Takachiho, a relatively obscure mountain village in southern Japan.[4] As of 1988, it had 18,800 citizens, with over 40 percent engaged in primary industries (principally agriculture) (*Jichishō*, 1988, p. 431).

Through most of the late nineteenth century, Takachiho villagers chose members of the traditional social and economic elites as their leaders. Few of these men had had any bureaucratic experience outside Takachiho, but all had had connections to the Tazaki house, the richest in the area. As the wealth available through the national and prefectural governments grew, however, so did the value of leaders who could exploit that potential. The traditional leaders did not meet that criterion, since most of them could tap governmental wealth no more effectively than anyone else. Consequently, voters began to reject them and to choose instead men who had cultivated their access to the bureaucracy.

The result was a major shift in power around the turn of the century. With large national and prefectural budgets, Takachiho benefited most if its leaders could manipulate the agents of those governments. To obtain a share of those budgets, its citizens now elected men with less wealth or status than the Tazaki men, but with better contacts in the bureaucracy. The men they chose were men who had already worked in the bureaucracy—and the men, therefore, who could best obtain the bridges and roads.[5]

Because prefectural and national bureaucrats continue to control large rents and subsidies, the successful Takachiho mayors have continued, in one anthropologist's words, to be people "who can use [their] relationships" with bureaucrats "to secure benefits for [the] municipality" (R. Ramseyer, 1974, p. 46). Dealing with bureaucrats is a large part of the mayor's mandate, and toward that end he "spends a great deal of his time in the prefectural capital and in Tokyo." By contrast, "the internal affairs of the town" are matters he leaves "in the hands of his administrative assistant" (p. 46). To be sure, all this pork-barrel manipulation remains subject to the constraints imposed by the LDP leadership. Because some room for bureaucratic interventionist services nonetheless remains, elite MOF and MITI bureaucrats can often translate their knowledge about the bureaucracy into national electoral prominence. For the same reason, village-level bureaucrats can transform their connections into local political power.

The Political Control of Elite Bureaucrats

Tanaka manipulated the Construction Ministry more than any other. The ministry has long obliged politicians, and even some scholars who consider many Japanese bureaucrats autonomous characterize the Construction Ministry as a politically driven pork wagon. When scholars argue over Japanese bureaucratic leadership, they focus mainly on "independent" agencies like the Fair Trade Commission (FTC) and the two ministries most often credited with Japan's allegedly "plan-rational" economic growth: MOF and

MITI. In fact, MOF, MITI, and the nominally independent agencies all regulate by a political logic explicitly tied to LDP electoral success.[6]

MOF

Consider the repeated attempts by MOF bureaucrats to consolidate the financial services industry. For decades, they have implicitly guaranteed deposits against bank failure. Wary of the potential liability, for decades they have also sought a more streamlined and profitable banking industry. Toward that aim, they have regularly tried to consolidate the banks to make them both better diversified and more easily monitored. In this they have consistently failed. Although the Japanese financial services industry today boasts a dozen or so world-class banks, it continues also to contain a vast array of small, local financial institutions.

MOF bureaucrats have failed because of the support financial institutions give the LDP. The recent segment of this story begins with the last years of the American Occupation, when the LDP's two predecessor parties were actively catering to the banking sector. One of the parties allied itself with the banks; the other courted the smaller credit-union-like institutions (the *mujin*). The former had the ministry's implicit deposit guarantee; the latter did not. But the latter calculated that they could obtain the guarantee if the government would merely license them. MOF bureaucrats agreed that licensing probably would carry with it that implicit guarantee. For that very reason, they opposed it. They wanted to streamline the industry, after all, not support its proliferation (Rosenbluth, 1989a, p. 118; 1989b).

The fight with the credit unions was but one of the first of the postwar battles MOF bureaucrats would lose. They lost it because the credit-union representatives took their case to the politicians, and the politicians listened. Through them, the credit unions obtained the licensing scheme they wanted and, with it, their implicit deposit guarantee. Given the political influence of the various financial institutions, MOF bureaucrats could not revoke the implicit guarantee they had given the banks, could not now deny it to the credit unions, and could not even convert it into an expanded formal insurance system and charge them all for the coverage.[7]

In 1951, MOF bureaucrats proposed a new banking law to mitigate some of their problems. With it they hoped to acquire the power to ban the compensating-balance requirements banks used to circumvent interest-rate ceilings; to limit bank dividends and salaries; to raise capital requirements; and to restrict the amounts banks could lend to any one borrower. The banks did what the credit unions had done: they complained to the politicians. To depoliticize the issue, the MOF invited banking leaders to a conference on the issue, but that invitation was too little and came too late. Other party politicians had already sided with the banks, and the bureaucrats had to abandon their bill.[8]

Five years later, MOF bureaucrats were ready to try again. In their new proposal, they focused more narrowly on the smaller banks and gave themselves the power to replace bank managers if the latter broke the law, ignored MOF directives, or took actions they (the bureaucrats) thought contrary to the public interest. Again, it was no contest. Bankers turned to the politicians, the latter listened, and the bill failed (Rosenbluth, 1989a, p. 120; 1989b).

By 1964, MOF bureaucrats opted for a different tack: encourage the weaker financial firms to merge with the stronger ones. As the bureaucrats gave the firms little reason to merge, however, not much changed. To be sure, the Daiichi Bank acquired an affiliated bank, and the Sumitomo Bank absorbed a partial subsidiary. But the massive spate of mergers that the bureaucrats wanted never materialized.[9]

Under the rubric of an "efficiency campaign," the bureaucrats tried again a few years later. This time they provided incentives for the mergers, including tax and antitrust advantages, and had more success. Between 1968 and 1973, the smaller financial institutions participated in many mergers, some of them thereby graduating to "bank" status. But many of the smaller institutions still preferred to forego the mergers and use their political clout to enhance the benefits they already enjoyed: the branch restrictions, for example, or the legal segmentation of the market and the fixed interest-rate structure. These small firms retained their political power because their role in the local community and their ties to their clients gave them a vote-gathering ability the politicians could not ignore. The money they donated to political coffers augmented that power.[10]

By the mid-1970s, MOF bureaucrats were ready once more to

eliminate the hold-out firms. Thus MOF Banking Bureau Director Hiroshi Tokuda announced in 1977 that "there are too many banking institutions," and launched a "new efficiency campaign." The campaign went nowhere, though, for Tokuda began by supporting Sumitomo Bank's proposal to acquire the reluctant Kansai Mutual Bank. The association of mutual banks rallied to defend Kansai Mutual, and an association of small financial institutions soon followed suit. The politicians remembered their debts and sided with the firms: in November 1978 Prime Minister Takeo Fukuda assured the mutual bank association that he supported their cause. Within a week Tokuda told Sumitomo Bank to cancel the merger.[11]

Three decades, a foiled banking law, and two efficiency campaigns later, MOF bureaucrats still had not consolidated the industry (see Table 7.1).[12] *Sic biscuitus disintegrat,* as Iris Murdoch once put it. Granted, Japan's top banks were among the largest and safest in the world. But the smaller firms remained in business too, many of them just barely. These were the firms that most worried the bureaucrats, for MOF remained their implicit guarantor. In 1979 the bureaucrats launched yet another campaign, this time for more consolidation, stronger regulatory powers, higher net-worth ratios, and stricter disclosure rules. But, again, the firms turned for help to the politicians. The financial firms were heavy contributors to the LDP, and the party leaders were worried about the inroads opposition parties were making among them. The LDP leaders again opposed the bureaucrats and the legislature passed only a drastically weakened version of MOF's bill.[13]

The conflict continues, of course. In 1984 MOF bureaucrats proposed a bill that would give them power to force financial firms to merge; the bill failed. They proposed a sturdier formal deposit insurance system; the banks transformed it into one that raised the coverage without proportionately raising the charge to the financial firms.[14] If MOF bureaucrats ever do obtain the consolidation they want, it will only be when the LDP itself lowers its reliance on the small business sector.

The point is not that the interests of MOF bureaucrats are identical to those of LDP politicians. As this history of the banking industry illustrates, bureaucrats often push policies that politicians seem not to want. The basic point is that the LDP always has the last word: if the party does not like a bill, it need not pass it.

Table 7.1 Financial institutions in Japan

Year	City banks	Regional banks	Trust banks	Long-term credit banks	Mutual banks[a]	Credit associations[a]
1945	8	53	18	4	58	312
1950	11	56	6	3	64	620
1955	13	65	6	2	71	553
1960	13	64	7	3	72	538
1965	13	63	7	3	72	526
1966	13	63	7	3	72	523
1967	13	63	7	3	72	521
1968	14	62	7	3	71	520
1969	15	61	7	3	71	507
1970	15	61	7	3	72	502
1971	14	61	7	3	71	484
1972	14	63	7	3	72	485
1973	13	63	7	3	72	484
1974	13	63	7	3	72	476
1975	13	63	7	3	72	471
1976	13	63	7	3	71	470
1977	13	63	7	3	71	468
1978	13	63	7	3	71	468
1979	13	63	7	3	71	462
1980	13	63	7	3	71	461
1981	13	63	7	3	71	456
1982	13	63	7	3	71	456
1983	13	63	7	3	71	456
1984	13	64	7	3	69	456
1985	13	64	7	3	69	456
1986	13	64	7	3	68	455
1987	13	64	7	3	68	455
1988	13	64	7	3	68	455
1989	13	64	7	3	68	454

Sources: Nihon ginkō chōsa tōkei kyoku, *Keizai tōkei nempō* (Economic Statistics Annual) (Tokyo: Nihon ginkō, various years); Zenkyoku shin'yō kinko kyōkai (1977, p. 968).
a. "Mutual bank" refers to *sōgō ginkō*; "credit association" refers to *shin'yō kinko*.

This friction between the LDP politicians and the banking bureaucrats mirrors the conflict between LDP leaders and backbenchers detailed in Chapter 5. When bureaucrats promote policies that LDP politicians resist, the politicians object because the policies harm the members of their particular support groups. Yet these policies would often promote the collective welfare of the party.

In substance, the conflict between the bureaucrats and the LDP politicians replicates the ongoing push-and-pull that takes place between LDP leaders and their backbenchers. Although backbenchers do monitor bureaucrats at the local level, the party leaders exercise far more comprehensive control. These party leaders use that control to force bureaucrats to design and implement policies that enhance the welfare of the party *as a whole*. The resulting policies (particularly at the MOF) frequently involve public goods, and their provision often limits the private goods on which individual LDP politicians so often rely. As a result, an *apparent* conflict between bureaucrats and politicians ensues.

MITI

MITI bureaucrats regulate at least as much by a political script as do their counterparts from MOF. Take the recent construction of a nuclear power plant in Fukushima Prefecture.[15] The presence of a port at the city of Soma made the prefecture ideal for a power plant. At issue, therefore, was where within the prefecture to put it. Soma had a Socialist mayor, while the surrounding towns—including one called Shinchi-machi—were LDP. In Japan, as here, voters like it when the government dispenses cheap electricity and subsidies, but dislike it when nuclear plants move into their neighborhoods.

The job of finding the site fell to MITI bureaucrats, who performed with marvellous political creativity: they placed the plant on the Shinchi-machi side of the border with Soma. Because the plant was on the border of the two towns, half the risks fell on the Socialist-controlled city. Because it was technically within Shinchi-machi, the bulk of the contracts and subsidies that accompanied it went to the LDP-controlled town.

The retail industry provides yet another example of the political logic underlying MITI's policies. Small businesses have long supported the LDP, and small retailers—collectively employing some 9.7 million workers (*Chūshō*, 1991, p. 265)—have long been part of that constituency. During the 1960s, these retailers faced increasing pressure from newer, larger, and cheaper supermarkets. To retain their support, Prime Minister Yasuhiro Nakasone promised to reduce that pressure (Upham, 1991, pp. 50–51). Toward that end, MITI drafted and the Diet passed the Large Stores Act.[16]

The Large Stores Act was a typical MITI statute, both in its super-ficially neutral design and in its fundamentally political logic. For-mally, it invoked all the platitudes orthodox scholars ascribe to Japanese regulation. The opening section, for example, described the goal of the Act as "the healthy development of the national economy." It instructed MITI to "consider the protection of con-sumer interests" and to promote the "appropriate development of the retail industry," while yet "guaranteeing the business opportu-nities of local small- and medium-sized retailers" (§1).

But such rhetorical flourishes mean no more in Japan than they do in the United States—perhaps even less. At root, the Diet passed the statute to help the local retailers because they had faithfully supported the LDP.[17] Many of these local merchants did eventually benefit from the statute. To be sure, their relief came only after some delay, as the initial regulatory program did not stop development as effectively as they had hoped. Consequently, they continued to demand more stringent regulation during much of the 1970s. By the early 1980s, however, MITI bureaucrats had solved the "prob-lem." In effect, they did so by assigning retailers a property right in their existing market share. Under the scheme, developers could not build a supermarket unless they first bought out the local retailers; only with the consent of the local merchants would the bureaucrats let them proceed. Predictably, this consent took years to obtain (Table 7.2), and sometimes over a decade.[18]

Developers now opened far fewer stores. From 1979 to 1983, the annual number of new supermarket construction notices fell from 576 to 125. It stayed under 200 until the late 1980s (Tsūsan shō, 1989, p. 190). Developers who did manage to open a supermarket typically did so only after contributing large amounts of money to local merchants and consenting to drastic reductions in floor space (see Table 7.2) as well as limits on discount sales, advertising, and levels of service.[19] "Whatever else one might say about this scheme," legal scholar Frank Upham (1991, p. 50) concludes, "it is not what one would expect of regulation by an elite bureaucracy regulating the market in the national interest." No, indeed. But it is fully consistent with what one would expect of regulation by an elite bureaucracy regulating the market in the LDP's electoral interest.[20]

Table 7.2 New supermarket openings

Announced opening date	Number of stores	Announced mean floor space (m²)	Mean reduction in floor space (%)	Mean opening delay (mos.)
1972	11	8,002	10.1	48
1973	10	9,848	23.2	49
1974	9	11,189	10.2	36
1975	24	13,515	36.3	50
1976	18	13,032	39.6	54
1977	27	11,471	32.8	39
1978	24	11,774	42.7	52
1979	27	11,609	36.9	56
1980	21	13,064	37.2	62
1981	27	12,007	36.7	67
1982	17	8,701	31.7	44
1983	9	11,725	23.7	54
1984	8	11,782	31.3	49
1985	4	8,623	13.5	39
1986	3	9,484	36.9	36
Mean	—	11,552	33.6	51

Source: Tsuruta and Yahagi, in Miwa and Nishimura (1990, p. 300). The figures are based on data from six large supermarket chains: Daiei, Itōyōkadō, Seiyū, Jasco, Nichii, and Yunii.

FTC

Because LDP leaders can trust bureaucrats to further the party's political advantage, they also delegate to them a wide variety of anticompetitive programs through the Japanese "antitrust" scheme. American occupational authorities imposed on Japan an Antimonopoly Act in 1947.[21] That original statute, however, has been but a small part of the antitrust program. Soon after the occupation ended, the Diet amended the Act to let majority legislators sell cartels for money and votes (Law No. 259 of 1953). More properly, it amended the Act to let firms cartelize their industry if they could convince the FTC that theirs was a "failing industry." Under the terms of this newly revised statute, they could then fix prices and coordinate production cuts (§24–3).

The official reason for this 1953 amendment was to prevent

"excess competition"; the effective result was to begin to convert the antitrust program into a pork barrel that the LDP could manipulate through the bureaucracy to its electoral advantage.[22] The program's beneficiaries were to be the business supporters of the LDP—particularly, for much of the postwar era, the small firms. Since 1953, politicians and bureaucrats have used this antitrust pork barrel aggressively. As of 1983, the FTC had approved 71 depression cartels. They involved 4 to 174 firms each, and 50 of the cartels had been renewed at least once. Most lasted from one half to two years.[23]

The government also inserted "recession cartels" into the Antimonopoly Act. Under this more modest designation, firms can share technology and transportation facilities, and buy and sell products collusively (§24–4). As of 1983 the FTC had only authorized 13 such cartels, but those approved had lasted long—an average of 105.5 months. The cartel in the rayon yarn industry had lasted from 1955 to 1971. The one in the iron and steel scrap industry lasted from 1955 to 1974 (Uesugi, 1986, p. 413).

More important than either depression or recession cartels have been those the LDP authorizes through MITI under various ad hoc anticompetitive statutes. As of 1989, 37 of these cartel-authorizing statutes were in place (*Kōsei*, 1989, p. 106). Potentially, the exemptions may have had a massive effect. In 1966, when the LDP still identified itself closely with the small firms, 1,079 exempted cartels were in place. By 1980, demographics had begun to shift the party's focus away from the small-business sector, and the party had begun to reduce the number of cartels it sanctioned. Accordingly, the number had fallen to 491. By 1989 the number was 276. Nonetheless, of the cartels in place in the early 1980s, almost half had been in effect for twenty-five years and over two-thirds for more than twenty years.[24] According to the FTC's and MITI's own studies, 17.6 percent of all domestic product shipments in 1973 involved goods produced under a statutorily authorized cartel. In the textile industry the figure was 42.2 percent, and in the iron and steel industry, 66.3 percent. For a bureaucracy pursuing economic growth, these were bizarre measures to implement. For a bureaucracy rewarding loyal LDP constituencies, they were what one might rationally expect.[25]

Bureaucrats and Policy Change

Although the control politicians exercise over the way bureaucrats handle many politically sensitive issues is fairly clear, their control over more basic national policies has been less obvious. Two reasons account for this. First, LDP leaders have never collectively lost control of the Diet. Had they traded power with politicians committed to different policies, scholars could measure the extent to which bureaucrats resisted the politicians. After all, any agency slack between politicians and bureaucrats will be clearest in times of disequilibrium: when either bureaucrats or legislators change their collective preferences. If the standard accounts of Japanese government were true—and bureaucrats were pursuing an independent vision of the commonweal—then bureaucrats would ignore such political shifts and follow their own instincts. Conversely, if they were regulating in the shadow of politics, they would follow these shifts carefully. Since LDP leaders have never collectively lost power, the issue is moot.[26]

Second, on many of the most basic policy (*non*pork) issues, the legislative-dominant and bureaucratic-dominant accounts yield an overlapping set of predictions. Suppose bureaucrats did pursue the independent vision modern academics ascribe to them. In general, they would promote economic development. But if they promoted the LDP's electoral advantage, they would still (subject to the electoral need for some pork) often do the same. Many observers forget, in other words, that what is good for the country is often good for the LDP. Ultimately, voters like governments that keep them employed, reduce inflation, and steadily raise living standards. To the extent their real incomes rise under LDP control, they will tend to choose LDP candidates. In the end, whether bureaucrats try independently to promote economic growth or try instead to promote LDP success, they will pursue many of the same policies.

Autonomous bureaucrats and responsive bureaucrats will pursue divergent policies only when LDP leaders, *for exclusively political reasons*, promote programs that *retard* economic growth. Accordingly, how much do LDP leaders rely on bureaucrats when—faced with declining electoral margins—they see a need to alter policy? Even under these circumstances, we hypothesize that they rely on the bureaucracy. Were bureaucrats formulating and implementing policy independently, LDP leaders could not use them to make these politically motivated shifts; were bureaucrats acting according to a nonpolitical logic, they would not respond to any distinctly electoral needs. As a result, if Japanese bureaucrats are as autonomous as traditionally asserted, then whenever LDP leaders find it necessary to move policy away from growth-oriented goals, one of two phenomena should ensue: LDP leaders should either ignore bureaucrats and formulate the new policy themselves, or replace senior bureaucrats and create more responsive ministries.

To locate these shifts in party policy, we turn to recent studies of the LDP. Political scientist Kent Calder (1988), for example, carefully identifies three postwar "crises" for conservative Japanese politicians: 1949–1954, 1959–1963, and 1971–1976. During these years the ruling party faced declining electoral majorities, increasingly successful and assertive opposition parties, and a variety of domestic and international pressures for change. Eyeing impending political disaster, conservative politicians each time repositioned themselves in the electoral market by changing the portfolio of policies they offered.[27]

As the first crisis (1949–1954) began, the conservative parties faced aggressive leftist opposition, economic disorder, and internal disarray: the labor and farm unions were strong and the Communists were growing militant; inflation was high and the Americans had ordered painful deflationary policies; and the Occupation had purged the conservative ranks of many of its most effective leaders. The second crisis (1959–1963) followed balance of payments problems, rampant opposition to the United States-Japan security treaty, increasing opposition success among small-business owners, and several long and bloody labor strikes. The third (1971–1976) came after several environmental disasters, the OPEC oil embargo, a series of American foreign-policy snubs, and the widespread leftist municipal victories detailed in Chapter 3.

To each of these crises, the conservatives responded with policies keyed not to growth but to the opposition's electoral strategies. More specifically, in each case the conservatives responded with policies that redistributed wealth to the organized groups to whom the opposition was trying to appeal. In the early 1950s, for example,

Table 7.3 Number of ministerial statutes compared with number of all
statutes, 1945–1985

Date of Diet dissolution	Total statutes (A)	Ministerial statutes (B)	B/A
12/18/45	25	25	1.000
12/25/46	71	69	.972
3/31/47	80	71	.888
12/9/47	156	148	.949
12/13/48	287	250	.871
12/3/49	277	247	.892
12/9/50	290	242	.834
11/30/51	314	225	.717
8/28/52	313	241	.770
12/8/53	334	233	.698
12/9/54	228	188	.825
12/16/55	196	146	.745
12/13/56	179	147	.821
11/14/57	185	161	.870
12/7/58	189	156	.825
12/27/59	223	207	.928
12/22/60	172	153	.884
10/31/61	238	219	.920
12/23/62	164	153	.933
12/18/63	182	170	.934
12/18/64	185	170	.919
12/13/65	146	132	.904
12/20/66	164	150	.915
12/23/67	147	140	.952
12/21/68	111	102	.919
12/2/69	97	92	.948
12/18/70	146	126	.863
12/27/71	147	116	.789
11/13/72	131	114	.870
9/27/73	118	103	.873
12/25/74	124	108	.871
12/25/75	98	78	.796
12/28/76	85	73	.859
12/10/77	91	76	.835
12/12/78	113	96	.850
12/11/79	72	63	.875
11/29/80	115	100	.870
11/28/81	95	77	.811
12/25/82	103	83	.806
11/28/83	81	70	.864
8/8/84	78	70	.897
12/21/85	119	101	.849

Source: Satō and Matsuzaki (1986, pp. 277–79).

they gave major benefits to farmers and small firms. During the late 1950s and early 1960s, they established national health insurance and pension plans and expanded the subsidies to farmers and small firms. In the early 1970s, they enhanced welfare and health plans, legislated radical environmental protection schemes, and again augmented their aid to small firms.[28]

The LDP that emerges from these recent studies is a party of quintessentially rational and effective politicians. If their position in the electoral market stays secure, they keep their programs intact. If observable phenomena like election results, financial contribution levels, or opinion polls signal a new political precariousness, they shift their policies to recapture that electoral strength.

At stake is the extent to which bureaucrats shift *with* conservative politicians. Suppose, on the one hand, that the traditional picture of high-handed and independent bureaucrats were accurate. Such bureaucrats would further their own preferences, which (by hypothesis, given their independence) will sometimes diverge from LDP preferences. If so, then bureaucrats will sometimes cooperate with LDP attempts to shift its programmatic focus, and sometimes not. In designing and implementing the shifts, the LDP leaders will be unable to rely on them.

Suppose, on the other hand, that bureaucrats are the faithful agents that we propose. At the very least, they will implement LDP policy changes relatively accurately. At best, they will do much more: they will gauge which programmatic shifts will best preserve an LDP majority, and then help party leaders design those programs. If bureaucrats are loyal agents they will plan policy, in short, but they will plan it according to a political logic.

Table 7.3 suggests that LDP leaders trust bureaucrats to design and implement the programmatic shifts they need. The table measures how frequently ministry bureaucrats draft the statutes the politicians pass. According to the table, the percentage of bureaucratically drafted statutes has stayed constant at 75 to 95 percent. Occasionally, the LDP leaders may decide to pass a politically popular measure as a floor bill for extra political credit.[29] More commonly, though, whether during times of stability or during times of change, they entrust ministry bureaucrats with the job of designing programs and drafting statutes. Consider again Calder's periodization:

1949–54 (conservative policy shifts):   .784 ministerial statutes.
1955–58 (conservative policy stability):   .814 ministerial statutes.
1959–63 (conservative policy shifts):   .920 ministerial statutes.
1964–70 (conservative policy stability: .916 ministerial statutes.
1971–76 (conservative policy shifts):   .842 ministerial statutes.
1977–85 (conservative policy stability):   .849 ministerial statutes.

During the past forty years, almost all statutes passed have been ministerial bills. If bureaucrats resisted the LDP's vote-seeking agenda, one would expect an increase in nonministerial statutes during times of crisis. No such result occurred. Instead, Table 7.3 suggests that bureaucrats are the relatively faithful agents that the earlier analysis led one to expect.

Table 7.4 suggests that LDP leaders also trust ministry bureaucrats to implement the statutes they pass. The table shows the number of regulations that the various ministries have promulgated. Although the numbers fluctuate widely—from 465 (in 1957) to 793 (in

Table 7.4 Number of ministerial regulations (Shōrei), 1951–1989

Date	Regulations	Date	Regulations
1951	655	1971	723
1952	793	1972	790
1953	702	1973	680
1954	708	1974	603
1955	634	1975	571
1956	579	1976	521
1957	465	1977	485
1958	651	1978	576
1959	593	1979	515
1960	515	1980	527
1961	639	1981	606
1962	665	1982	570
1963	693	1983	539
1964	724	1984	547
1965	665	1985	578
1966	666	1986	597
1967	699	1987	607
1968	643	1988	616
1969	605	1989	650
1970	649		

Source: Ōkura shō, *Hōrei zensho* (1951–90).

1952)—they show no systematic change during times of policy shifts. They show no systematic evidence, therefore, of either an attempt by bureaucrats to undo the policy shifts through increased regulations, or an attempt by the LDP to curb ministerial control by reducing the opportunity for regulations. Granted, the test is imprecise. Nonetheless, the data suggest—however tentatively—that even when the LDP changes its programmatic agenda for political reasons, it trusts the bureaucracy to implement its changes. To see the point more explicitly, consider again Calder's periodization:

1951–54 (conservative policy shifts):	715 regulations per year.
1955–58 (conservative policy stability):	582 regulations per year.
1959–63 (conservative policy shifts):	621 regulations per year.
1964–70 (conservative policy stability):	664 regulations per year.
1971–76 (conservative policy shifts):	648 regulations per year.
1977–90 (conservative policy stability):	570 regulations per year.

Last, Table 7.5 suggests that the LDP finds no need to fire senior bureaucrats to produce a ministry that will respond to the political exigencies it faces. The table shows the number of bureaucrats leaving the ministries to take jobs in firms under that ministry's jurisdiction. The figures are available only since 1967, and we have divided the period into five-year terms. The second of these periods roughly coincides with Calder's third period of LDP programmatic shifts.

Were the ministries unresponsive to politically driven policy changes, one would expect the leaders to "clean house" at the ministries and "ease out" recalcitrant bureaucrats during transitional periods.[30] If so, then the number of such lateral moves during the 1972–1976 period should exceed the number during other periods. No such personnel exit occurred. Apparently, the LDP leaders did not find the existing bureaucrats a barrier to their proposed changes.

During the past forty-five years, conservative leaders have several times changed their programmatic aims to boost their electoral performance. Independent autonomous bureaucrats (that is, a bureaucracy with extensive agency slack) would not aid such changes. Apparently, Japanese bureaucrats have been neither independent nor autonomous. Even during times of politically induced change, the LDP has been able to trust them to draft statutes and implement programs without replacing the senior bureaucrats.

Table 7.5 Bureaucrats moving laterally to business firms

Ministry	1967–71 mean	1972–76 mean	1977–81 mean	1982–86 mean	1987	1988	1989
MOF	47.2	59.6	65.8	67.4	66	61	64
Agriculture and Forestry	24.6	26.2	34.4	43.2	52	31	41
Transportation	22.2	22.6	32.6	46.8	30	34	41
MITI	25.4	20.2	22.0	33.0	30	21	28
Construction	15.8	18.6	23.4	26.4	20	21	22
Posts and Telecommunications	8.0	8.6	16.2	24.0	24	28	19
Education	0.0	0.8	3.8	11.2	10	18	15
Health and Welfare	3.0	6.2	5.0	6.2	7	6	1
Labor	2.2	2.6	1.8	2.2	2	2	3
Justice	0.0	0.2	0.0	0.2	0	0	0
Foreign Affairs	0.0	0.2	0.0	0.0	0	0	0
Internal Affairs	0.0	0.2	0.0	0.0	0	0	0
Total	148.4	166.0	205.0	260.6	241	222	234

Source: Jinji in (various years).
Note: Number of bureaucrats taking positions of officer or consultant in business firms pursuant to permission from the National Personnel Office under Kokka kōmuin hō (National Public Servant Act), Law No. 120 of 1947, §103(b).

Conclusion

By definition, rational politicians will create and use organizations that further their electoral advantage. Also by definition, they will manipulate the institutional structure of the electoral market to enhance that advantage further. In the process, majority party leaders will necessarily try to control the thousands who staff the government apparatus. Ultimately, they have little to gain and much to lose by letting bureaucrats flout politically necessary policies to flaunt instead their idiosyncratic personal visions.

LDP leaders have been nothing if not politically successful, and rational political strategy has been part of their winning formula. They have organized their party to facilitate both a coordinated response among themselves and control over their bureaucratic agents, and they have manipulated government institutions to augment that bureaucratic control. As we examine the success they have achieved, three points stand out.

First, voters prefer political candidates who can manipulate the bureaucracy to those who cannot. Second, LDP leaders both set the basic contours of economic regulation and constrain their bureaucratic agents effectively enough so that they can rely on them to perform politically sensitive jobs. Third, LDP leaders constrain their bureaucrats enough to entrust them with fundamental policy shifts. Although the party has never lost political control, from time to time it has come perilously close. During those periods, it has shifted its policies toward those of the opposition parties and toward, therefore, the median voter. In doing so, it has necessarily relied on the bureaucrats in office. Were bureaucrats pursuing independent, exclusively growth-oriented visions of the commonweal, LDP leaders would not be able to use them to implement those changes. Were bureaucrats the responsive agents that we suggest, LDP leaders could indeed safely trust them. According to our evidence, LDP leaders do.

Upon reflection, perhaps we have taken Japanese bureaucrats a bit too seriously. LDP leaders do use them, and use them successfully. By all odds, they do accomplish well that which those leaders care most about. But on issues that affect the LDP only peripherally, their accomplishments may sometimes be peripheral as well. American academics tend to collect their data by interviewing bureaucrats. Between the two of us, we too have interviewed dozens of bureaucrats; indeed, some of our best friends are (or were, until they read this book) bureaucrats. We also talk with others, however. And depending on whom we interview and what we ask, we obtain a rather different picture—a picture of bureaucrats far less effective than the "plan-rational" engineers who inhabit most political science monographs.

"We just wrote new memos for them." The young executive took his eyes off the road momentarily to explain how things work to one of us. It was night, and he was driving as fast as he could around the speed-traps. For months his company had been trying to list its stock on the prestigious Section 1 of the Tokyo Stock Exchange. Before letting it do so, though, MOF bureaucrats wanted proof that it had been making appropriate risk assessments over the past several years. In fact, it had made some assessments, but nowhere near what the bureaucrats wanted.

"You back-dated memos?" one of us naively asked.

"No, no," he replied. "We just keep date-stamped blank memo paper around. When the MOF people want an old memo, we go back and find the paper with the right date stamped on it. Then we write them the memo they want."

"Think about it, though," he smiled. "Memos you write the night before won't look like memos you crammed into a file cabinet several years ago."

"So what do you do?"

"We keep the date-stamped blank sheets in a file drawer," he explained. "We jam 'em in just like we would real memos. That way, when we take a piece of paper out to write a memo on it, it looks wrinkled and dog-eared just like a real one." It worked, for the company soon proudly traded its stock on Section 1. And it represents the gist, we suspect, of much of the Japanese "plan-rational" state.

8

Political Structure and Judicial Incentives

The late 1800s were risky times for the men who would be king in Japan. Not only did they face political opponents at home; they also faced Western leaders intent on carving and recarving East Asia into manageable, governable, expropriable units. By 1894 one of these men, Aritomo Yamagata, would march the Japanese First Army onto the continent and defeat the Chinese. By 1904 the Japanese navy would sail up to the Russian Pacific Fleet, the army would once again march onto the continent, and both would beat the Russians. But in May 1891 matters seemed quieter, and the future Czar Nicholas II thought he could still safely visit Japan, as he was in East Asia already to break ground for the Trans-Siberian Railway. He was mistaken: a small-town policeman named Sanzō Tsuda decided the Russian prince had come to spy. Rather than let him do that, Tsuda attacked and stabbed him.

Tsuda worried the Russians, but he also irritated the autocrats like Yamagata, who found his attack a very bothersome complication. To placate the Russians, they wanted him dead. To kill him legally, they prosecuted him. Fortunately for Tsuda, Supreme Court Chief Justice Iken Kojima reminded them that the law did not provide the death penalty for attempted murder, and Nicholas did not die. Neither therefore should Tsuda. Because Kojima controlled the courts, Tsuda lived. In the process, according to the standard histories, Kojima installed the "principle of judicial independence" in Japan. And there the standard accounts end (see Takayanagi, 1964, pp. 9–10; Saitō, 1985, p. 307).

A positive theory of principal-agent relations in government should leave one suspicious of this story. Even if democratically elected legislators might cut judges this much agency slack for the sake of electoral advantage, autocrats have little reason to do so. Should judges act this independently, most rational autocrats would punish them. In fact, that was exactly what they did in Japan, for the standard histories skip the end to this story. After the trial the autocrats discovered that Kojima and six of his fellow justices frequented geisha houses. As the law permitted some prostitution, the justices could safely have retained licensed prostitutes. As it sanctioned mistresses, they could safely have kept as many women as they could afford. As it allowed debauchery generally, they could safely have sung and danced and drunk themselves into a stupor.

Aside from these pastimes, Kojima and his friends, like American Supreme Court justices, played cards. It was their downfall, for in 1892 gambling was illegal. The prosecutors used the games to impeach them, and paraded fourteen geishas as witnesses. Alas for the prosecutors, the law required them to prove their case before several other Supreme Court justices. Notwithstanding incentive structures, agents do not *always* follow their principal's wishes. The Supreme Court justices stood by their colleagues and loyally dismissed the charges against them for lack of evidence. Not that this show of insubordination stopped Yamagata. He was now Minister of Justice, and when he fired his prosecutors, he made sure Kojima left too. Because he controlled the army, neither the technicalities of evidence nor Kojima's legal right to stay on the bench were at issue, and Kojima knew this. Yamagata told Kojima he should leave, and Kojima left (Kusunoki, 1989, pp. 11–44).

In the modern variant of the Kojima story we seek to find out whether and how much "agency slack" (that is, how much "judicial independence")[1] exists between political leaders and judges today. At the outset, we review two prominent choice-theoretic hypotheses about why vote- or wealth-maximizing politicians might choose to cut their judges substantial slack. According to these scholars, that slack would both help legislators credibly to make long-term commitments to their constituents, and reduce the potential for slack in the legislative-bureaucratic relationship.

Whether or not these hypotheses apply elsewhere, they do not apply to Japan. We have outlined several ways Japanese legislators commit themselves and monitor bureaucrats; given the various solutions they have devised, LDP legislators have few reasons to allow judges extensive slack.

Without having either significant reasons to give judges slack or a constitution that *effectively* prevents constraints on the judiciary, rational political leaders will not permit judges that slack. Independent judiciaries (courts that are relatively free of control by political elites) are notoriously expensive. By placing judges beyond review for any but the grossest misdeeds, political leaders who sanction judicial independence simply let judges indulge their own tastes for leisure and idiosyncratic ideology (Epstein, 1990). If the leaders can otherwise mitigate the problems of maintaining the credibility of election promises and of monitoring bureaucrats, one would thus expect these politicians to try to minimize the independence of the courts.

We intend to show why and how LDP leaders have tried to minimize the agency slack in their nominally independent judiciary. After reviewing the theoretical scholarship on judicial independence, we outline the institutions that Japanese party leaders can manipulate to monitor and constrain judges (see appendix to this chapter for other indices of judicial performance, like university diploma). Subsequently, a comprehensive set of career records for all Japanese judges educated after the war (the *Zen saibankan keireki sōran*—abbreviated ZSKS) will help us to illustrate how the party leaders have manipulated those institutions to control their judges.

Positive Theories of Judicial Independence

By tradition, Anglo-American legal scholars argue more about the normative implications of judicial independence than about its positive aspects.[2] They all agree that independence is a good thing, but do not explain why it is a likely thing. At least one possibility is obvious enough. If voters think an independent judiciary would be a good thing, they will want it. If they want it, vote-maximizing legislators may offer it.

The argument may explain why the LDP would not today fire someone in Kojima's spot, but it explains little else. Independence, in our formulation, refers to the agency slack in the relationship between the majority party and the judiciary—to the degree judges act autonomously of the political leaders. At issue, therefore, is the extent judges ignore LDP policy preferences when deciding cases. In effect, to argue that judicial independence would maximize votes requires the assumption that the voters (who elected the LDP in the first place) would prefer that judges randomly flouted LDP preferences. Yet voters do not want politicians who merely enact policies and programs. Instead, they want politicians who deliver them systematically and coherently. Judges who decide cases by ignoring LDP policy preferences obstruct this process. If voters have no reason simultaneously to want their politicians to reflect their preferences and their judges to ignore them—and we know of no such reason in ordinary cases[3]—the argument does not work.

Apologists for the American constitutional tradition argue that voters want an independent judiciary because they want to protect democratic government. Absent an independent judiciary, they assert, elected politicians could use their institutional monopoly on violence to arrogate more power to themselves than voters want them to have. Voters might want an independent judiciary, in other words, to keep their own elected agents in line.

As the story of Kojima and Yamagata illustrates, the argument does not take us very far. More than anything else, voters who fear unlimited government fear unchecked military power. Unfortunately, people who control the military—whether Yamagata, Hitler, or a South American junta—need never obey judges. In any showdown between the military and the judiciary, the military almost always wins. But there are two better theories of judicial independence.

Credible Commitments

In 1975, William Landes and Richard Posner advanced independent judges as a solution to what scholars have since come to call the Williamsonian (1983; 1985) "credible commitments" problem: in order to extract rents, rational legislators will want to commit themselves to long-term statutory bargains; they will not be able to do so without institutional constraints because of their incentive to renege after the fact. To extort money, they will want to promise credibly that the statutes they enact will stay in force for some minimal amount of time. Once they have collected the money, however, they necessarily have an incentive to renege. Knowing their representatives have that incentive, constituents will pay less cash at the outset (McChesney, 1991).

According to Landes and Posner, independent judges make legislative promises credible precisely because they stand apart from legislators. Because judges need not answer to legislators, judges can enforce legislative bargains by the terms the enacting coalition promised. By preventing legislators from reneging on their deals afterward, they can help legislators maximize their rents and votes beforehand.[4]

Although Landes and Posner identify the right problem, their answer does not quite work. First, as Cass Sunstein (1990, pp. 13–39) and others note, if a statutory provision is ambiguous, a judge is not likely to know what the enacting coalition would have chosen. In a significant fraction of cases, that choice would have depended on the vagaries of agenda manipulation. Because the coalition did not actually negotiate the issue, a judge will have to imagine how the parties might have manipulated the agenda. It is no easy feat. Except where the state is trying to renege on deals against a statutory mandate that—for whatever reason—happens to be clear, judicial "solutions" probably solve very little.

Even if judges knew what the enacting coalition wanted, independent judges need not enforce rent-extracting bargains by that coalition's terms. To be sure, Richard Posner (1985, p. 287) and Frank Easterbrook (1984), distinguished federal judges themselves, have urged judges to do so.[5] Oliver Wendell Holmes (1953, p. 249) did once assure a friend that if Americans "want to go to Hell I will help them. It's my job." But those are probably not the views of all or even most American and Japanese judges. And the judges who see their jobs in other terms have few institutional constraints to stop them from following their instincts (see Epstein, 1990). Landes and Posner's model "works" only when independent judges feel constrained enough to follow the enacting coalition's rent-extracting mandate, provided the mandate is at all clear. The irony of an independent judiciary is that it constrains judges not at all.[6]

Landes and Posner (1975, p. 885) do suggest that legislators might punish courts that do not enforce rent-extracting bargains; they suggest, as a result, that judges might enforce the enacting coalition's deal to avoid those penalties. Several scholars do show that American legislators seem to punish the judiciary for decisions they do not like (Anderson, Shugart, and Tollison, 1989; Toma, 1991). Even so, however, neither they nor Landes and Posner explain why *individual* judges would abandon their personal preferences for the sake of the common judicial good. Absent a way to penalize judges individually for ignoring the good of the greater judiciary, intra-judicial problems of collective action necessarily remain.

In any case, the most common rent-extracting deals are not deals the courts enforce. Suppose a legislator promises to help enact bill S-1954 in exchange for a PAC's contribution. If the legislator simply takes the money and gives nothing in return, the PAC cannot sue. Suppose that 51 percent of the legislators promise to help enact S-1954 for PAC support. They do, but repeal it the next term after receiving contributions from a rival PAC. Again, the cheated PAC cannot sue. No matter how independent a court may be, legislators can freely cheat on many deals.

Ultimately, therefore, the problem Landes and Posner identify remains real, but an independent judiciary may not solve it. In Japan, the solutions lie instead in the various aspects of party structure and bureaucratic organization described earlier in this book. LDP members delegate control over the party to leaders from relatively stable districts who earn large rents through their leadership. Because the leaders anticipate large future rents, they have less of an incentive to renege on legislative deals now. Because those rents derive from their control over the party and bureaucracy, they also have an incentive to ensure that backbenchers and bureaucrats do not renege (see Kreps, 1990, p. 111). The rents to the party leaders constrain those leaders, in short, and the leaders constrain the backbenchers and bureaucrats.

Bureaucratic Monitoring

Mathew McCubbins and Thomas Schwartz take a different approach, and argue that independent courts mitigate bureaucratic slack by serving as "fire alarms" (1984; see Bishop, 1990; McCubbins, Noll, and Weingast, 1987). Legislators routinely allow bureaucrats discretion over programs. In the process, however, they must try to ensure that the bureaucrats implement the programs as they intended. Hypothetically, they could constrain the bureaucrats by monitoring them routinely through what McCubbins and Schwartz call "police-patrol" monitoring. Instead, they often find it more efficient to give constituents ways to publicize their complaints through what they call "fire-alarm" monitoring.

McCubbins and Schwartz outline several variants of these fire alarms. One is the independent court. Legislators could establish procedural and substantive rules, they suggest, that let aggrieved constituents challenge bureaucracies in court. When constituents sue, the independent courts would force the bureaucrats to implement the initial legislative deal.

Unfortunately, McCubbins and Schwartz's positive theory of judicial independence raises the same problem that plagues Landes and Posner's theory. For litigation to work as a fire alarm, courts must enforce statutes in the spirit the politicians drew them up. Yet for the same reasons discussed in the context of Landes and Posner, little reason exists to think independent judges necessarily know what politicians wanted or would choose to enforce it if they did.

The LDP instead mitigates agency slack in the bureaucracy through a combination of at least the following three factors. First, LDP backbenchers resolve many cases of bureaucratic slack themselves. They do so because they thereby attract voters to the party and share them out among the LDP candidates. Rather than let judges earn credit for forcing reluctant bureaucrats to respond, they do the work and take the credit themselves.

Second, LDP backbenchers appoint their leaders as designated monitors for any residual slack in the bureaucracy. When problems of collective action prevent backbenchers from constraining bureaucrats, the leaders intervene to do the job. In fact, so long as LDP backbenchers and leaders do their jobs reasonably well, those who take complaints about the bureaucracy to court will disproportionately include supporters of other parties. As a result, the LDP can increase the value of LDP loyalty simply by disabling the courts as a mechanism of administrative review.

Third, Japan's parliamentary structure itself, combined with the LDP's stable majority and strong party leadership, helps the LDP leaders constrain bureaucratic agency slack. Consider again Figures 6.1 and 6.2. In divided governments such as that of the United States, strategic bureaucracies can sometimes insulate themselves from legislative correction. Suppose, for example, that the President and the legislature hold different policy preferences (P and L, respectively) but negotiate a program at point x. So long as the bureaucracy implements the program at any point on the contract curve $C(LP)$, it can effectively ignore the instructions to locate it at x. Because the President and the legislature have different prefer-

ences, one of the two will always prefer the bureaucratically implemented *b* to the originally enacted *x* and will refuse to help correct
the misimplementation. Effectively, their different preferences prevent the President and the legislature from reassembling the initial
coalition to relocate the program at *x*. The same problem can occur
in a parliamentary system, if one or more policy-based groups exist
within the majority party. In governments like Japan's, with a
stable and centralized parliamentary majority party, the problem
largely disappears.

According to McCubbins and Schwartz, legislatures and presidents can use the courts to prevent the strategic misimplementation
that occurs in divided government. In Figure 8.1, suppose the President and legislature negotiate a program at *x*, but a strategic bureaucracy implements it at *b*. Although the legislature and President will
not be able to correct this misimplementation, a court that enforced
legislative deals by their original terms could do so. Disgruntled
constituents would sue, and the court would force the bureaucracy
to implement the program at *x*. The legislature and President would
rely on the courts to do what they could not do themselves.[7]

Nonetheless, centralized parliamentary majority parties do not
need these fire-alarms; not needing them, rational party leaders
will not impose them—for independent judges can use litigation to
shift programs toward their *own* ideal points.[8] In Figure 8.1 the
court's own ideal point is *C*. Suppose the legislature and President
agree to a program at *x*, the bureaucracy implements it at *b*, and a
disgruntled constituent sues. The court can now shift the program
to *c*, the point on the contract curve closest to its ideal point but
even farther from the initial negotiated program at *x*. For the same
reason that a divided government could not correct the bureaucratic
misimplementation at *b*, it cannot correct this judicial misimplementation at *c*. Worse yet, if the court can cite the Constitution to
justify its opinion, it can even shift the outcome off *C(LP)* to *C*.

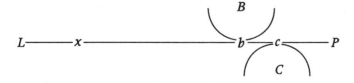

Fig. 8.1   Bureaucratic implementation and judicial correction

Unless the legislature and President can amend the Constitution, they will be unable to respond. Once again, the problem is relatively minor in a centralized and stable parliamentary system like Japan's, but more basic to American-style divided government. It is also a problem that judicial independence creates.

Judicial Review in Japan

Apparently, the LDP does not use the courts to create either Landes and Posner's check on legislative opportunism or McCubbins and Schwartz's fire alarms. Admittedly ambiguous, the evidence for this proposition is drawn from how people use the courts in Japan, and what the courts do when people try to use them. First, note that Japanese citizens seldom sue the government. In 1989 they filed about 650,000 civil suits in the national district courts and 1,150,000 in national summary courts (there are no prefectural or municipal court systems). By contrast, in district courts they filed only 1,100 administrative suits, and in summary courts only 250 (*Saikō*, 1989, pp. 6–9). Second, note that Japanese courts seldom void legislation. In the forty-odd years since the war, the Japanese Supreme Court has rarely held a statute unconstitutional. Once it voided a provision that imposed a heavier penalty for patricide than for general murder, once a provision that granted local monopolies to drug stores, twice a provision that overrepresented some electoral districts, and once a provision that prevented some forest owners from partitioning their land.[9] No other statutes have been overruled.

This evidence does not rule out, however, bureaucrats' administering in the shadow of the statutes, and legislators' passing statutes in the shadow of the Constitution. In other words, knowing that the courts ruthlessly reverse illegal dispositions, bureaucrats would make a point of staying within legal bounds, while legislators would draft laws within the limits of the Constitution. To determine whether forceful courts are imposing their will on docile bureaucrats and legislators, or conversely, whether bureaucrats and legislators are ignoring passive and obedient courts, one would need to examine specific disputes. Involving as it would an elaborate array of administrative, procedural, and constitutional doctrines, the exercise would not be an easy one to complete. Fortunately, however, few subjects in Japanese law have been studied by so many fine legal scholars as the subject of the relationship between law and government, and none has generated as much agreement.[10]

Scholars routinely note the deference Japanese courts extend to the legislature and even to bureaucrats. Dan Henderson, for example, writes that "ordinary citizens under Japanese law simply cannot bring the bureaucracy into court to measure administrative action by statutory or constitutional standards" (1990, p. 90). Michael Young finds that courts declare most Japanese administrative dispositions nonjusticiable (1988, p. 90). And Frank Upham, in his classic study of law and social change, provides a marvellously cynical summary (1987, p. 15):

> In those exceptional cases where a plaintiff is determined enough to overcome the doctrinal and practical obstacles and succeeds in getting judicial scrutiny of discretionary acts, the courts almost invariably do two things: first, they reject the government's claim that the decision is totally discretionary and assert the court's right and obligation to review for abuse of discretion, no matter how broad; second, they determine that, in this case, the government's decision was within its scope of discretion.

Incentive Structures within Japanese Courts

Because LDP leaders have ways to make legislative bargains and police their bureaucrats, they have little reason to allow their judges extensive independence. As a result, so long as they can cheaply reduce that judicial independence, rational LDP leaders will constrain their judges by manipulating the institutional apparatus.[11]

At a superficial level, the institutional framework seems to ensure considerable agency slack. The Constitution guarantees independence: "All judges shall be independent in the exercise of their conscience and shall be bound only by this Constitution and the laws." It promises them "adequate compensation which shall not be decreased during their term of office."[12] And the courts remain administratively distinct from the bureaucracy and seemingly impervious to anyone in the cabinet or legislature. As Bradley Richardson and Scott Flanagan (1984, p. 59) put it, "[t]he postwar constitution completely transformed the judiciary into an independent coequal branch of government."

Despite this nominal independence, Japanese judges are not as free as, for example, their American federal peers. Like senior American politicians, LDP leaders decide who will become a judge. Unlike American politicians, they can also manipulate the system to reward and punish those they have made judges. More specifically, they mitigate the agency slack that would otherwise inhere in the judiciary through the following ploys:

1. They appoint to the Supreme Court only those judges whose policies are consistent with their own, and appoint them late enough in life (close enough to their mandatory retirement age) to prevent their growing substantially more independent over time.

2. They assign their Supreme Court appointees the job of monitoring the performance of lower-court judges, and of rewarding and punishing them appropriately. In practice, these justices delegate much of this administrative task to the Secretariat (the courts' administrative offices). To ensure that the Secretariat itself remains responsive, however, party leaders maintain on the Supreme Court at least one justice who has headed the Secretariat and understands closely how the system works. Thus:

(a) Party leaders appoint to the lower courts only those people whom their Supreme Court nominees (using the Secretariat) recommend to them as appropriate.

(b) They assign their Supreme Court justices the job of stacking the Secretariat with politically reliable judges.

(c) They then assign the judges in the Secretariat the job of manipulating the careers of the other lower court judges in a way that minimizes agency slack.

(d) Less frequently, they also let the Secretariat judges generate the desired decisions by manipulating case assignments.

The Supreme Court

The cabinet directly appoints Japanese Supreme Court justices. By tradition, it appoints several of the fifteen justices from the career judiciary. It usually appoints as justice at least one person who has served as Secretary General of the Secretariat. The rest of the justices it names from the bar, the university law faculties, the prosecutorial ranks, and the career bureaucracy. The justices face a popular referendum at the first lower-house election after their appointment, and every ten years thereafter.[13] No one has ever failed one of these popular votes. Only 4 to 15.17 percent of the people voting at these referenda have ever voted to dismiss a justice.[14]

Despite security of tenure, Japanese Supreme Court justices do not last long on the job. Because the LDP holds solid control over the legislature, it can afford, as American presidents cannot, to appoint quite elderly justices—even though the law forces justices to retire by age 70 (*Saibansho hō*, §50). By so doing, it avoids the risk of the Earl Warren type of agency-slack: the chance that a politically reliable appointee will shift, over time, to very different positions. Justice Matasuke Kawamura served the longest tenure of any Japanese Supreme Court justice. Appointed in 1947, when he was a 54-year-old university professor, by the first and last Socialist cabinet, he served until age 70. By contrast, among the last 20 justices appointed, the age at appointment has ranged from 60 to 67. The mean appointment age has been 64.[15]

The Lower Courts

The cabinet appoints lower-court judges from a list of nominees prepared by the Supreme Court and Secretariat. Almost all appointees are young men (and a few women) who have decided to become judges immediately upon graduating from the national law school, the Legal Research & Training Institute (the LRTI). For Japanese lower-court judges, the decision to join the bench is thus made early in their career. This transforms the court system into an institution very different from the federal court system in the United States and closer to the model of continental Europe.[16] Although federal judges also obtain their jobs through politicians, they generally join the bench in middle age. Some federal trial judges hope to obtain an appellate post, others a Supreme Court spot (Cohen 1991). But most federal judges' initial post is their last, and they know it. Their position is one they can keep for the rest of their working lives.

Tenure apart, whether Japanese judges live well or live humbly depends on their status with the LDP leaders in the cabinet and the LDP agents in the Secretariat.[17] Basically, the judges serve 10-year terms, which the cabinet can freely decide to renew (*Kenpō*, art. 80;

Saibansho hō, §40). Generally, that decision will depend on the judges in the Secretariat. If renewed, a judge may work until his or her sixty-fifth birthday, though some retire earlier (Table 8.1).[18]

On some of the minute details of job assignment, the Secretariat may defer to High Court presidents and district court chief judges (Tsukahara, 1990, p. 27). With each assignment, for example, a judge also takes a post in a division within the local court. Each such division is composed of three to five judges, one of whom chairs the division and handles administrative matters. The local court then allocates cases to these divisions according to its own internal rules.[19]

Most important, the issues of when judges receive promotions, where they work, and what they do are all decided by the judges at the Secretariat. In theory, these assignments are something the LDP appointees to the Supreme Court determine (*Saibansho hō*, §47). In practice, the justices delegate the task to the judges in the Secretariat, who then determine the basic assignments. Crucial to agency slack is thus the composition of the Secretariat: by appointing politically reliable justices to the Supreme Court (including at least one who knows first-hand how the Secretariat works), and by having these justices pick reliable judges for the Secretariat, LDP leaders can keep considerable control over the entire judiciary.[20]

How much money Japanese judges make depends on how highly the Secretariat judges regard their work. As Table 8.2 shows, the

Table 8.1 Age of retirement for judges who began their careers in 1951

Age	Number retiring	Age	Number retiring
64	26	55	1
63	5	54	2
62	4	53	0
61	14	52	1
60	5	51	0
59	4	50	0
58	0	40–49	4
57	4	30–39	11
56	1	20–29	0

Source: Nihon minshu hōritsuka kyōkai (1990, pp. 38–45).

Note: The table excludes the 14 members who either died in office, were still working at the end of 1990, or whose birth dates were unavailable.

Table 8.2   Monthly salaries of judges (in yen)

Supreme Court Chief Justice	1,892,000
Supreme Court Associate Justice	1,319,000
Tokyo High Court president	1,222,000
Other high court presidents	1,125,000
Full judge (high end)	1,115,000
Full judge (low end)	494,000
Assistant judge (high end)	405,000
Assistant judge (low end)	190,600

Source: Nihon minshu hōritsuka kyōkai (1990, p. 471).

Note: Current as of April 1, 1989, when $1.00 equalled ¥132.5. To allow for the customary Japanese bonuses, assume a 17-month year (Hattori and Henderson, 1983, pp. 3–35).

pay scale ranges from ¥190,600 per month to ¥1,892,000. These are relatively good wages for a professional, as a comparison with Table 6.4 illustrates.[21]

More important for issues of judicial independence, the Secretariat can use this pay scale to reward and punish judges. Judicial pay is not a matter of lock-step seniority. A judge's place on the pay scale depends on the Secretariat, and considerable variance within each age cohort develops over time.[22] From top to bottom of the pay scale, judges face a pay multiple of 9.93.[23] Of course, as Table 8.3 shows, Supreme Court appointments and High Court presidencies are not realistic goals for most judges.[24] Even the full-judge pay scale has a pay multiple of 2.26.

Table 8.3   Highest judicial positions attained by class of 1951

Position	Number attaining
Supreme Court Justice	1
President (high court)	2
Chief judge (district court or family court)	50
High court judge	9
District court judge	13
Family court judge	4
District court branch office head	1

Source: Nihon minshu hōritsuka kyōkai (1990, pp. 38–45).

Note: The table shows the highest judicial (nonadministrative) position held by judges who began their career in 1951 and remained in their job for at least 20 years.

Job prestige and geographical location also matter to judges, and the Secretariat can use its control over these issues to punish and reward. Indeed, the Secretariat can probably use this power *more* effectively than its power over the purse, for it can *de*mote. By article 80 of the Constitution it is not permitted to lower a judge's pay. Nothing, however, prevents it from transferring a Tokyo High Court judge to a small branch office or a back-mountain family court.

Most judges share basic preferences about the type of appointment they want. Granted, a few judges will prefer small-town life and some will dislike appellate work. In general, though, most Japanese judges prefer an urban post to a rural post. They prefer a family court to a branch court, a district court to a family court, and a high court to a district court. They prefer a chief-judgeship to associate-judge status. And they hope for an occasional administrative position in the Secretariat or at one of the ministries. According to Table 8.3, most judges can realistically hope for at least one stint as a chief judge in a district or family court. Generally, they will obtain it near the end of their career. As 58 of the judges in this class of 1951 also served at least once on a High Court, they can also realistically hope for an appellate position.

Although the lengths of assignment vary, judges generally work for three years in each post. Before reassignment, they can request preferred appointments (Tsukahara, 1990, p. 27). Nominally, they can even refuse transfers they do not want (*Saibansho hō*, §48). In fact, however, they refuse them at their peril. By 1969, Judge Shigeharu Hasegawa had worked in Hiroshima for 17 years, and his wife was sick. When he declined an out-of-town transfer that year, he was out of a job: the cabinet refused to reappoint him to his next 10-year term.[25]

The Fast Track

Consider two examples of "fast-track" careers. As of early 1991, Ryōhachi Kusaba was chief justice of the Supreme Court (*ZSKS*, 1990, pp. 40–41). Kusaba was born in November 1925, attended the University of Tokyo, and began his judicial career in 1951 in a large metropolitan (Yokohama) family court. He then spent three years in a branch office of a provincial (Nagano) family court. From

Table 8.4 Positions held by class of 1951 judges in December 1988

Position	Number holding
High court president	2
High court judge	19
Chief judge, district court or family court	2
District court judge	1
Dead or retired[a]	73

Source: Nihon minshu hōritsuka kyōkai (1990, pp. 38–45).
a. The category includes judges who retired but returned as summary court judges.

there, however, he moved to a three-year administrative post at the Secretariat. After another three years in family court, he returned to an administrative position; in 1966 he moved to the Tokyo District Court. Several more years passed, and he again left the bench for various administrative positions. Subsequent rewards came quickly: he became a district court chief judge at the young age of 54 (1980), joined the Tokyo High Court (1982), headed the Secretariat (1986), became president of the Tokyo High Court (1988), and finally joined the Supreme Court (1989). Table 8.4 shows the positions his classmates held at the time he was High Court president.

Supreme Court Justice Katsumi Teika spent even less time on the bench. He too attended the University of Tokyo, but began his career in the Chiba Family Court in 1950. Three years later he moved to the Ministry of Justice, and from there he worked through a series of administrative jobs outside the judiciary until he returned in 1977 to sit on the Tokyo High Court. He then became head of the Civil Affairs Bureau of the Ministry of Justice, chief judge of two district courts, and president of the Hiroshima and Osaka High Courts before joining the Supreme Court in 1988. Although nominally a career judge, Teika had served on the bench for only seven years (other than in the administrative posts of chief judge and president) before becoming a Supreme Court justice.

Continuity

The war had less effect on the situation than one might expect. Granted, the principals have changed: a democratically elected LDP controls the government instead of the autocrats who controlled it before. This may indeed change the government's response to a case like Tsuda's attempt on Nicholas II's life. But some of the other differences matter less.

Scholars routinely note, for example, that the prewar courts were under the Ministry of Justice, whereas modern courts are nominally the equals of the legislative branch. But no one has ever explained why the difference is more than nominal. Before the war, the Ministry of Justice picked the judges; now the cabinet picks them. Before the war, the Ministry of Justice rewarded and punished judges; since the war ended, the senior judges at the Secretariat, who are beholden to the Supreme Court justices, who in turn are beholden to the cabinet, reward and punish them. Prewar judges at least had life tenure, whereas, since the war, the cabinet has had the option every 10 years of firing a judge.[26]

Moreover, to integrate the courts into the rest of the political apparatus, the judges at the Secretariat routinely send their best judges on temporary jobs to various ministries (Shioya, 1991). As of October 1990, 98 of the judges (about 4.6 percent) held administrative posts outside of the courts, 77 of them with the Ministry of Justice (ZSKS, 1990, pp. 462–63). All told, 15 percent of the judges had worked at one time at the Ministry of Justice (ZSKS, 1990, p. 464). Upon returning to the courts, these judges most often took jobs at the major courts of Tokyo and Osaka. Indeed, 68.1 percent of the judges returning to the courts in 1975–1987 took jobs at the Supreme Court, the Tokyo High Court, or the Tokyo District Court. As a result, 21.8 percent of the judges in the civil section of the Tokyo District Court had worked in nonjudicial government jobs. Of the divisional chairs in that civil section—the judges heading the panels with the most important cases—45.9 percent had Ministry of Justice experience (Mizuno, 1988, p. 33).

Conclusion

An independent judge might do several things. For example, an independent judge might help self-interested legislators increase their rent-extracting potential by enforcing their legislative deals. An independent judge might even help legislators monitor and constrain their bureaucratic agents.

None of these potential virtues flowing from judicial independence matters much in Japan. LDP legislators make their promises
credible by delegating broad powers to party leaders, who stand to
lose large rents if the LDP reneges on its deals. Party backbenchers
monitor bureaucrats to win votes, and assign any residual monitoring to their party leaders. And the Japanese governmental structure—a stable parliamentary system run by a centralized and disciplined party—helps legislators constrain bureaucrats.

To the extent judges are independent, they introduce enormous
problems of agency slack of their own. Accordingly, where—as in
Japan—legislators can devise extra-judicial ways to make their
commitments credible and to constrain their bureaucratic agents,
one would expect them to limit the independence of their judicial
agents. The LDP leaders have fashioned a judicial organization that
is susceptible to such control. Lower-court judges join the court at
a young age, and stay for most of their working lives. Where they
work, what they earn, and what cases they decide all depend on
what their superiors at the Secretariat think of their work. In turn,
judges at the Secretariat answer to the Supreme Court. And the
Supreme Court includes only recent LDP appointees.

Through all this the LDP could—if it chose—maintain tight control over the ways judges decide cases. We predict that, as an
organization that competes successfully in a volatile political market, it does choose to keep control. In due course we will investigate
just how tight a control it maintains.

Appendix: Indices of Career Promise

For judicial careers, two of the most basic early indices of ability are
undergraduate university and age of appointment. The University
of Tokyo (and to a lesser extent a few of the other national universities) has always maintained the most selective admissions policy.
Predictably, its graduates are very successful among their fellow
judges.

Eighteen of the 97 judges in the class of 1951 failed to obtain at
least a High Court position by the end of 1990 (Table 8.3). They
make up a "career failure" rate of 18.6 percent. Of these 18 judges,
three were from the University of Tokyo, four from the University
of Kyoto (generally ranked second), three from Chuo University (a
large private university), and two from other universities. The ZSKS

provided no university information on the remaining six—either they did not graduate from a university (one need not graduate from college to attend the LRTI) or the university information was not available. Given that the class included 29 Tokyo graduates, 24 Kyoto graduates, 12 Chuo graduates, 10 graduates of other universities, and 22 apparent nongraduates, the career failure rates are: Tokyo—10.3 percent, Kyoto—16.7 percent; Chuo—25.0 percent; other universities—20.0 percent; apparent non-graduates—27.2 percent.[27]

Age of appointment often shows how quickly a judge passed the college and LRTI entrance examinations; it is thus used as another index of intellectual ability. Many people study several years before successfully entering the University of Tokyo or University of Kyoto law faculty, and continue to study several more years after graduation before successfully entering the LRTI. As a result, the average LRTI entrant is now over 29 years old (Ramseyer, 1986: 524). All else being equal, therefore, the younger the LRTI graduate, the smarter he or she is assumed to be.

Consider again the 18 low-performing judges in the class of 1951. Eight were in the oldest quartile, nine in the middle two quartiles, and only one was in the youngest quartile. This yields failure rates of 33.3 percent for the oldest quartile, 18.4 percent for the middle quartiles, and 4.2 percent for the youngest.[28] Note that the number of years on the bench before retirement do not explain these differences, for the age differences are—as a fraction of a judge's total career—minor. Within the class of 1951, the youngest quartile was born after July 1925, the oldest quartile before 1921. Judges who *neither* attended a national university nor were in the youngest 3 quartiles seldom did well: for them, the failure rate was 60 percent.[29]

9

Judicial Manipulation

"The Supreme Court seems awfully obsequious toward bureaucrats these days," observed Ebato to Taniguchi. Tetsuo Ebato was a freelance journalist. His interlocutor, Masataka Taniguchi, had retired from the Supreme Court a year earlier (Ebato, 1990, pp. 60–61).

"You're right. I wonder why," replied Taniguchi.

"Maybe it's because the Prime Minister has the last word in appointing chief and associate justices," said Ebato.

Taniguchi was not sure. "Professor [emeritus and former Supreme Court justice] Dandō says so too, but I wonder. I thought judges just had to follow their conscience and the law, and issue opinions. But when I said so to [Tohoku University professor] Odanaka, he wouldn't have it. 'You're wrong,' he told me. 'The judges I know who're conscientious and write good essays spend all their time circulating through provincial district courts.'"

If they were looking for agency slack in the legislative-judicial relationship, Ebato and Taniguchi identify the right issue: whom does the Secretariat promote fastest, and whom does it circulate through provincial district courts? We argued early on that the eagerness with which political principals monitor and constrain their agents will correlate inversely with the costs to doing so. In that vein, the more cheaply politicians can police judges, the more tightly they will do so. With regard to the legislative-judicial relationship, the usual positive explanations for agency slack ("judicial independence") do not apply to Japan. Whatever the case elsewhere, we know of few reasons LDP leaders should generally want to encourage judicial independence in Japan. They have many ways to constrain judges, and in this chapter we will use judicial career records (the *ZSKS*) to determine how closely they manipulate various judicial institutions in order to control their judges.[1]

The judicial career records suggest—however anecdotally—that LDP leaders, acting through their agents in the Supreme Court and the Secretariat, do use their control over job assignments to police judges. Most obviously, they punish judges who publicly criticize the way they manage the courts. They also punish some judges who decide controversial cases in ways that threaten vital LDP positions.[2] They do not punish *all* deviant judges—but they do not need to do so: in England, as Voltaire reminds us, "it [was] thought well to kill an admiral from time to time to encourage the others." So long as principals set the punishment high enough, they can constrain their agents with less than full enforcement.[3]

The Supreme Court sets the tenor for the courts by deciding most politically charged cases in ways that protect important LDP interests. It expects lower courts to do the same. Like the U.S. Supreme Court, it reverses lower-court judgments that go against the grain. Unlike the U.S. Supreme Court, it also punishes these judges in their careers. It does not, through these ploys, constrain its agents perfectly; a few judges continue to flout LDP control. Yet some slack almost always inheres in any agency: so long as principals incur nontrivial costs in monitoring and disciplining their agents, one would not expect full compliance. The point is that Japanese legislators not only *try* to discipline their judicial agents, but they also largely—however imperfectly—succeed.

The Fukushima Incident

According to many observers, it was not until the late 1960s that the LDP began to manipulate judicial careers toward political ends. Before then few judges asserted any political independence, so the Secretariat could assign them to judicial posts without considering their politics (*Zadankai*, 1959, pp. 13, 16; Shioya, 1991).

Most scholars of the Japanese judiciary locate a judicial "crisis" in the late 1960s. Right-wing ideologues, they argue, began attacking judges for their leftist bias (Saitō, 1971, p. 66; Hanada, 1970, p. 5). Eager to placate these conservative constituents, the LDP launched a witchhunt. It criticized recent court decisions, and urged the cabinet to make independent judges pay for their independence (Saitō, 1971, p. 66). By March 1969 the Minister of Justice could declare that the time had come "to jam the cogs of the courts" (Hanada, 1970, p. 5).

The man who would take center stage in this controversy was one Shigeo Fukushima, a Sapporo district judge born in 1930.[4] He had joined the judiciary in 1959, and had just begun his second 10-year term in 1969 when he found an explosive issue on his docket.[5] Nearly 200 local citizens had sued the Japanese government over a planned missile base. Article 9 of the Constitution banned military force, they claimed, and the base was thus unconstitutional.[6]

Fukushima was a leader in a leftist organization of lawyers, law professors, and judges called the Young Jurists' League (YJL). By its own terms, the group was dedicated to preserving the 1947 Constitution (Seinen, 1969, p. 58). Given the LDP's persistent attempts to remove Article 9, this slogan was code for fighting the Japanese military. The implications worried local chief judge Kenta Hiraga. Lest Fukushima ban the proposed base, Hiraga wrote him a letter explaining why, were *he* deciding the case, he would refuse the injunction. But to no avail. Fukushima ignored the letter and enjoined the base.[7]

Although Japanese academics vilified Hiraga, he followed a noble tradition. The man considered to be the patron saint of judicial independence, prewar Justice Iken Kojima, often told lower-court judges how to decide their cases (Kusunoki, 1989, p. 2). Even when he fought the Ministry of Justice over executing Tsuda, for example, the issue was not properly his—for he was not on the panel hearing the case. To him, and apparently to Hiraga, "judicial independence" meant that judges judged independently of the executive and legislative branches. It did not mean that they did so independently of other judges *within* the judiciary.

Fukushima did not keep Hiraga's efforts quiet. Instead, he circulated copies of Hiraga's letter to his friends in the YJL, and some of them circulated copies to the press. Within a few days, the letter was in the newspapers. The press and professoriate accused Hiraga of subverting judicial independence, and the Diet launched impeachment proceedings. Nonetheless, Hiraga emerged relatively unscathed. On October 19, 1970, the impeachment committee reprimanded him but dismissed the charges.[8] After additional reprimands from the Sapporo District Court and Supreme Court, he joined the Tokyo High Court.

Fukushima fared worse. He too faced impeachment proceedings, for leaking the letter to the press. But where the committee dismissed Hiraga's charges, it ruled against Fukushima. It did let Fukushima stay on the Sapporo bench,[9] however, and Fukushima himself remained adamantly "independent." He railed against the judicial bureaucracy in public (see Fukushima, 1971). And notwithstanding Supreme Court decisions to the contrary, in 1973 he held the entire Japanese military unconstitutional.[10] Although the Secretariat eventually brought him to the Tokyo District Court for a time, it soon dispatched him to the Fukushima and later the Fukui family courts. By 1989, he was 59 years old and had served without relief in provincial family courts for over 12 years. Rather than continue, he quit (*ZSKS*, 1990, pp. 86–87).

The Young Jurists' League

What happened to the other YJL members is just as controversial. Academic writers persistently claim that the LDP and its politically reliable judges in the Supreme Court and Secretariat launched an antileftist crusade. Because the League had over 200 judges on its rolls (Table 9.1), they say, the Court and Secretariat fought desperately to eliminate it from the courts.[11] To be sure, the LDP had made ominous statements: Japan, "as a constitutional nation, could never allow" its judges to join the League (quoted in Ushiomi, 1971, p. 3). The secretary general of the Secretariat himself declared that judges should not join activist political organizations. And the chief justice of the Supreme Court announced that the judiciary should exclude political extremists of all sorts (quoted in *Zadankai*, 1971b, p. 69).

But talk is cheap. More interesting is what the judges at the Supreme Court and Secretariat did. In 1970, they refused to hire several League members who wanted judicial jobs. While they never explained their refusal, they did hire other League members. But most observers accused them of violating the candidates' civil rights. In turn, the frustrated applicants railed against the "Gestapo tactics" of the Supreme Court in legal journals, extolled the plans they had made to revolutionize the judiciary, and criticized the pressure on young judges to avoid red-light districts and pinball parlors (judges would thereby lose touch with the common man; see Saibankan, 1971, p. 12). None of this moved the Supreme

Court, of course. It continued to hire selectively, and by 1979 had rejected 34 graduates; twenty-four of them were members of the League.[12]

Equally controversially, in April 1971 the cabinet and Supreme Court refused to reappoint League member Yasuaki Miyamoto. Critics immediately accused the LDP of politicizing the courts. Miyamoto had been an assistant judge on the Kumamoto District Court, and had served on panels that issued several mildly left-leaning opinions.[13] Yet they were hardly so aberrant as to warrant this unusually draconian treatment. In contrast to the critics, some observers suggested that Miyamoto was simply a mediocre and slow judge. After all, not every slight is political harassment. As Freud put it, sometimes a cigar is just a cigar.

Because the Court steadfastly refused to explain why it did not reappoint Miyamoto, the public can only speculate about its reasons. Lawyers and law professors claimed political harassment, but to no avail. The Court insisted that 10-year contracts were 10-year contracts: it could offer judges another term or it could let their contracts expire, and in either case it owed no one an explanation. The next year, League member Toshio Konno of the Nagoya Family Court heard that the Court might not reappoint him either. Rather than risk that fate, he resigned.[14]

Contrary to almost all accounts of the subject, however, the Supreme Court did *not* generally punish leftist judges for joining the League. Its message seems instead to have been: "Think whatever you want, but don't let personal politics interfere with your work." Table 9.1, which describes the composition of the League's judicial branch in 1969, shows that most members had begun their career in the 1960s. Theirs was a generation radicalized by the massive 1960 riots over the United States-Japan security treaty negotiations. Joining the League was not much of a nonconformist act, for close to a third of them had joined.

According to Table 9.2, listing the highest jobs attained by 1990 for the judges in the classes of 1960 and 1961, the Secretariat judges promoted League members as high as their non-League colleagues.[15] If by joining the League a judge showed serious ideological heterodoxy, then the judges in the Secretariat might also have hesitated to assign League members to the sensitive administrative jobs in the Secretariat or the Ministry of Justice. Again,

Table 9.1   1969 Young Jurists League membership, by entering class
(percentages in parentheses)

Class	League members	Class	League members
1950	3 (2.70)	1960	31 (35.2)
1951	0 (0)	1961	20 (22.7)
1952	2 (2.94)	1962	26 (34.2)
1953	0 (0)	1963	28 (30.8)
1954	0 (0)	1964	28 (44.4)
1955	1 (1.41)	1965	25 (32.9)
1956	0 (0)	1966	20 (27.8)
1957	8 (9.76)	1967	5 (6.49)
1958	7 (10.4)	1968	10 (11.6)
1959	10 (13.2)		

Sources: Biographical data: Nihon minshu hōritsuka kyōkai (1990, pp. 30–143).
League membership roster: Shisō undō kenkyū sho (1969, pp. 61–70).

Table 9.2   Highest judicial positions attained by classes of 1960 and 1961
(percentages in parentheses)

Position	Non-League class member	League member
President (high court)	1 (1.27)	1 (2.63)
Chief judge (district or family court)	6 (7.59)	4 (10.5)
High court judge	48 (60.8)	24 (63.2)
District court judge	22 (27.8)	7 (18.4)
Family court judge	2 (2.53)	2 (5.26)
Total	79 (100)	38 (100)

Sources: Biographical data: Nihon minshu hōritsuka kyōkai (1990, pp. 72–77).
Note: The table shows the highest judicial (nonadministrative) position held by
judges who began their careers in 1960 or 1961 and remained in their job for at least
20 years. The two classes are aggregated because of the relatively small numbers of
League members.

however, they showed no such hesitation. By late 1990, 42.1 percent of the League members in the classes of 1960 and 1961 and
41.7 percent of the others had held administrative jobs (*ZSKS,*
1990, pp. 90–101). Moreover, some League members had held
extraordinarily important positions: Kōzō Tanaka had headed the
Ministry of Justice's litigation bureaus for Fukuoka and Osaka;
Naoyuki Kuroda had headed the litigation bureaus for Hiroshima
and Nagoya; Akira Machida had served in the Cabinet's Legal Af-

fairs Bureau; and Yoshio Ōsaka had held two chief judgeships and the presidency of the Osaka High Court (*ZSKS*, 1990, pp. 90–101).

Although Table 9.2 suggests League members did well in the long run, we wanted to find out whether the Secretariat penalized them at its first chance after the "crisis" of the late 1960s. To test for such a penalty, we graded judicial positions by status and geography, and compared judicial jobs on September 1969 (when a conservative group published the League's membership roster [Shisō, 1969]) with those held two years later. These calculations yield the results in Table 9.3; a positive figure indicates a net promotion, a negative number a net demotion. At least by this crude index, League members did not suffer. Members of the class of 1960 did mildly worse than their non-League colleagues, but that difference is less than the amount by which 1961 and 1962 members did *better* than their colleagues. Because of the arbitrariness of the index and the large variance involved, Table 9.3 does not prove the Secretariat was partial toward League members. The message is more basic: the calculations yield no evidence of any bias *against* them.

The evidence also shows the extent to which the LDP targets the median voter rather than right-wing voters. To test how closely the Secretariat sympathized with fringe right groups, we compiled

Table 9.3 Mean promotion index from September 1969 to September 1971 for classes of 1960–1962

Class of 1960	
Non-League members	+.178
League members	0
Class of 1961	
Non-League members	+.240
League members	+.429
Class of 1962	
Non-League members	−.700
League members	+.560

Sources: Biographical data: Nihon minshu hōritsuka kyōkai (1990, pp. 90–107). League membership roster: Shishō undō kenkyū sho (1969, pp. 61–70).

Note: We graded judgeships as follows: high court appointments and administrative positions—8 points; district court judgeships—6 points; family court judgeships and district court or family court branch office headships—4 points; branch office judgeships—2 points. In addition, we added 1 point for moves into Tokyo or Osaka and subtracted 1 point for moves out of the two cities.

biographies for the 21 League members named in a prominent 1969 right-wing book as having participated in "problematic" panels (Shisō, 1969, pp. 246–50). Of these, two had bad careers: Miyamoto, fired in 1971, and one eccentric Haruhiko Abe, described below. Of the other 19 judges, only two among the 16 who served at least 20 years in the courts had not had a high court appointment, a chief judgeship, or a series of fast-track administrative jobs by 1990 (ZSKS, 1990, pp. 30–131). In short, only four had done poorly. The fraction is higher than the analogous rates for the entire class of 1951 (see Table 8.3 and Appendix to Chapter 8), but not by much.

More to the point, some of the 21 judges fingered by the ultra-rightists did spectacularly well. Yoshio Okada took a chief judgeship at age 55, Tatsunori Shishidō at the unusually young age of 53, and Takeo Kojima retired after four chief judgeships and two high court presidencies (ZSKS, 1990, pp. 96–97, 104–05, 32–33). Of the 21 judges, two had participated in more than one "problematic" opinion: Yasuhisa Tanaka (eight such opinions) and Akira Takayama (nine opinions) (Shisō, 1969, pp. 249–50). Yet Tanaka spent 13 years with the Ministry of Justice, then took an administrative position with the cabinet before returning to the Tokyo District Court. Takayama spent 10 years in high court appointments, including four with the Tokyo High Court and three with the Osaka High Court (ZSKS, 1990, pp. 122–23, 80–81). Fundamentally, the evidence confirms the middle-of-the-road character of the LDP. Complaints from the fringe-right in fact counted for very little.

Secretariat Critics

Granted, not all League activists fared well. For example, those who directly and publicly criticized the Supreme Court and Secretariat's administrative policies often paid a price. Take Masamichi Hanada, appointed in 1957. His own reappointment was not an issue: the Supreme Court had already renewed his contract for another 10 years before the 1969 "crisis." And Hanada had at least started his career right. A University of Tokyo graduate, he had begun at the Tokyo District Court, done a stint in Hokkaido, and returned to Tokyo by 1963. Hanada was a leader in the League, however, and when the Supreme Court refused to reappoint Miyamoto, he became a public spokesman for those opposing the Court.[16] For this he paid a price. In 1972 the Secretariat transferred him to a branch office, in 1976 to a family court, and in 1979 back to a branch office. By 1987 he was 56 years old and had spent the last 15 years in branch offices or family courts. Like Fukushima, he quit (*ZSKS*, 1990, pp. 74–75). His principal co-signer on a petition to the Court over the Miyamoto affair was Minoru Takeda. In 1972, the Secretariat transferred Takeda from the Tokyo District Court to a branch office. He stayed in branch offices for the next 11 years (*ZSKS*, 1990, pp. 80–81).

The severity with which the Secretariat treated Hanada is illustrated in Table 9.4. The table details what the members of Hanada's class were doing at the time he was working in family courts and branch offices. Of class members still working in 1981, 16 were high court judges, 21 were district court judges, and six held administrative posts. Only two others were ordinary judges in branch offices. By April 1987, when Hanada resigned, of the remaining 43 class members six were chief judges, 12 were High Court judges, 13 were district court judges, three were family court judges, and six held administrative posts. Only two were branch office heads and only one was an ordinary branch office judge (*ZSKS*, 1990, pp. 72–77). The person who eventually replaced Hanada in one of his branch office posts was a judge 16 years his junior (*ZSKS*, 1990, pp. 9–10).

Others who protested the Supreme Court's treatment of Miyamoto also found their career paths blocked. Take the four judges who contributed to a 1972 book on the Miyamoto affair entitled

Table 9.4   Positions held by class of 1957 judges in December 1981

Position	Number holding
High court judge	16
District court judge	21
Family court judge	4
District court branch office head judge	3
District court branch office judge	3
Administrative post	6

Source: Nihon minshu hōritsuka kyōkai (1990, pp. 72–77).
Note: 21 judges had either died or retired.

Security of Status for Judges (Ikeda and Moriya, 1972). One was
Hanada. A second was Katsuhiko Moriya. The year after the book
appeared, the Secretariat transferred him to the northern Sendai
Family Court, and as of 1990 he had spent the last 11 years on
family matters, four in a branch office (*ZSKS*, 1990, pp. 100–101).
A third was Tsuneo Suzuki. The year after the book appeared, the
Secretariat demoted him from the Tokyo District Court to a branch
office (*ZSKS*, 1990, pp. 100–101). Moriya and Suzuki were both
national university graduates (see Appendix to Chapter 8), and
both have since spent at least some time on a high court. But the
fourth, Masahiro Tanaka, went to a private university and suffered
worse. The year after the book appeared, the Secretariat moved
him to a branch office. As of 1990, he had stayed in branch offices
for the entire 17 years since the book was published (*ZSKS*, 1990,
pp. 98–99).

Controversial Court Decisions

The Campaign Cases

Although it does not do so consistently,[17] the Supreme Court Secretariat can also penalize judges for writing politically incorrect opinions—most readily when the decisions threaten vital LDP positions.
The various judges who held the Japanese campaign rules unconstitutional provide a good example. The Public Offices Elections Act
drastically restricts the tactics candidates can use. These restrictions
benefit incumbents because incumbents obtain media coverage
through their official functions, while challengers do not. Because
the LDP has the most incumbents, they benefit the LDP. To one
Japanese academic they seem "part of a partisan strategy of the
ruling party to hinder the election of reformist local governments
supported by opposition parties."[18]

Section 138(a) of the Elections Act bans door-to-door canvassing.
In 1950 the Supreme Court had held a similar ban constitutional,[19]
but by the late 1960s people had again started challenging it as a
violation of their free-speech rights (Kenpō, art. 21). In the first
of these cases, a 1967 Tokyo District Court decision, the court
suggested—gingerly—that 138(a) *might* be unconstitutional.[20]

The Supreme Court responded almost immediately: 138(a) was

indeed constitutional.[21] But that did not satisfy judge Haruhiko Abe. A University of Tokyo graduate who started his career at the Tokyo District Court, Abe was one of the most able members of the YJL. He was also one of the most outspoken. In 1971, for example, he wrote (Abe, 1971, p. 194):

> Trials must also be fair politically. To make them politically fair, some people claim that we judges should be politically neutral . . . But suppose we interpret this to mean that we should be neutral toward all political ideologies, and should not let our political value judgments affect our work. Given these tumultuous days, is this possible? Clearly, to avoid political value judgments would cause us uncritically to support and blindly to follow the preferences of the establishment. Clearly, to avoid political value judgments would cause us to abandon our quest for fairness.

In 1968, sitting temporarily in a summary court as an assistant judge with less than 5 years' experience, Abe held the canvassing ban flatly unconstitutional[22]—the very ban the Supreme Court had upheld against the same challenge a few months earlier. When his initial 10-year term expired in 1972, observers rumored that the Court would not reappoint him (Odanaka and Sasaki, 1972, p. 98), but not so. It did reappoint him—into oblivion. The Secretariat gave him family law responsibilities for several years, and then moved him to a branch office. By 1990, 35 members of Abe's class had already served one or more terms on a High Court. Abe had been in branch offices since 1979 (*ZSKS*, 1990, pp. 102–03).

Since its 1967 decision, the Supreme Court has held the canvassing ban constitutional at least another seven times.[23] The ban's political importance is obvious and, perhaps for that very reason, some lower-court judges persist in fighting it. When they do, they suffer badly. Wholly aside from politics, one would not expect the Secretariat to promote quickly judges who ignore Supreme Court precedent. But politics are not an aside—for by all odds the Secretariat punishes more harshly the judges who ignore precedent in these politically controversial cases than it does those who ignore it in more mundane disputes.

One-time League member Tetsurō Sō, for example, held the ban unconstitutional in 1978.[24] As of late 1990, he was still in a branch office. He had spent three of the 13 years since the decision in

Table 9.5 Years that judges of the class of 1968 spent in district court
branch offices by 1990

Years	Number of judges	Years	Number of judges
0	5	8	6
1	2	9	4
2	1	10	3
3	12	11	1
4	4	12	2
5	5	13	0
6	10	14	1
7	8	15	1

Source: Nihon minshu hōritsuka kyōkai (1990, pp. 138–43).
Note: 21 judges had either died or retired.

family court and five in branch offices (*ZSKS,* 1990, pp. 122–23).
Judge Kunio Ogawa held the ban unconstitutional in early 1979,[25]
and as of 1990 still had not left branch offices (*ZSKS,* 1990, pp.
120–21). Only one-time League member Shigemi Anazawa es-
caped branch offices for voiding the canvassing ban. He held it
unconstitutional in 1980,[26] and spent the years since handling family law cases in various northern provincial courts.

The punishment is most evident for judges who show the most
promise. Take Judge Masato Hirayu, who held the same canvassing
ban unconstitutional in September 1979.[27] A star University of
Tokyo recruit like Abe, he too began his career in the Tokyo District
Court. Although not a League member, he had overlapped with
Miyamoto at the Tokyo District Court and participated in a study
group with him (Tsukahara, 1990, pp. 30). After holding the ban
unconstitutional, Hirayu stayed in a branch office until 1987. He
then returned to a district court, but still with only family law
responsibilities. By the end of 1990, he had spent 11 of his 23 years
on the bench in a branch office (*ZSKS,* 1990, pp. 142–43). As Table
9.5 shows, that placed him in the last 8 percent of his class. Among
his University of Tokyo peers, it placed him at the very bottom.

The Tokyo Five

It is instructive to learn how the Secretariat eventually handled the
bizarre affair of five Tokyo judges (taking turns on a panel of three)

who, in the late 1960s, took judicial agency slack to new lengths. The incident shows that a judge need not necessarily flout Supreme Court precedent to earn the Secretariat's ire. In 1967, the Tokyo Public Safety Committee (TPSC) told a group planning to march through central Tokyo that they could indeed demonstrate, but only if they stayed away from the Diet building. On June 9, this panel—then consisting of judges Ryōkichi Sugimoto, Kenkichi Nakahira, and Fujio Senda—held that the Committee violated the demonstrators' free speech rights, and cancelled the order.[28] In a rare move, Prime Minister Eisaku Satō immediately intervened to challenge the decision.[29] Dutifully, the court (judges Sugimoto, Senda, and Keiichi Murakami) retracted its decision.[30]

The lesson did not sink in, however, and the court did exactly the same thing the next month. On July 10, 1967, the same panel (Sugimoto, Nakahira, and Senda) ordered the TPSC to cancel an order requiring another group of demonstrators to avoid the Diet building.[31] On the 11th, Satō intervened, and later that day the court again retracted its order.[32]

The leader of the first group routed away from the Diet then sued the city of Tokyo for damages. He was traumatized, he claimed, by his inability to protest in front of the Diet. On December 2, 1969, the panel, now with Sugimoto, Nakahira, and Shun Iwai, awarded him ¥100,000 for his emotional distress.[33] The city of Tokyo had violated his freedom of expression and caused him anguish. It now owed him money.

For several more months, this agency slack continued unabated. The panel continued, for example, to harass the TPSC.[34] In 1968 the maverick threesome (now Sugimoto, Iwai and Akira Watanabe) held that the Ministry of Education violated the rights of authors when it certified textbooks for high schools.[35] And in 1969, they barred the government from implementing the COCOM Agreement, an American-led embargo of communist countries. Under the Japanese Constitution, the judges explained, "the freedom to export is a fundamental human right." If the government refuses its citizens the right to sell militarily sensitive equipment to the People's Republic of China, it violates that fundamental right.[36]

The judges most involved in these opinions paid for their independence. As Table 9.6 shows, Watanabe and Senda were on relatively few of the panels and were never on a panel together. Indeed,

Table 9.6 Sitting judges in selected problematic cases before the Tokyo
District Court

	Judges				
Cases	Sugimoto	Nakahira	Iwai	Senda	Watanabe
Demonstrations					
(a) Hoshino I	X	X		X	
(b) Hoshino II	X	X	X		
(c) Horii	X	X		X	
(d) Kō	X	X	X		
(e) No name	X		X		X
Textbooks					
(f) Ienaga I	X	X	X		
(g) Ienaga II	X	X	X		
COCOM (h)	X		X		X

Sources: (a) Hoshino v. Tokyo kōan iinkai, 483 *Hanrei jihō* 3 (Tokyo D.C. June 9,
1967); (b) Hoshino v. Tokyo kōan iinkai, 575 *Hanrei jihō* 10 (Tokyo D.C. Dec. 2,
1969); (c) Horii v. Tokyo kōan iinkai, 487 *Hanrei jihō* 18 (Tokyo D.C. July 11, 1967);
(d) Kō v. Tokyo kōan iinkai, 501 *Hanrei jihō* 52 (Tokyo D.C. June 9, 1967); (e) (no
names given), 483 *Hanrei jihō* 3 (Tokyo D.C. June 9, 1967); (f) Ienaga v. Monbu shō,
530 *Hanrei jihō* 12 (Tokyo D.C. Sept. 27, 1968); (g) Ienaga v. Monbu shō, 597 *Hanrei
jihō* 3 (Tokyo D.C. July 17, 1970); (h) 1969 nen hokkyō jōkai nippon kōgyō
tenrankai v. Kuni, 560 *Hanrei jihō* 6 (Tokyo D.C. July 8, 1969).

because lower-court opinions never disclose how the judges voted,
they may have been dissenters. In any case, they received relatively
ordinary assignments and eventually became chief judges (*ZSKS*,
1990, pp. 86–89).

The judges who served most often on these panels were Nakahira,
Sugimoto, and Iwai. Nakahira was the most senior of the three and
retired in 1972 (Tsukahara, 1990, p. 31). Sugimoto and Iwai fared
poorly. The Secretariat moved Sugimoto from the civil division
of the Tokyo District Court to the bankruptcy division. When it
eventually promoted him to the Tokyo High Court, it put him in
the patent division and kept him away from all administrative
responsibilities (Tsukahara, 1990, p. 31). From 1970 to 1986, Sugimoto spent three years in family court and 10 in district court
branch offices (*ZSKS*, 1990, pp. 132–33).

Although Iwai too eventually received a High Court appointment, he was on a much slower track than the one on which he

had started. Iwai was born in 1942 and began his judicial career in 1967 at the Tokyo District Court. Apparently, he passed the entrance exam to the University of Tokyo on the first try, and the entrance exam to the LRTI while still in college (see Appendix to Chapter 8). Of the 77 judges in Iwai's class, only four others passed the Institute exam so young, and only one was a University of Tokyo graduate. Because the only University of Tokyo graduate as young as Iwai quit the bench within five years, by all odds Iwai was the class star (*ZSKS*, 1990, pp. 132–37). By 1990, however, he had spent 10 years in branch offices. According to Table 9.7, that placed him in the last third of his class. Of the University of Tokyo graduates, he was at the very bottom.

Stacking Cases

The Nagara River

Harder to prove is the way the Secretariat and local senior judges use the personnel apparatus to fix the outcome of controversial cases. Two law suits against the national government for flood damages may illustrate this strategy. In September 1976, a powerful typhoon hit Gifu prefecture. The water level in the Nagara River rose and, under the pressure, the 80-meter-high dike burst and flooded the neighboring towns. Because the national government maintained the dike, the citizens sued the government. Although

Table 9.7 Years that judges of the class of 1967 spent in district court branch offices by 1990

Years	Number of judges	Years	Number of judges
0	2	9	2
1	1	10	4
2	3	11	5
3	7	12	4
4	4	13	1
5	0	14	1
6	7	15	1
7	5	16	0
8	5	17	2

Source: Nihon minshu hōritsuka kyōkai (1990, pp. 132–37).
Note: 22 judges had either died or retired.

they all sued in one court, they brought their claims in two separate cases.

The first group reached trial first and won. In December 1982 a three-judge panel held that the nation had maintained the dikes negligently, and awarded the plaintiffs ¥14 billion.[37] The same court did not reach the second group of plaintiffs until May 1984. When it did, it denied their claims outright.[38]

One could try initially to explain the radically different outcomes by precedent. In the time that elapsed between the two opinions, the Supreme Court issued an opinion on the standards that applied to the maintenance of river facilities.[39] Thus the court may have held for the first plaintiffs under its own understanding of the law. In view of the new Supreme Court precedent, it held otherwise in the second case.

Yet the circumstances may be more complex. As several commentators noted at the time, the Supreme Court opinion involved a case where the river overflowed its banks. Whether its logic applied at all to cases where dikes collapsed was far from clear (Katō, 1984; Saikawa, 1984). At the same time, the country's potential liability in flooding cases was enormous. Since 1974 courts had decided 13 mass tort cases for flood damage, and the government had lost all but one.[40] At the time of the Nagara River trials, 30 to 40 flood cases were still pending (Katō, 1984, p. 23; Saikawa, 1984, p. 50). Accordingly, rather than leave the nation's liability to the vagaries of judicial interpretation, the Supreme Court held a judicial conference to tell judges how to decide these cases (as well as how it intended to decide its own pending case) (*Zadankai*, 1990, pp. 10–11, 19). Rather than leave the second Nagara River case to judges who awarded the first plaintiffs ¥14 billion, moreover, the Secretariat replaced the senior judge on the panel.

The judges who heard the first Nagara River case were Junko Ikadatsu, Shinmei Matsunaga, and Takao Akimoto. Born in 1950, Ikadatsu was the junior. She was still an assistant judge, and this appointment was her second. Technically, she sat on the Gifu Family Court, and heard this case by designation (*ZSKS*, 1990, p. 180). Matsunaga was born in 1945, and he too was still an assistant judge (*ZSKS*, 1990, p. 173). As a result, the judge who set the tone for the case was Akimoto. Born in 1935, Akimoto was a University of

Table 9.8 Positions held by class of 1960 judges in 1990

Position	Number holding
Chief judge (District court or family court)	6
High court judge	11
District court judge	12
Family court judge	4
District court branch office head	6
District court branch office judge	4
Administrative appointments	6

Source: Nihon minshu hōritsuka kyōkai (1990, pp. 90–95).

Tokyo graduate promoted to the Tokyo District Court within three years of his initial appointment (*ZSKS,* 1990, pp. 90–91).

But it was Akimoto who had awarded the plaintiffs ¥14 billion, and the Secretariat moved him to another provincial district court before the court even issued the decision publicly. From there it transferred him to a Shizuoka branch office (*ZSKS,* 1990, p. 91). As of late 1990, the others in his class who had not yet retired held the positions shown on Table 9.8. Stuck as an ordinary judge in a branch office, Akimoto sank to the bottom of his class.

Takeo Watanabe, the man the Secretariat brought to replace Akimoto, had also been born in 1935 and served on the Tokyo District Court. But Watanabe was a man with ties to the Ministry of Justice. From the Tokyo District Court he had moved to the Ministry's litigation section at the very time that it was handling several flooding suits. From there, he went to the Tokyo High Court, and the Secretariat then moved him to the Gifu flood-claims panel. After deciding the second Nagara River case, Watanabe returned to Tokyo within four years (*ZSKS,* 1990, pp. 100–101). His transfer from the Tokyo High Court to the Gifu District Court was out of the ordinary, for the Secretariat generally moves high court judges with Watanabe's seniority to inferior courts only when the lower court lies with*in* that high court's jurisdiction. In other words, the Secretariat tries to reduce the discomforts of mobility for judges who have that much seniority. Only in extraordinary cases like this does it move its senior judges across the country to inferior posts (*ZSKS,* 1990, p. 11; Miyazawa, 1991, p. 12).

Kanemi PCBs

Judges who hold against the government do not always jeopardize their careers. In 1968 the Kanemi chemical firm accidentally mixed PCBs with its cooking oil and chicken feed. When in 1984 the Fukuoka High Court held the Japanese government liable for ¥1.4 billion for its regulatory lapses,[41] the three judges involved seem not to have suffered. The senior judge, Kazuyoshi Miyama (age 56 at the time) next became chief judge of the Miyazaki District Court (*ZSKS*, 1990, pp. 54–55). Hiroshi Tanimizu, age 49, went to the Fukuoka District Court, returned to the Fukuoka High Court, and then became chief judge of the Kumamoto District Court (*ZSKS*, 1990, pp. 86–87). Only the most junior judge even arguably suffered: Shōji Adachi went to a branch office for three years before returning to a district court (but most judges do spend *some* time in branch offices, as Tables 9.5 and 9.7 show).

Yet the Secretariat may have done here what it apparently did in the Nagara River cases. Another case involving the Kanemi PCB disaster was still working its way through the Fukuoka appeals system at the time, and in 1984 the Secretariat reassigned all three judges on the first decision. As a result, an entirely different panel decided the second case. The senior judge on this reconstituted panel was again a fast-track judge with five years in the executive branch (*ZSKS*, 1990, pp. 42–43). On essentially the same facts as the 1984 decision, and with no intervening Supreme Court precedent, the new Fukuoka High Court panel held that the government owed nothing.[42]

Conclusion

A positive principal-agent approach to government suggests that political leaders will try to restrain their agents from flouting their policy preferences. Although they are nominally equals, Japanese legislators and judges are not so in fact, for LDP leaders have access to an array of devices to control the judiciary. In substance, Japanese judges are agents of LDP principals; in practice, LDP principals treat Japanese judicial agents much as principal-agent theory suggests. LDP leaders use their direct control over judicial appointments and indirect control over the Secretariat to shape judicial decisions.

Given the inherently anecdotal character of the available evidence, our conclusions are no more than tentative. Moreover, even by this anecdotal evidence, LDP leaders do not penalize judges just for joining leftist organizations, and not necessarily just for deciding controversial cases controversially. But they do punish judges who criticize court management; and they sometimes punish those who write opinions that flout LDP preferences, particularly when they ignore stated Supreme Court preferences. Because of the nontrivial costs political principals incur in monitoring judicial agents, one would not expect perfect compliance by Japanese judges, and one does not find it. However much they try, LDP leaders do not make their judges into automatons. Yet they do aggressively manipulate the institutional apparatus of the courts and they do, thereby, largely obtain the loyalty they want.

In considering judicial independence the norm, American legal scholars may have paid too much attention to their own tradition. As comparativist Martin Shapiro (1981, p. 20) put it, "the universal pattern is that judging runs as an integral part of the mainstream of political authority rather than as a separate entity." Such a pattern fits a coherent theory of principal-agent relations in politics. It also fits the phenomenon one finds in Japan.

Appendix: Judicial and Bureaucratic Independence—Comparative Statics

A. Judicial Independence

Wide-ranging comparisons of different judicial systems go beyond the logistics of this study. Nonetheless, the discussion above suggests several overlapping predictions about judicial independence.

1. Credible Commitments. To the extent Landes and Posner's (1975) analysis holds, judges should be more independent where politicians cannot credibly commit themselves to rent-extracting bargains. Accordingly, judges should be most independent (a) where the regime in power cannot realistically expect to stay in power long, and (b) where the regime is not controlled by a powerful set of leaders earning efficiency wages.

2. Fire alarms. To the extent McCubbins and Schwartz's (1984) analysis holds, judges should be more independent where politicians cannot effectively constrain the bureaucracy. In agreement with Landes and Posner's analysis, therefore, judges should be most independent where regimes cannot expect to stay in power and are not controlled by effective leaders. Because a divided government necessarily increases bureaucratic independence, this analysis also suggests that independent judges should be more common in presidential systems (like the United States) than in parliamentary systems (like Japan).

3. Risk-aversion. In a situation where politicians are risk-averse, the degree of judicial independence will again inversely correlate with the expected tenure of the party in power. If a party (like the LDP) can expect to stay in power long, it has much to gain and little to lose by controlling the judiciary tightly. All else being equal, it will adopt institutions that let it do so. If a party (like the American parties) has no such expectations, it may (if risk-averse) prefer institutions that extend its control over the judiciary *into the future*. To do so, however, it necessarily must reduce the government's present ability to constrain the judiciary (Easterbrook, 1992).

Whether parties in power maintain independent judiciaries depends on the strategies they play in what is effectively an indefinitely repeated game. Although some aspects of judicial independence (like life tenure in the United States) are constitutional, many are not. Arguably, the U.S. Congress could abolish the circuit structure of the federal courts and transfer its judges the way the Japanese Secretariat does. That neither Democratic nor Republican regimes have done so suggests that both parties (as risk-averse parties) may be using cooperative strategies in a repeated game. As in any indefinitely repeated game with low discounting, the cooperative outcome is but one of many possible results.

B. Bureaucratic Independence

Our analysis also points to the essential equivalence between courts and bureaucracies. Notwithstanding two centuries of American political theory to the contrary, fundamentally courts *are* bureaucracies. Consequently, many of the arguments above about judicial independence apply equally to bureaucratic independence.

1. By the logic of A.1 above, politicians trying to commit themselves credibly to rent-extractive bargains could—hypothet-

ically—do so by delegating the administration of their bargains to bureaucrats over whom they have no further control. Thus, all else being equal, civil service protection should be strongest where the expected political tenure is shortest and the control of the party leadership the weakest.

2. By the logic of A.3 above, risk-averse political leaders should maintain not only an independent judiciary but also an independent bureaucracy. Again, civil service protection should be strongest where the expected tenure of the ruling party is shortest.

10

Conclusion: Political Markets and Electoral Change

"There are those who argue . . . that Japan is moving toward genuinely democratic politics in which the political parties are predominant, but that argument seems out of proportion to reality . . . The superficial commitment of politics . . . to economic issues . . . is partly due to the fact that the bureaucracy traditionally exercised direct control over industry and industry groups" (Sasaki, 1991, p. 1). These are not the words of a demoralized foreign journalist frustrated one too many times in her efforts to pry a good story out of Japanese bureaucrats. Nor is it the opinion of some American scholar more impressed by how Japan differs from the American political system than how it resembles it. They were written by a well-known professor at Japan's preeminent educational establishment, the University of Tokyo Law Faculty. As creative as they may be, foreign journalists and scholars did not invent the story about Japan's powerful and autonomous bureaucracy. It is a story that, in various guises, is told by Japanese themselves.

A central aim in this book has been to show why this assessment is wrong, and to explain how so many intelligent observers could believe it. Most basic to their argument is that Japanese bureaucrats not only draft most legislation, but micro-manage the economy through thousands of nonstatutory measures. Unfortunately, they confuse activism with autonomy.

In the preceding chapters we argued that members of the LDP, not bureaucrats or judges or even LDP faction leaders, control Japan's policymaking process. We outlined what the LDP members want, and how they structure their party organization and government processes to generate the policies they seek. Ultimately, the

LDP members' desire to enhance their reelection chances drives Japanese government policy—not, say, any "statist" interest in national economic development.

If we take reelection to be a reasonable goal for politicians, we should keep in mind that different electoral rules alter how politicians go about seeking reelection. As we pointed out, Japan's multi-member district and SNTV electoral rules force the LDP to field multiple candidates in most districts to defend its Diet majority. The resulting personal-vote strategy drives the party to reward producer groups with favorable regulatory policies.

In more recent decades demographic and economic changes were forcing the LDP to shift its policy mix toward policies that favor the urban voter. This shift has not been easy for the party. Given current electoral rules, the party still needs to divide the vote, and has found it hard to target urban voters with particularistic policies. The possibility exists that electoral calculations will lead the LDP to abandon the multi-member district electoral system altogether.

The LDP has also organized itself to maximize the electoral chances of its members. Although its factional organization has been blamed for the huge expense of Japan's elections, the blame is misplaced and should be directed instead at the electoral rules. Given the need to divide the vote, the decentralization of financial and personnel matters along factional lines makes sense. Granted, hypothetically the LDP could do all this by fiat: it could decide at headquarters which candidates would get access to which types of policy favors to woo particular types of constituents. But, like multi-divisional firms, it has chosen instead to encourage intra-party competition and innovation by decentralizing the process.

If factional organization has its advantages, it also creates risks. The most obvious pitfall is that factions will promote their own interests at the expense of the party. To prevent this, and thereby to protect the benefits of majority party membership, LDP members delegate certain crucial decisions in a *trans*-factional party leadership.

The LDP monitors and polices its bureaucratic agents in various ways. The party's most powerful, if bluntest, means of getting what it wants is its legislative veto over any bureaucratic action. The party also has independent sources of expert information among its constituents, bureaucrats who have their eyes on political office, and bureaucrats of competing ministries. Finally, the LDP leadership can block the promotion of uncooperative bureaucrats. This is of particular concern to Japanese government employees because of their back-end-loaded pay scales.

Bureaucrats in fact serve their political principals well. The first bit of evidence is that voters reward representatives who can bring home regulatory and budgetary favors.[1] If bureaucrats were the principals rather than the other way around, voters would be foolish to expect such rewards in exchange for votes. The regulatory protection accorded to small banks and small retailers, for example, is good politics but makes very little economic sense. The record suggests that the LDP continually bases such regulatory decisions on calculations of support gained and lost. Finally, the percentage of bureaucratically drafted statutes and the number of nonlegislative ministerial regulations have not correlated positively with periods of large LDP electoral margins. If the LDP were uncertain of its ability to hold the bureaucracy to legislative intent, it would not allow the bureaucracy the same wide latitude in times of electoral crisis as in periods of electoral safety.

A similar logic applies to the ability of the LDP to control the judiciary. Two reasons that the LDP might actually *want* an independent judiciary are: either the LDP would need the courts to enforce bargains and hence to help it make "credible commitments" to campaign supporters, or the LDP would need courts to serve as "fire alarms" against the possibility of bureaucratic sabotage of legislative intent.

In the Japanese context neither reason for an independent judiciary applies. In the first place, ensuring the judiciary's independence would give the party no guarantee that courts would enforce the bargains struck with campaign supporters; independent courts, by definition, could do as they pleased. LDP party members are better off delegating authority to party leaders, over whom they have ultimate control. As for giving courts a "fire-alarm" function, the potential risks outweigh the costs in a parliamentary system, because bureaucrats have no separate executive to play off against the legislative branch. Where for structural reasons the possibilities for bureaucratic slack are fewer, political principals are wiser to monitor and police bureaucrats in cheaper, safer ways.

The career patterns of judges involved in court decisions that affected LDP interests show that uncooperative judges cannot act with impunity. The evidence corroborates the notion of a judiciary effectively controlled by the LDP. In numerous instances judges who held against LDP interests, despite earlier indications of their being on the "fast-track," found themselves rerouted into long stints in branch offices. Not all judges who hold against the LDP's interests are punished so blatantly. But by all indications, enough judges are sanctioned for the threat to be effective.

All along we have stressed the importance of institutions in shaping incentives. Here we will discuss the role institutional analysis plays in comparative work, outline the institutional basis of power, and speculate on the stability and persistence of institutional systems in Japan. We then compare contemporary Japanese political institutions to those of prewar Japan, to consider the consequences of institutional change. For the postwar period, we examine the effect that exogenous changes have on the pace at which the LDP alters the institutional framework to politics and conclude by speculating on the effect of electoral reform.

The Institutional Approach

In the wake of the "behavioralist revolution" of the 1970s, many political scientists considered it passé to study a country's institutions. Their "politically correct" research agenda was to measure the values voters held and to model and quantify voting behavior. During much the same period, neoclassical economists extended rational-choice assumptions to politics and developed the "public-choice" approach to political inquiry. Although clearly different from the behavioralists, many public-choice writers shared their scorn for institutions (Eggertsson, 1990, p. 349).

Country Specialists and Theory

Most comparativists never believed that institutions were unimportant. Most could never bring themselves to ignore the differences among countries or to treat foreign systems as trivial variants of the American case. But they also could never agree about which institutions to study, or how they should analyze those they did study. As a result, country specialists worked with an eclectic set of assumptions and approaches. When all else failed, they tossed in vague and undefined notions of "culture" to make up the difference. In the words of the distinguished historian Carol Gluck, "culture [became] the repository of our collective ignorance."[2] No wonder country specialists came to be called, somewhat disparagingly, "area-studies people." At least the term distinguished them from the "theorists" who made their assumptions, however specious, explicit.

We are not the first to notice this theoretical gap and to try to rectify it. Indeed, a central concern among many scholars studying Japan—whether Japanese or Western—has been to explain its national patterns in ways that make the comparison to other countries explicit and analytically coherent.

The Institutional Basis of Power

Although we build on the work of a large number of scholars, many others will object to our approach. Some anthropologists and legal scholars, for example, ask whether the Constitution, and the formal authority it accords the Diet matter in Japanese politics (see Inoue, 1991). Even we cast some doubt on the Constitution's Article 81, which calls for an independent judiciary. As we saw, the LDP has a variety of ways to limit challenges from the courts to its interests. How then does one examine the effects of institutions without resorting to the tautological claim that whatever appears to matter must matter?

Ultimately, nothing substitutes for a close analysis of the institutional incentives that the political players face. Upon that close analysis, some institutions will turn out to be more restrictive and others more malleable. The Constitution itself is relatively hard to change, and this does give it a certain prominence in the institutional landscape. It can be amended only by a two-thirds majority of both houses of the legislature and a simple majority in a national referendum.

Yet because the Constitution ultimately means what the Supreme Court says it means, the political party that controls the Diet can manipulate the document by picking the people who interpret it. The LDP has done this with striking success. For example, the Constitution's Article 9 bans all "land, sea, and air forces, as well as other war potential." Despite this text, the Court has consistently deferred to the LDP's claim that the Article permits a large military force. It is not likely to challenge the party's recent decision to place some of those forces under the command of U.N. Peace Keeping Operations. Although in 1985 it did hold the malapportionment of electoral districts unconstitutional, the effect remained consistent with LDP interests.[3] The Court ordered the LDP to reduce the gap in the voter-to-representative ratio by some unspecified amount, and the party complied. Given the Socialist gains among rural voters, the resulting reapportionment hurt the Japan Socialist Party as much as the LDP.

The LDP Dietmembers' institutional advantage derives not just from the letter of the Constitution and law, but also from the party's ability to change the law to the detriment of its competitors—whether bureaucrats, judges, or Socialist legislators. For instance, as the legislative majority in a parliamentary system, the LDP can in many ways affect the careers of judges; judges, however, have no way to affect the party members. The Diet not only has sovereign power in principle, but also the *sole* power to pass or not to pass the laws that govern all other political players. The LDP's ultimate weapon, therefore, is its ability to legislate its preferred solutions to disputes with other actors if it so chooses. That it has rarely elected to use this weapon—to reorganize the judiciary, for example, or to fire its elite bureaucrats—is a sign not of its uselessness but of its overwhelming power.

The Persistence of Institutions

At one level, the origins of modern Japanese political institutions are easy enough to discover. The postwar Japanese Constitution, for example, was imposed by reform-minded Occupation forces. But institutions, being manmade, are changeable; the challenge is to understand why some persist and some disappear. We have argued that the institutions which endure are those that solve the problems of the political players. LDP backbenchers, for example, retain institutions that constrain their options primarily when the institutions mitigate self-defeating collective-action and coordination problems.

We confess to functionalist reasoning insofar as we generally expect the institutions that solve political problems to survive and the others eventually to disappear. But we reject the Panglossian claim that an institutional structure evolves into the "best of all possible worlds." In the first place, one might ask, best for whom? Institutions serve those with the most resources to shape them. In democracies, voters have the final say through their power to punish the politicians who control political institutions. But, we have argued, agency slack can persist in that mechanism for extended periods of time.

Second, as Douglass North and others have noted, institutional development is "path-dependent." Each generation faces a range of options that is limited by past choices. Institutional choices may not be the most efficient, even for those who possess disproportionate resources. But they are likely to be the most feasible.

The Stability of Japanese Politics

Senior Japanologists sometimes quip that nothing ever changes in Japanese politics; they tell their juniors that Nathaniel Thayer's 1969 classic *How the Conservatives Rule Japan* leaves nothing more to be written. They have a point: Japan's postwar political institutional structure has indeed produced patterns of policymaking that have changed only incrementally, and one would hate to answer to a Higher Power for all the trees felled in the cause of tenure. In Shepsle and Weingast's terms (1981), Japanese political institutions (but not American universities) have produced structure-induced equilibria.

Given this institutional stability in Japan, the persistence of some basic patterns in political behavior is not surprising. Except for opposition victories in the Upper House in 1989, the LDP has consistently controlled both houses. It still controls the far more important Lower House. Even if politicians have become more interventionist since the mid-1970s, they still delegate considerable authority to the party leadership in order to economize on the transactions costs of multiple one-shot bargains. In turn, the LDP delegates policymaking and implementation to the bureaucracy in order to consolidate its political advantage. And in all these cases, the delegation has remained conditional: party backbenchers can vote their leaders out of office, and the leaders can override and punish bureaucrats.

The usual explanations for this equilibrium invoke coincidence. With their great stores of wisdom, for example, perhaps the bureaucrats simply chanced upon policies that voters happened to like. Alternatively, perhaps bureaucrats simply happened to be of like minds with LDP politicians and independently implemented policies that pleased LDP constituents. In either case, however, the bureaucrats are the principals. The politicians are merely the agents they use to "legitimize" their reign to the benighted public.

We agree with Kent Calder that the two central features of Japanese politics—LDP longevity and bureaucratic delegation—are anything but coincidence. Instead, they represent the result of rational political actors pursuing their self-interest under institutional constraints. The LDP remains in power because it adapts to and manipulates the electoral rules effectively. In turn, its leaders delegate to the bureaucracy because they know they can keep bureaucrats in line. Strategy, not happenstance, explains the equilibrium.

The Consequences of Institutional Change

Much is made of Japan's economic success, past, present, and probable future. Indeed, Japan has enjoyed almost consistently above-average economic performance since the mid-1920s. It is this performance, of course, that has enabled academics skeptical of market processes to cite Japan to extoll the virtues of smart bureaucrats. We caution against their leap in logic. For all the pages written about Japanese bureaucrats, a closer look at Japanese economic policies reveals their fundamentally political logic.

The alternative and more overtly political account of Japanese economic regulation we offer begins with a brief institutional sketch. For it is, we believe, the differences in the relative institutional power of pre- and postwar legislatures that explain much of the subsequent regulatory difference. From 1925 to 1945, elections were conducted under the same multi-member district electoral rules that govern contemporary Japanese elections. In both pre- and postwar Japan, majority-seeking parties had to divide the vote, and in both, therefore, they developed personal-vote strategies. Expensive electoral campaigns cultivating personal followings were common in both periods.

Radical differences, however, existed in the latitude of policy available to politicians. Postwar LDP politicians have been able to manipulate government resources to cultivate their electoral support, whether among small business proprietors, farmers, or major business firms. Although before the war politicians sometimes tried to do the same, they lacked the institutional authority to do so successfully. Instead, the popularly elected Lower House was held in check by a variety of electorally unaccountable bodies: the Upper House, the Privy Council, the military leadership, and the senior advisers to the Emperor. Because the Emperor rather than the Diet held sovereign authority, the legislature could not use the threat of a legislative veto to impose its will. And because these democratically unaccountable officials had no interest in supporting politicians, they routinely prevented them from using the government to transfer wealth to farmers or small business proprietors.

Two patterns ensued: money passed from the larger firms to the people in government, and legislation disproportionately favored those larger firms. The men in the senior positions, who were electorally unaccountable, had the power to create rents through government; the popularly elected politicians had the power to delay the process. As a result, the two groups together were able to extract rents from the larger firms by "selling" competition-inhibiting regulation. The regulation was valuable, and the larger firms were able (and willing) to buy it.[4]

The senior, nonaccountable officials were particularly interested in selling statutes that favored these firms, for many had a direct financial stake in the businesses. In 1930 over a third of the members of the Upper House were managers or part-owners of *zaibatsu* firms (Tiedemann, 1971, p. 281). The smaller businesses and farmers had far fewer supporters among the unelected officials. Even if they had had that support, they faced larger collective-action costs. As a result, the most politicians could do to win their votes was to recycle some of the money they raised from the zaibatsu into local bribes.

The Second World War changed all this. Most basically, McArthur's staff destroyed the institutional power of the democratically unaccountable officials. Consequently, Lower House legislators could now use government resources to their private electoral advantage. The LDP leaders have done so in spades. They have manipulated the government with two aims: to gather votes directly, and to obtain the money they need to gather votes indirectly. Under their control, the government has favored numerous small producer groups with policies ranging from subsidies and tax breaks to barriers to entry and trade protection. These policies have not promoted efficiency—whether of the directly affected sectors or of the economy as a whole. Instead, the policies have simply transferred wealth to groups with easily organized constituents who will reliably vote LDP.

Under LDP control, the government has also favored groups that donate generously to LDP Dietmembers. Big contributors (in the 1960s and 1970s, the steel industry, utilities, and banks; in the early 1990s, electronics, construction, and financial institutions) regularly obtain government-enforced protectionist barriers and other regulatory breaks. Even so, these cartels have been unstable. Because they enjoy government sanction, however, they last longer and are established more often than they would in a country where apprehended cartel organizers go directly to jail.

Two points drive our comparison between pre- and postwar Japan. First, Japanese economic regulation is seldom apolitical: an electoral logic governs the process from the outset. Second, political institutional authority shapes Japanese economic regulation. Before the war, a few large firms bought favorable regulatory regimes for their private benefit. After the war, other groups have been able to compete in this regulatory market as well—largely because of the increased authority the postwar Constitution gives the Diet.

Exogenous Change and the Pace of Evolution

Institutions, we have suggested, can produce structure-induced stable outcomes. The LDP has adopted a personal-vote electoral strategy in response to Japan's electoral rules, while LDP backbenchers have delegated extensive authority to the party leadership to overcome the collective-action problems inherent in one-shot bargains. In another balancing act, the LDP's legislative veto allows the party to delegate a substantial policymaking role to the bureaucracy without fear of the party's intentions being subverted, while a cooperative bureaucracy leaves the LDP uninterested in an independent judiciary.

From these stable patterns of policymaking and the thirty-five-plus years of uninterrupted LDP rule one should not deduce stasis in Japanese politics. Changes in Japan's demographics and in its international environment have forced the LDP to adjust its policies (see Chapter 3). Note, however, that as of this writing in summer of 1992 the LDP has chosen to operate within the existing rules rather than to use its Diet majority to change them. The LDP has shifted the *content* of its policies without abandoning a process that has worked for it so well.

The most significant change the LDP has faced is the steady urbanization of the Japanese electorate. In 1990, more than three quarters of Japan's population lived in areas classed as urban, up from 68 percent in 1965 (Japan Statistical Yearbook, 1991). As we suggested, this posed several problems for the LDP. First, fewer rural dwellers meant fewer members of Nōkyō, the well-organized network of agricultural cooperatives that mobilized the vote for LDP candidates at election time. The loss of rural voters signified an increase of urban, typically white-collar workers who were more likely to vote as consumers than as producers.

The LDP steadily lost its vote share through the 1960s and 1970s. Its votes did not go to the Socialist Party, however—by then it had become even more dependent on its rural supporters than had the LDP—but to the smaller middle-of-the-road parties such as the Democratic Socialists, the Kōmeitō, and for a time the LDP splinter group, the New Liberal Club. By shifting policy emphasis at the margin to programs like social security, medical insurance, and urban infrastructure, the LDP was able to stem the emigration of its supporters to the opposition. But this also prompted a rearguard reaction among LDP backbenchers eager not to lose their traditional constituents. We attribute the often-noted "rise of LDP interventionism" in the 1970s to backbencher dissatisfaction with the party leaders' new policy mix rather than to any real change in the power of the LDP relative to the bureaucracy.

A second pressure the LDP began to feel in the 1970s and 1980s was foreign insistence that Japan limit its current account surplus, or open its markets to greater foreign competition, or both. Being Japan's most important ally gives the United States considerable diplomatic weight. The greatest pressure from the United States on the LDP, however, was indirect. As the larger Japanese firms gained important stakes in the American market, they increasingly urged the party to reduce its protection of agriculture and the less efficient segments of the small business sector.

Accordingly, the LDP's policies began to shift at the margin away from protecting agriculture and small business. But the current electoral rules made fundamental policy shifts expensive. Even though farmers represent less than 12 percent of the population and only a fourth of them actually farm full-time, multiple-candidate districts place a premium on organized voters who will vote in a predictable fashion. This, more than lingering malapportionment, gives farmers clout beyond what their numbers alone would suggest. As a result, although the LDP leadership has gradually opened the citrus and beef markets and hinted at opening the rice market, it has moved slowly.

The same slow pace of reform characterizes the policies designed to protect small businesses. Since 1982 the government has gradually reduced its subsidies for small firms, despite the blow a stronger currency dealt to small manufacturers whose goods compete with imports. But government has continued to let these firms under-report their income, even as it has initiated the sales tax described in Chapter 3. And it has imposed significant restrictions on banks, even as it has nominally permitted them to enter the credit card market.

Yet another example of the LDP's slow pace in changing its policies toward small business is the Large Stores Act. With its roots in the prewar regulatory regime, the law both protects small retailers from their larger and more efficient competitors, and lets existing retailers cartelize their local markets. The LDP had pledged to cut back this regime once the law reached the priority list of American trade negotiators. As amended in 1990, it did weaken the entry barriers to the industry. Notwithstanding the amendment, however, change remained incremental, and small firms retained much of their ability to exclude large competitors.

What accounts for the LDP's inability to act more decisively in the face of domestic and foreign pressures for change? The immobility is not born of the party's factional organization. There are no significant factional differences over agricultural or small-business policy. The battle lines are drawn between the party leaders, responsible for the party's longer-term electoral prospects, and backbenchers concerned with their own immediate survival. It is a battle in which the backbenchers hold a decisive advantage. For despite their delegated powers, the leaders answer to backbenchers in two ways. First, a majority of backbenchers can oust the leadership at any time. Second, in order to remain in power the leaders need to ensure the election of an LDP Diet majority—the election, in short, of several hundred backbenchers.

It is the backbenchers who have consistently slowed the pace of reform. Out of concern for the investments they have made in their personal support networks among farmers, local merchants, and small-scale producers, they have consistently fought radical policy change. As a result, the real constraint on the LDP has remained the personal-vote strategy caused by the multi-member district system. Short of a drastic revision of that system, the structure-induced outcome, even in response to serious exogenous pressures, is incremental change.

Electoral Reform

The LDP seemed content with its ability to muddle through, albeit with perennially thin electoral margins and a constant risk of U.S. trade retaliation, until its loss of the Upper House majority in July 1989. It is ironic that an Upper House electoral defeat should have been the decisive prod to action, since the Upper House is governed by electoral rules that give less play to the personal vote strategy needed for Lower House elections. The shares-for-influence Recruit scandal had also taken its toll. Although of only passing interest to voters, the scandal highlighted to the business world the dangers of funneling the huge sums of illicit money required to oil the LDP's political machine. Businesses now began to question more seriously their net gains from an LDP majority.

Changing Business Interests

Businesses have always complained to the LDP that Japanese elections, and hence the campaign contributions the LDP requires of them, are too costly. For decades business contributors have prodded the LDP to rid itself of its factional organization, in hopes that a centrally coordinated LDP election campaign would be cheaper.

But when pressed, the businessmen have never failed to bankroll the LDP's lavish multi-member campaigns. For them, a non-LDP administration was always worse than the election expenses. Particularly during the decades when Japan's was a relatively closed economy, the protection LDP policies afforded businesses was apparently worth considerable sums.

In more recent years, large export-oriented manufacturing and service firms have had less use for government-managed cartels. Cartels are of little value in foreign markets where most competitor firms are unbridled. The large exporters are also the most vulnerable to trade retaliation, even if the ire of foreigners is directed at import-competing firms in Japan, because exporters have the most to lose in the event Japanese firms are denied access to foreign markets. So long as the big contributors obtained policies of value to themselves, they willingly underwrote the LDP's cultivation of the agricultural and small business vote. Now that agricultural and small-business protection has increased the likelihood of trade retaliation, they seem to have recalculated their net gain.

Owners and managers of large firms still value a conservative government. They prefer stable property rights, low corporate taxes, low inflation, stable exchange rates, weak labor unions, and an otherwise generally positive business environment. But they have strongly voiced their desire for a reorganization of the LDP's coalition, even if that entails changing the electoral system. They want cheaper elections and less protection to the inefficient sectors of the Japanese economy.

The Legislative Process

Soon after the Recruit scandal hit the tabloids in 1988, the LDP established a Political Reform Task Force *(Senkyo kaikaku hombu)* within the party to clean up the party's tarnished image. Prime Minister Takeshita's public approval rating had fallen to an unprecedented two percent, forcing him to resign and setting off an internal leadership crisis. Veteran LDP politician Masayoshi Itō refused the party presidency, pleading poor health, but also complaining that the party wanted him for his squeaky-clean image and not for serious work. Nonetheless, Itō did agree to chair the Task Force, and to undertake the job of reforming the electoral system.

Voters greeted the reform plans with a cynicism bred of repeated disappointment. A political reporter for one of Japan's large dailies epitomized the public reaction when he privately chided one of us: "Don't take it seriously. The LDPers are just using this talk of electoral change to distract people from campaign finance reform. They don't really plan to go through with either. What they want, instead, is to propose electoral reforms that will never pass, blame the opposition for torpedoing them, and find that—by that time—the public has forgotten about the campaign finance mess."

The skepticism may have been warranted. But the LDP leadership did continue to explore electoral change. It renamed a subgroup of the Task Force the PARC Electoral System Research Committee *(Senkyo seido chōsakai)* and told it to work on radical change. The group represented every faction in rough proportion to factional size, and Tsutomu Hata, a sixth-term star in the Takeshita faction, chaired it. Over the next two years, with help from the Ministry of Internal Affairs and the Electoral System Advisory Council *(Senkyo seido shingikai)* in the Prime Minister's office, the group drew up plans for a complete restructuring of Japan's electoral rules.[5]

The Advisory Council produced a midterm report in April 1990. Not surprisingly, the planned reforms cleverly favored the LDP. Instead of electing 512 representatives from 130 districts, voters would be allocated to 300 *single*-member districts. Simulations on the basis of past elections showed the LDP would win a majority by a large margin, but most likely the margin would be temporary. In the longer run, opposition parties would merge into a single counterforce to the LDP and forge a majority in most districts.

To forestall this possibility, the report gave voters a second ballot for the party of their choice. One hundred seventy one additional seats, for a total Lower House membership of 471, would be allocated to the parties on the basis of proportional representation in eleven large districts (Kawamura and Matsui, 1990, p. 17). The proportional representation portion of the ballot would give small parties an incentive not to merge with the larger parties. If all worked according to plan, the LDP would win a majority of single-member districts on the basis of a plurality, and keep its opposition splintered by giving all parties a chance to win seats on the proportional representation ballot.

Consequences of Electoral Reform

Social scientists rarely have a chance to test one variable at a time. Particularly in postwar Japan, where a single party has stayed in control for over thirty-five years, scholarly debates have relied heavily on causal assumptions that have never been put to the test. If the LDP abandons plans for electoral reform, our arguments too will rest on logic and circumstantial evidence. But if it does change the electoral system, we would have a vivid test of our hypothesis that the present system radically shapes the LDP's internal organization, electoral strategy, and policy choices.

We predict that electoral reform in favor of single-member districts and party lists would have major consequences for Japan and its trading partners. In its organization and functioning, the LDP would grow to resemble more closely British parties. Personnel, electoral strategy, and policy decisions would be centralized. Factions would atrophy because they would no longer serve an important function for LDP members. PARC committees would grow relatively inactive, as members lost their need to scramble for budgetary and regulatory favors for their constituents. Instead, LDP Dietmembers would form loose policy-based and regional groupings as the members strove to ensure that their respective districts' interests were reflected in the party's policy platforms.

Without a need to divide the vote among several candidates in most districts, the LDP would be free to compete electorally with other parties on the basis of a party platform. Its candidates would appeal to voters more on the basis of issues, and less with constituency favors. That is not to say the LDP would forfeit its advantage as incumbent party. At the margin, it would still have an incentive to target budgetary and regulatory favors strategically. In deciding how far off the median voter's preference point to pitch its policies, it would weigh how much the business sector was willing to pay for pro-business policies and calculate how those contributions would translate into votes. Nonetheless, a set of policies as favorable to producers and protectionist as it was under the old system would be unlikely. At the very least, the LDP would reduce its dependence on farmers and small business owners, whose main attraction remains their ability to help the LDP to get its vote spread evenly.

The relationship between the LDP and the bureaucracy would change as well, though more subtly. Because LDP backbenchers would have less need for pork, the party's primary contact with the bureaucracy would be through the party leadership. Some observers may infer from this that, just as the party seemed to gain influence in policymaking in the 1970s, the party would now be losing influence because it would appear less interventionist. Obviously, we think this would be precisely the wrong conclusion to draw. Because the party would be more centralized, it would be better able to speak with one voice. If anything, the LDP would be able to monitor its agents more effectively.

The Reaction of Opposition Parties

The opposition parties objected to the reform proposal for the very reason the LDP conceived of it: the new electoral system would give the LDP a maximal electoral advantage. As the second largest party, the Socialists would potentially benefit from single-member districts. In a straight single-member district system, they could expect to absorb the smaller parties as voters abandoned a hopeless cause. But the party-list portion of the ballot gave smaller parties the ability to survive on their own, and reduced the attractiveness of the new system to the Socialists. That, of course, was the idea. By contrast, the smaller parties—the Democratic Socialist Party, for example, or the Kōmeitō and the Communist Party—welcomed the party-list element of the new plan, but objected to the high ratio of single-member to party-list seats. After all, the LDP wanted just enough party-list seats to keep the opposition divided, but not enough to vitiate the LDP's large party advantage in the single-member districts.

The LDP probably has room for compromise. To buy off one of the smaller parties, for example, it may increase the ratio of party-list seats to single-member district seats. But at some point, the party will lose more from making concessions than it would gain from reforming the system. As one would expect, the LDP backbenchers (whose careers are on the line) have peered over the shoulders of their leaders to ensure that their interests were not being sold out.

Opposition within the LDP

It is the LDP backbenchers who ultimately control the party. That the party does not decide everything by party caucus, we have argued, is by design. To provide themselves with collective goods, party members delegate to their leaders the power to make certain decisions on behalf of all, and the means to reward and punish the membership. But the condition for the leaders to retain their delegated powers is that they serve the interests of the party membership. Ultimately, a majority of members can always revoke those powers.

Typically, the established backbenchers were more leery of reform than the younger party members. For those who had invested huge sums in developing a reliable personal following, the idea of campaigning on a party label had less appeal. In addition, incumbents whose personal following was geographically dispersed across their district were most uncomfortable about running in a single-member district carved out of a portion of that district.

The party leaders tried to reassure reluctant members. They promised that no "independent" running against the party-endorsed candidate in single-member districts would be accepted into the party retroactively upon election. They also promised to include on the party list, wherever possible, incumbents with widely dispersed constituencies. But some backbenchers continued to fear that their political futures would be less secure without personal followings. All of the bargaining chips under the new rules would be in the leadership's hands. More seriously, the party leaders had trouble making credible their promises to restrict the party's options.[6]

In June 1991 the reform plan passed the PARC Electoral System Research Committee, the PARC Advisory Council, and the party's Executive Council. But under pressure from worried backbenchers, the Executive Council agreed in advance to resubmit the electoral reform laws to party scrutiny should party leaders have to amend the bill to get it through the opposition-controlled Upper House.[7] In other words, backbenchers withheld from their leader-agents the authority to change the reform plan in a way that would affect the reelection of backbenchers.

This concession to the backbenchers effectively tabled the plan. Backbenchers knew that the reform, designed to further LDP interests, would encounter fierce resistance from the opposition parties. Given the opposition's control of the Upper House, the fate of electoral reform rested on the LDP leadership's ability to find a scheme that would both satisfy the LDP backbenchers in the Lower House and pass the Upper House. It would all take years—so Toshio Kōmoto, head of Prime Minister Toshiki Kaifu's faction, privately assured one of us in August 1991—just as it had done with the sales tax. Within the LDP, change comes slowly.

Conclusion

We began our analysis with simple rational-choice assumptions about political behavior. Through our investigation, we concluded that political markets operate about as one would expect given the way incentives are structured. Granted, we did not explicitly test the hypotheses of strong bureaucracy or cultural tendencies. Nonetheless, once we had accounted for the incentives that the key institutions created, we found such alternatives unnecessary to explain what one finds in Japan.

Of the principal-agent relationships that we examined, the weakest appears to be that between voters and their political representatives. For this, we argue, voters have the multi-member district electoral system to thank. Voters have tolerated policies skewed toward special interests, in exchange for personal attention and constituency services from their representatives. We also found, however, that the LDP has gradually shifted its policies toward the median voter as the electorate has urbanized. The agency slack in this relationship has diminished over time, and visibly so since the 1970s.

Perhaps the LDP will now change Japan's electoral system. Whether it succeeds will depend on how party members calculate their electoral fortunes under the various alternatives. Whatever the party chooses to do, we expect one thing to remain the same: self-interested but institutionally constrained behavior by all the major players involved—constituents, politicians, bureaucrats, and judges. In the process of outlining how institutions like the electoral rules constrain each group of players, and the latitude each group has for altering those constraints, we implied that any changes in the rules could have broad-ranging ramifications.

The current talk of institutional change presents a rare opportunity. For thirty-odd years, Japan has given us a stable set of structure-induced outcomes. Because so much has stayed the same, most of the evidence we describe has been circumstantial. Soon, however, that could change. If the LDP does adopt new electoral rules, readers will have a chance to test the claims so many observers have made about Japanese politics: to examine the resulting changes in the LDP's internal organization, in its electoral strategy, in its relations with bureaucrats and judges, and in its basic policies. It is an opportunity not to be missed.

Notes

1. Introduction

1. The story has become known as "the fable of the barge." See McManus (1975, p. 341n3) (paraphrased by Ramseyer and Rosenbluth).
2. Geertz (1973, pp. 249–50); see Stigler and Becker (1977).
3. Readers unfamiliar with the literature on principal-agent theory may wish to turn to Eggertsson (1990, pp. 40–45); Jensen (1983); McMillan (1992); Moe (1984); Rasmusen (1989, chs. 6, 7). For an explicit application of principal-agent models to Japan, see Kohno (1991).
4. We borrow Douglass North's definitions: that institutions are "humanly devised constraints" (1990, p. 3), while organizations are "groups of individuals bound by some common purpose to achieve objectives" (1990, p. 5).
5. Denzau and Munger (1986); Jacobson (1987); Noll (1988).
6. For the equivalent issue in economic markets, compare David (1985) with Liebowitz and Margolis (1990); for a generalization of the role of expectations, see Krugman (1991).
7. On drafting contracts based on the agent's effort, see Holmstrom (1979) and Shavell (1979).
8. Becker and Stigler (1974); Rasmusen (1989, 7.3); Shapiro and Stiglitz (1984).
9. As to what they maximize, see Chapter 2, note 3.
10. For a survey of this literature, see Haley (1978); Ramseyer and Nakazato (1989); Ramseyer (1991).
11. Compare similar phenomena described by Bates (1981, pp. 119–20; 1983, p. 41).
12. For example, see Bates (1983, p. 122); Magee, Brock and Young (1989, p. xiii); Downs (1957). For a contrary view, see Peltzman (1990).
13. Coase (1960). In fact, however, in such a transactions-costless world voters would probably engage in endless cycling (Aivazian and Callen, 1981; Arrow, 1950).

2. Electoral Rules and Party Strategy

1. Recruit is an employment-information and publishing company that issued millions of dollars worth of its own stock at below-market prices to politicians in the late 1980s.

2. Cox (1989); Grofman and Lijphart (1987); Taagepera and Shugart (1989).

3. As is customary in the rational-choice tradition, we assume that politicians maximize their chances for reelection subject to a budget constraint. Like all humans, legislators have a variety of goals. But they first must be reelected before they can achieve many of their second-order goals, be they income, status, or policy preferences. Aware of its limitations, we adopt the simple reelection-maximizing assumption for tractability (Demsetz, 1990, pp. 144–60; Strom, 1990, pp. 565–98). On the budget constraint to vote maximization, we refer readers to Joseph Kennedy's instructions to his son: "Don't buy one more vote than necessary. I'll be damned if I'll pay for a landslide." Of course, in 1960 his son almost lost . . .

4. *Kōshoku senkyo hō* (Public Offices Election Act), Law No. 100 of 1959, *fuzoku* (appendix).

5. Note that this contrasts with the spatial voting models which posit that politicians tailor their policy platforms to the interests of the median voter (Downs, 1957; Cox, 1990).

6. Gary Jacobson (1987) disputes the apparent incumbency advantage. He argues that incumbents are "running scared" and therefore provide their constituents with the policies they want before would-be challengers have a chance to find weaknesses. But Jacobson's argument is agnostic as to whether or not the policies are skewed in the direction of private goods.

7. Gary King (1991) provides empirical evidence for the link between constituency service and incumbency advantage for state legislators, but there is no comparably rigorous treatment of this issue in congressional elections.

8. To some extent, politicians should be able to exchange outlier policies for campaign funding (Congleton, 1989; Baron, 1989). Rhetoric may suffice to keep some voters satisfied some of the time in a world of seriously asymmetric information. But the problem should be ameliorated at least partially in a competitive electoral system by challengers who have a strong incentive to expose empty rhetoric in order to get elected. See also Denzau and Munger (1986, p. 89) and McChesney (1991) for other ways unorganized groups might get their interests represented.

9. This and the following section draw heavily from McCubbins and Rosenbluth (1991).

10. While approval of both houses of the Diet is required for the passage of ordinary legislation, the Lower House alone has the power to elect the Prime Minister, pass the budget, and ratify treaties.

11. David Laitin suggested this cue-giving as a hypothetical method of vote division.
12. Richard McKelvey (1976) has shown that in a setting where many issues are politically live, a politician or party theoretically can forge a new majority coalition around an alternative mix of policies, however slightly different from the mix it is competing against.
13. Senior LDP politicians often have many more. Kakuei Tanaka is said to have maintained over 300 personal-support organizations in his district.
14. Sasago, Abe, and Muraoka (1990, pp. 59–60); Ishikawa and Hirose (1989, pp. 14–28); Kitaoka (1985, pp. 50–63).
15. A recent amendment to the Public Offices Election Act bans contributions by politicians to weddings, funerals, and festivals, but the Ministry of Internal Affairs has apparently turned a blind eye to money given in the name of Diet secretaries. The provision at issue is §249–2 of *Kōshoku senkyo hō* (Public Offices Election Act), added by Law No. 81 of 1989, effective February 1, 1990. See Tajima (1991, p. 9); *Jichishō senkyo bu* (1991, pp. 131–35).
16. Iwai (1990, pp. 138–43); Kitaoka (1985, pp. 56–62); Inō (1984, pp. 22–215); Curtis (1968, pp. 153–78).
17. See Chapter 6 for a further discussion of staffing.
18. Allocating relatively more staff members for constituency service work in the districts parallels the policy of Democrats in the House of Representatives (Zupan, 1990).
19. The Ministry of Internal Affairs compiles the reported campaign contributions and releases the figures every year in the fall. See, for example, "Seiji shikin, saikō no 1733 oku en," *Nihon keizai shimbun* (September 14, 1990), p. 1.
20. *Kokkai hō* (Diet Act), Law No. 79 of 1947, §41; see also Baerwald (1979).
21. A similar argument appears in Johnson (1989, p. 199) and Okimoto (1989, p. 123).
22. In British politics the two main parties' backbenchers do exert some influence on their party leaders by means of their respective party committee systems, but the contrast with Japan in the extent of this influence is stark. See, for example, McKenzie (1963, pp. 56–57) for a description of the Conservative party's Committee of 1922.
23. Although the LDP has changed the official English translation of *Seimu chōsakai* to Policy Research Council (PRC), we prefer PARC to avoid confusion with the more widespread use of PRC to refer to China.
24. *The Constitution of the Liberal Democratic Party* (English transl., June 1990) p. 15.

25. MOF and MITI bureaucrats, for example, refer to certain senior members of PARC committees who "have a veto" over policy decisions (interviews with mid-level and high-ranking bureaucrats, February 19–27 and August 19–23, 1991).

26. For a similar argument in the European context, see Strom (1990).

27. A structural generalization akin to Duverger's law is that a country will have $M + 1$ effective parties, where M is district magnitude (Duverger, 1963). Reed (1990) has shown that this is borne out in Japan.

28. The experiment is not perfectly controlled, since the lesser policy importance of the Upper House may cause voters to take their Upper House votes less seriously.

29. As poor as the LDP's party list performance sounds, the LDP did even worse before the SNTV nationwide district (where each voter named a single *candidate*) was changed to the party list system in 1983. The LDP's biggest problem before 1983 was in dividing the vote among candidates at a nationwide level. See Horie and Umemura (1986).

3. Demographics and Policy

1. Watanuki, Miyake, Inoguchi, and Kabashima (1986, p. 139); Kawato (1987, pp. 369–84); Flanagan (1984, pp. 163–68).

2. Recently, the party adopted as its official English name the Democratic Socialist Party of Japan. To avoid confusion with the Democratic Socialist Party, we retain the traditional names for the parties.

3. The *Sōkagakkai* is in fact a lay organization of the Buddhist sect, *Nichiren shōshū*. In recent years a well-publicized dispute has surfaced between the religious sect and the lay organization: *Nichiren* priests charge *Sōkagakkai* leader Daisaku Ikeda with arrogating to himself too much authority, religious and otherwise. See Fujimoto (1991).

4. Campbell (1991); MacDougall (1989); Samuels (1983).

5. *Nihon keizai shimbunsha* (1986); Inoguchi and Iwai (1987); Muramatsu and Krauss (1987).

6. Anderson (1987); Campbell (1991); Katō (1991); McKean (1981); Upham (1987).

7. See Peltzman (1991) for an argument and some empirical evidence that voters punish politicians in the United States for spending, even when much of it is in their districts.

8. Murakawa (1979) and (1986); Kakizawa (1985); Sakakibara (1991); Ohkawa (1985).

9. Iwai (1990, pp. 147–48); Sone and Kanazashi (1989, p. 51). The LDP Secretary General and the Chairman of the Diet's Legislative Affairs Committee (always an LDP member) share the task of "purchasing,"

if necessary, the cooperation of opposition parties in hastening a bill's passage.

10. One has to be careful in deciphering numbers in the budgetary allotments to public-sounding programs. LDP members in the PARC division concerned with health and welfare, for instance, manage to direct money to doctors, nurses, public bath houses, and restaurants in exchange for electoral support. For a classic study of the political clout of the Japan Medical Association, for example, see Steslicke (1973).

11. *Maruyama chōsa kai* (1985, p. 16). The LDP established the Maruyama Tax Research Committee in 1985 under the chairmanship of former MOF bureaucrat and veteran LDP politician Tatsuo Maruyama to study tax reform.

12. The relative burden to consumers and investors of sales and corporate income taxes will depend on supply and demand elasticities. Nonetheless, the corporate world seems to have believed that large firms would gain from a revenue-neutral tax package that simultaneously reduced corporate income taxes and imposed a sales tax.

13. Shindō (1989, pp. 40–53); see also *Seifu zeisei chōsa kai,* ed. (1986); and *Jiyū minshu tō,* ed. (1986).

14. A group of backbenchers formed an anti-sales-tax group within the LDP, but they quickly disbanded upon threat of sanctions from the LDP leadership (Ishikawa and Hirose, 1989, pp. 208–13).

15. See *Jiyū minshu tō* (1989; 1990).

16. *Nihon keizai shimbun* (April 24, 1991), p. 3.

17. See generally Chapter 7; see also Johnson (1982) on the steel cartel in the 1960s and Samuels (1988) on the oil refinery cartel. MITI's failure to rein in maverick automobile producers in the early 1970s is also well documented (Cusumano, 1985), and Noble (1989) describes the failure of the steel industry to keep out competition from mini-mills in the early 1980s.

18. The small credit card companies and credit associations have been regulated by the MITI according to the *Kappu hanbai hō* (Installment Credit Act) of 1961. Section 1 para. 2 of the law states that "the stability and growth of the small businesses that offer installment credit shall be taken into consideration in the implementation of this law." See *Chūshō kigyō chō* (1990).

19. Paragraph 4 of the Diet's resolution stated, "In the interests of the growth of the small firms in the credit-installment business, the entry of banks and bank-affiliated credit card companies into this business shall not be permitted to hurt the small credit installment companies" (May 10, 1984).

20. See, for example, *Kappu hanbai shingikai kurejitto sangyō bukai* (Install-

ment Credit Advisory Council [to MITI], Credit Industry Subcommittee) (1989).

4. Party Factions

1. Nakane (1967, p. 132). See also Yamamoto (1986), and Thayer (1969).
2. The *Jiyūtō* was renamed the *Seiyūkai* in 1900, and eventually became the postwar Liberal Party. The *Kenseikai* called itself, over the years, the *Minseitō*, the *Minsei hontō*, the *Shimpōtō*, and, after the war, the Democratic Party.

   Until universal male suffrage was adopted in 1925, only men over the age of 25 could vote, provided they had been registered residents in the district for the previous full year and paid land taxes of 15 yen or more, or had paid income tax of 15 yen or more for at least three years. The tax requirement was gradually relaxed, increasing the electorate from about 1.14 percent to about 5 percent of the population by 1919. See Matsuo (1989, pp. 8–10).
3. Murase (1988, pp. 79–81); Kitaoka (1990, pp. 195, 234); Kiseki (1965, pp. 82–93).
4. For accounts of factional competition within districts, see Tsukuda (1973, pp. 226–27). According to Naohiko Seki, a politician during the 1920s in the Kakushin Club, political candidates easily spent as much as 70,000 or even 100,000 yen. At an exchange rate of about 2 yen to the dollar, this amounted to campaign spending on the order of about $35,000 to $50,000. Recounted in Hazama (1982, pp. 635–36). As a frame of reference, political campaign spending Britain during the 1920s was an average of about $20,000 per politician. See Pinto-Duchinsky (1981, pp. 314–15).
5. This was the first election in Japanese history in which women could vote. Thirty nine women were elected to the Diet, a number that has never been reached since.
6. Prime ministers often do not use their agenda-setting power to push through their private visions of Japan's destiny. The Prime Minister who still holds the record for number of years in office, Eisaku Satō, was jokingly referred to as *Musaku* [No Policy] Satō.
7. Virtually every Prime Minister, once in office, has commissioned an internal party group to consider how to rid the LDP of factions. For a detailed account of such groups and their reports, see Tanaka (1986).
8. Ōhira actually only won first place in the first round of the primary, at which point second-placed Fukuda bowed out rather than to face a run-off against Ōhira. Ōhira was selected as party president at the

LDP Party Conference on December 1 by acclamation (Masumi, 1985, pp. 307–308).

9. Despite Fukuda's opposition to the Ōhira prime ministership, Ōhira named four members of the Fukuda faction to his cabinet, in rough proportion to the Fukuda faction's size.

10. No-confidence motions from the opposition parties are common, but the LDP's failure to override them was unprecedented. The ostensible reasons for the motion were revelations that high officials in the public corporation for international telecommunications, KDD, had been diverting corporate money for political uses, and that an LDP member, Kōichi Hamada, had lost large sums of money gambling in Las Vegas.

11. Political historian Junnosuke Masumi (1985, p. 317) suggests that Fukuda was willing to compromise with Ōhira but that he was unable to convince the young hotheads in his group in time to override the no-confidence motion.

12. Article 69 of the Constitution gives the Prime Minister a choice between dissolving the cabinet or calling new elections within 10 days of a successful no-confidence resolution.

13. Williamson (1986). McAfee and McMillan (1991) argue that hierarchies and the agency costs that usually accompany them should not exist in competitive industries, since a firm with agency slack would not survive. But even owners of monopolies are interested in maximizing profits and should seek out ways of minimizing agency slack. Creating inter-divisional competition could be one such way.

14. For more on the benefits and drawbacks of centralization, see McMillan (1992).

15. Kakuei Tanaka summarized the essence of factional competition when he said, "politics requires power; power requires numbers; and numbers require money." Quoted by LDP veteran politician Masayuki Fujio in Kinoshita (1991, p. 66). We save a discussion of the fundraising function of factions and of the party for Chapter 5.

16. One reason the party is less concerned about having experienced cabinet ministers than one might expect is that the party does not need this particular form of monitoring bureaucrats. As we discuss in Chapter 6 and Chapter 7, the LDP has other more powerful ways to structure the incentives of bureaucrats in line with LDP interests.

17. See Holmstrom and Tirole (1989) and O'Flaherty and Siow (1991) for the "tournament" literature on competition for advancement among managers.

18. Occasionally, frustrated faction members or independents will attempt to form a following of their own without mustering quite enough

adherents to be considered a real faction. Examples include Ichirō Nakagawa, who had a group of about 15 until he committed suicide in 1983, and Shintarō Ishihara, who garnered 48 votes for the LDP party presidency in 1984.

19. The prime ministerial race alone does not produce the sort of factions that exist in the LDP. In countries where the electoral system does not require intra-party competition at the district level, such as Britain, divisions within the party are likely to be policy-based but relatively loosely organized.

20. We are grateful to Gary Cox for helping us work through this argument. Arye Hillman and John Riley (1989) offer an alternative explanation for the small number of contestants in political races in general. If different politicians attach different values to the contested office, those with lower valuations will select themselves out of the race before expending more resources than the office is worth to them. While this is logically plausible, we prefer an explanation that does not rely on their assumption about the asymmetry of office valuation.

21. Again, we thank Gary Cox for his suggestions.

22. Buchanan (1965); see Tollison (1972).

23. Masaru Kohno (1992) found that in the February 1990 House of Representatives election, members of the LDP's smallest faction (the Kōmoto faction) and independents were less likely to run in three-member districts and more likely to run in five-member districts than did members of the four larger factions.

24. Not surprisingly, the Japan Socialist Party, with its inability to win more than two or three seats in any district, tends to have two or three factions.

25. Ishibashi's remains the shortest prime ministership in LDP history: 48 days. His runner-up, Sōsuke Uno, held on to the job for 63 days, between June and August 1990, before stepping down amidst a barrage of public criticism over his sexual improprieties. The revelations were particularly embarrassing for the LDP because it had chosen Uno for his "clean" image following the Recruit scandal.

26. Some scholars, including the highly regarded professor of international politics at the University of Tokyo, Takashi Inoguchi, have claimed that factions have discernible policy differences. Inoguchi bases his claims in part on a survey of Diet members conducted by the *Ekonomisuto*, a business news weekly, in 1989. See Inoguchi (1989, pp. 84–91). But we question the significance of one-time policy biases without controlling for cabinet and party positions currently held. Because cabinet members are expected in part to represent the interests of the groups they regulate, their views change with their cabinet

and party positions. Faction leader Miyazawa, in an interview with columnist Minoru Ōmori (*Gendai,* 1991, p. 57), corroborates our view that factions are not distinguishable on policy grounds.

5. Party Organization

1. Rogowski (1990) explains some of the range of committee authority across countries by measuring the level and variance in opportunity costs—by which he means how easily politicians can find equally remunerative and satisfying work outside the legislature—and the level of preference-homogeneity among legislators in different legislatures. When legislators possess similar amounts of expertise but face unequal opportunity costs, they may delegate wide decision-making authority to a single committee of *party leaders,* (like the British cabinet) rather than to specialist committees of backbenchers. By contrast, in legislatures where members face uniformly high opportunity costs and have more or less similar preferences, legislators will be willing to delegate substantial decision-making authority to *specialized* committees comprised of backbenchers, because committees' choices are not expected to stray far from the legislature's median position. Party members delegate policymaking in both types of cases, but they are willing to delegate to each other—that is, to specialized committees not under strict party oversight—only when they agree with each other anyway. We expect legislators' preferences are rarely so homogeneous as to make this a realistic possibility.

2. In the American context, party leadership is not universally recognized among legislative theorists as an electorally necessary layer of organization. Much has been written about legislatures without ever mentioning party leadership. A number of scholars of American politics stress the importance of Congressional committees in the electoral calculations of legislative incumbents. These committees do substitute for party leadership to some extent, as these theorists claim, though we believe this may be exaggerated even in the American case. For arguments stressing the role of parties in Congress, see for example Rhode (1990), and Cox and McCubbins (forthcoming). Keith Krehbiel (1990, 1991), by contrast, argues that the apparent rise in partisanship is illusory and suggests that the rise in party-line voting reflects a growing homogeneity of preferences within the two principal U.S. parties rather than more binding partisan constraints.

3. An LDP member's vote-getting and fund-raising abilities are weighed in personnel advancement decisions, presumably because the party needs people who will be able to bring a long-term perspective to their

job. When politicians talk about the "price" for a good vice-ministerial position being so much, they are referring to their fundraising record on behalf of their faction. See, for example, Honzawa (1990).

4. In rural districts, only 38 percent of those asked said macroeconomic policies were important determinants of their vote. See Arai (1988, p. 109).

5. The LDP apparently miscalculated the public's reaction against the value added tax in 1979. Hakuo Yanagisawa, who had helped design the value added tax when he was a bureaucrat in the MOF Tax Bureau, claims to have been surprised when he failed to win a Lower House seat in the 1979 election (Yanagisawa, 1986, pp. 45–47).

6. *Tokutei fukyō chiiki chūshō kigyō taisaku rinji sochi hō* (Temporary Measures Law Governing the Policy toward Small and Medium-Sized Firms in Specified Depressed Areas), Law No. 106 of 1978; *Tokutei fukyō chiiki rishokusha rinji sochi hō* (Temporary Measures Law Governing the Policy toward Unemployed Workers in Specified Depressed Areas), Law No. 197 of 1978; Ramseyer (1981b).

7. A recent example of a "shadow endorsement" is the defeat of incumbent Bunsei Satō (Ōita 2nd, Nakasone faction) in February 1990 by Takeshi Iwaya, a former secretary of Kunio Hatoyama who ran as an "independent" with backing from the Miyazawa faction. Satō's election campaigns were the subject of Curtis (1971).

8. Prime Minister Ōhira violated this implicit rule during his first cabinet in 1978, over the protests of the Fukuda, Nakasone, and Miki factions. But Ōhira honored the rule in his second cabinet, and no Prime Minister has violated it since. The LDP has also adopted an implicit rule requiring that the head of the LDP's Finance Bureau belong to a faction other than the Prime Minister's or the Party Secretary's.

9. Our assumption here, of course, is that there is not a one-to-one correlation between money and votes. More money in the hands of the LDP without a way to share the votes at the district level could result in worse, not better, electoral performance.

10. *Nihon keizai shimbun* (July 5, 1991), p. 3.

11. The incentive device is known as "efficiency wages." See Rasmusen (1990); Shapiro and Stiglitz (1984).

12. Benjamin Klein and Keith Leffler developed the reputation-signaling argument to explain why service companies, such as law firms, could compete with leaner firms despite their seemingly wasteful use of clients' money to purchase expensive rugs and other office furnishings. Price competition by firms with strong reputations would only reduce the quality of their product and thereby squander their hard-earned reputation. Better to make the same profit as leaner firms, as

market forces ineluctably dictate, but spend some to signal reputation rather than giving clients lower prices.

13. Gary Jacobson (1980) has argued persuasively that favor-maximizing contributors must estimate the probability of politicians' reelection in calculating the expected return from their contributions. Contributions to an electorally vulnerable politician, no matter how willing to provide favors if elected, are ill-advised. Note that, for example, banking industry PACs give generously to strong Democratic incumbents, even though they would prefer Republican representatives to win in most cases.

14. Haruhiro Fukui (1978) points out that the rapid rotation of cabinet positions scarcely gives cabinet members time to learn their jobs.

6. Political Structure and Bureaucratic Incentives

1. Pempel's 1970s approach also shows in his contribution to an edited volume (Pempel [1987]) whose publication was badly delayed for other reasons. A similar argument is made by Richardson and Flanagan (1984, pp. 346–48), and Johnson (1975, p. 10). The most prominent Japanese scholar subscribing to this thesis is Kiyoaki Tsuji (1969).

2. See also Richardson and Flanagan (1984, pp. 348–50). The point is potentially misleading, as Table 7.3 makes clear. Despite large annual variations, the number of ministerial regulations has held relatively steady. The number of regulations has increased relative to the number of statutes only because the number of statutes has diminished (see Table 7.2).

3. For example, Fukui (1984, p. 432; see 1987) finds that, even if others do participate in the process, Japanese political policy is "made under the normally substantial and often decisive influence of LDP leaders." Muramatsu and Krauss (1984; see Muramatsu, 1981, 1990) survey politicians and bureaucrats and discover that both believe politicians play a major role in policymaking.

4. Wolferen (1990, p. 145); see Johnson (1985, p. 60) ("the bureaucracy makes policy and the Diet merely rubber-stamps it").

5. Calvert, Moran, and Weingast (1987, p. 501, original emphasis); see Calvert, McCubbins and Weingast (1989). The point has become standard in the modern literature on positive political economy. See, generally, Bagnoli and McKee (1991); Coate, Higgins, and McChesney (1990); Ferejohn (1987); McCubbins and Schwartz (1984); Weingast and Moran (1983); Weingast (1984); Wood and Waterman (1991), and the articles in the 1990 special issue of the *Journal of Law, Economics, and Organization*.

We find inscrutable Bishop's (1990, p. 499) comment that the "Weingast-Fiorina view of the regulatory agency as serving the political needs of congressmen and senators really has no ready application to a parliamentary system."

6. Campbell (1977, pp. 283–84). As Baerwald (1986, p. 157) notes, bureaucrats "cannot ignore the balance of political forces in the National Assembly." Curtis (1988, p. 108) likewise points out that in MITI "there had to be a considerable amount of anticipatory reaction underlying bureaucratic behavior."

7. The point is basic to the modern theory of the firm. See Coase (1937); Klein, Crawford, and Alchian (1978); Klein and Coffee (1990, pp. 17–19); Williamson (1975, p. 8; 1985, ch. 6).

8. *Kokkai hō* (Diet Act), Law No. 79 of 1947, §132. By contrast, each member of the U.S. House of Representatives is allowed $411,099 to hire up to 22 staff members (Wright and Dwyer, 1990, p. 39). On the use of privately funded staffers, see Chapter 2.

9. The recent Nomura securities scandal illustrates this dynamic. The LDP had opposed letting former Nomura Chairman Setsuya Kabuchi testify before the Diet's Special Committee on Securities and Financial Problems, for fear he would implicate LDP Dietmembers. They need not have worried. Without a large enough staff to help them prepare for the questioning, the opposition Dietmembers were unable to dislodge any information unfavorable to the LDP from Kabuchi.

10. Both LDP backbenchers and party leaders do a certain amount of monitoring. Backbenchers monitor to increase their personal support networks (Chapter 2); leaders serve as the designated monitors for any cases where collective-action problems among backbenchers prevent effective monitoring (Chapter 5).

11. For example, Haley (1982; 1988a; 1991, ch. 7), Johnson (1982, p. 255), and Ohyama (1989, pp. 100–108) each recount failed attempts to enact statutes that would have given MITI or MOF greater power over the economy.

12. On the traditional notion that the Cabinet Legislative Bureau is above politics, see Naikaku (1991).

13. In this regard, the use of informal measures (so called "administrative guidance") by Japanese bureaucrats is a red herring. Informal orders are enforceable in practice only if the ministry controls sufficient *concrete* incentives—whether penalties or rewards. Also, informal dispositions will be reported by constituents to Dietmembers if they contravene LDP policy, and they can then be overturned by statute.

14. We provide the following simplified example only for illustrative purposes. Readers interested in more rigorous, formal, and generalized

discussions should see Ferejohn and Shipan (1990); Gely and Spiller (1990); McCubbins, Noll, and Weingast (1989; 1990); Marks (1989); Shepsle and Weingast (1981).

15. Where there are more than two parties, the problem is potentially one of empty-core cycling (Aivazian and Callen, 1981; Telser, 1982).

16. *Kokka kōmuin hō* (National Public Servant Act), Law No. 120 of 1947, §55; Muramatsu (1981, p. 81).

17. Curtis (1988, p. 110); see Johnson (1982, p. 52); Richardson and Flanagan (1984, pp. 51–52).

18. Koh (1989, p. 208); to the same effect, see Sone and Kanazashi (1989, p. 151) and Takeuchi (1988, pp. 37–40). Note that even as powerful and well-connected a star bureaucrat as Shigeru Sahashi suffered significant career setbacks when he antagonized politicians (Park, 1986, pp. 72–73; Johnson, 1982, pp. 261–62).

19. Ministry of Internal Affairs bureaucrats also retire into local and regional politics. As of January 1989, 16 of the 47 prefectural governors were ex-bureaucrats from the Ministry of Internal Affairs (*Kokumin,* 1990, p. 664). See also Samuels (1983, p. 55); Reed (1981).

20. This argument is often reversed: that ministries "sponsor" bureaucrats who want to enter politics in order to have a representative for their interests in the Diet (Okimoto, 1989, pp. 220–22). Yet the point misses the exigencies of politics. Once bureaucrats have left a ministry, they have no reason beyond sentiment to support their old ministry. Conversely, they have every incentive to cater to their constituents and obey party leaders. For additional data on the backgrounds of Japanese politicians, see Youn (1981).

21. Johnson (1974); Blumenthal (1985). Most bureaucrats reach the level of section chief, generally at a mean age of 42.1. The few who become bureau chief do so at a mean age of 50.2 (Muramatsu, 1981, pp. 71, 78). Some prominent firms refuse to hire former bureaucrats (Upham, 1987, p. 177).

    The facts that the ministry locates the job for the bureaucrat (so that he or she does not have to seek it in the labor market), and that the law bans retirement to firms with which a bureaucrat has worked too closely, both suggest (however tentatively) that these post-retirement jobs do not represent late payment of a bribe—deferred compensation to the bureaucrat for pork routed to the constituent firm while in the ministry, paid by the firm upon retirement. For such a hypothesis outside the Japanese context, see Che (1990) and Spiller (1990).

22. Seifu (1991, pp. 212–20); see Ogawa (1984). The data on retirement benefits apply only to the 86 officers for whom such information was available.

23. Krueger (1974); Posner (1975); Tullock (1967, 1990).

24. This argument is often reversed to claim that the ministries place ex-bureaucrats in private firms to extend Japanese bureaucratic influence into the private sector (Sterngold, 1991). This ignores the exigencies of the labor market and the rudiments of principal-agent theory: ex-bureaucrats have no incentives to be loyal to their former ministries, and every incentive to maximize profits for their present employers.

7. Bureaucratic Manipulation

1. Law No. 130 of 1956; Law No. 82 of 1967; Law No. 55 of 1972; Law No. 58 of 1974; Law No. 34 of 1979. See Ramseyer (1981b, pp. 614–15).
2. Ike (1980). A more optimistic appraisal of the industry appears in Dore (1986, ch. 8).
3. Johnson (1986, p. 8); Kobayashi (1989, pp. 97–99, 102); Sasago (1988, pp. 76–82). The railroad also reached the districts of several other prominent LDP politicians.
4. The account that follows is based on Robert L. Ramseyer (1974).
5. R. Ramseyer (1974, ch. 6). Note that much of this change occurred *before* the introduction of universal suffrage—reducing the effectiveness of an alternative class-based explanation. See Chapter 4 n2.
6. For a nice description of the politically driven logic of the Ministry of Posts and Telecommunications' administration, see Weinberg (1991). Cargill and Hutchison (1991) find that even the Bank of Japan's monetary policies are designed to boost LDP electoral success.

   The more traditional approach is to assert that ministries like MITI are *generally* above politics, and to explain counterexamples as cases where the ministry either was not entirely successful "at protecting public policy from being dominated by parochial interests" or made "costly mistakes" (Okimoto, 1989, p. 5).
7. *Kin'yū zaisei jijō* Nov. 27, 1950, pp. 78–79; Dec. 4, 1950, pp. 29–31; Dec. 18, 1950, pp. 3–4; Feb. 19, 1951, pp. 7–8; Feb. 26, 1951, pp. 6, 39–44; *Tokyo shimbun* July 20, 1951; *Nikkei shimbun* Aug. 18, 1951.
8. *Kin'yū zaisei jijō* Sept. 2, 1951, p. 3; Oct. 1, 1951, pp. 10–12; Oct. 8, 1951, pp. 8–9, 20–21; *Sankei shimbun* Sept. 17, 1951; *Mainichi shimbun* Sept. 26, 1951.
9. Matsuzawa (1985, pp. 116–17); Nakajima (1979, pp. 143–44); *Kin'yū zaisei jijō* Jan. 4, 1965, pp. 56–57; *Zaikai* Oct. 1, 1972, pp. 34–37.
10. Rosenbluth (1989, pp. 122–25); Matsuzawa (1985, p. 118); Mondo (1985, pp. 34–42); Nakajima (1979, pp. 138–39, 226–27); *Asahi shimbun* Feb. 8, 1968; *Kin'yū zaisei jijō* Feb. 19, 1968, Mar. 11, 1968, pp. 25–27; *Kin'yū to ginkō* Apr. 18, 1980, p. 32.

11. Nakajima (1979, pp. 139, 146–50, 153–212); Horne (1985); *Kin'yū zaisei jijō* Apr. 17, 1978, p. 27; *Shūkan gendai* Sept. 24, 1981, pp. 52–56; interviews with Mr. Hiroshi Tokuda, June 1985 and June 1986.

12. In addition to the banks, mutual banks, and credit associations, a wide variety of other specialized financial institutions were part of the industry.

13. *Nihon keizai shimbun* Feb. 22, 1980, Dec. 18, 25, 31, 1980, Jan. 11, 14, 15, 22, 30, 1981, Feb. 3, 5, 11, 1981, Apr. 17, 1981; *Kin'yū to ginkō* Apr. 18, 1980, pp. 30–31; *Kin'yū zaisei jijō* Jan. 12, 1981, pp. 16–17, Jan. 19, 1981, pp. 14–20, Feb. 16, 1981, pp. 14–17, Feb. 23, 1981, pp. 22–34; *Tōyō keizai* Jan. 31, 1981, pp. 102–106.

14. *Nihon keizai shimbun* June 26, 1984; Oct. 2, 1984; *Zaikai* Sept. 18, 1984; *Zaikai shōhō* Mar. 31, 1986, pp. 2–6.

15. The account is based on the on-site research of Michael Thies, University of California, San Diego.

16. *Daikibo kouritenpo ni okeru kourigyō no jigyō katsudō no chōsei ni kansuru hōritsu* (Law Concerning the Adjustment of Retail Business Operations in Large Retail Stores), Law No. 109 of 1973; see generally Kohama (1991).

17. Contemporary department stores—powerful contributors to the LDP—also generally supported the Act. See Hosono (1991, pp. 37–38).

18. Ibid., p. 53; Tsuruta and Yahagi (1991, pp. 298–301).

19. Suzumura (1990, p. 6); Tsuruta and Yahagi (1991, pp. 305–306).

20. For recent changes to the Large Stores Act, see Chapter 10.

21. *Shiteki dokusen no kinshi oyobi kōsei torihiki no kakuho ni kansuru hōritsu* (Law Concerning the Prohibition of Private Monopoly and the Preservation of Fair Trade), Law no. 54 of 1947; Ramseyer (1981a); see generally Ramseyer (1992).

22. For an academic discussion that takes seriously the claim that Japan may have unusual problems with "excessive competition," see Okimoto (1989, pp. 38–48).

23. Uesugi (1986, pp. 410–15); Matsushita (1986, p. 385).

24. *Kōsei* (1989, pp. 225–33); Uesugi (1986, p. 401). MITI has also regularly approved informal cartel arrangements, though no reliable figures are available regarding these cartels. See generally Ramseyer (1981a; 1983; 1985).

25. Uesugi (1986, pp. 415, 418). Most orthodox scholars have attributed the inefficiencies caused by Japanese cartels to "unintended and perverse consequences" (Okimoto 1989, p. 7). For a highly unorthodox and theoretically coherent argument regarding the efficiency of cartels in Japan, see Dick (1991, 1992).

26. LDP factions have waxed and waned, to be sure. Given their nonideological character, however, even those shifts have not created significant policy transitions.

   Scholars of American politics have studied the agency slack in the legislative-bureaucratic relationship by measuring the impact on bureaucratic policy of changes in the party and personnel controlling the legislature, the presidency, or the key committees. See, for example, Calvert, Moran, and Weingast (1987); Faith, Leavens, and Tollison (1982); Moe (1982); Weingast and Moran (1983).

27. Calder's argument is also consistent with such studies as Muramatsu and Krauss (1990, pp. 301–302) and Okimoto (1989, pp. 186–93).

28. They were about to reduce their dependence on these firms, as detailed in Chapter 3.

29. For example, *Kashikin gyō no kiseitō ni kansuru hōritsu no ichibu wo kaisei suru hōritsu* (Law to Amend a Portion of the Law Regarding the Regulation, etc., of the Moneylending Industry), Law No. 74 of 1991 (limiting the ability of financial institutions to fund racketeers).

30. It is no reply to say that Japanese civil service law formally makes dismissals difficult (*Kokka kōmuin hō* [National Public Servant Act], Law No. 120 of 1947, §§89 to 92–2). Personnel reviews are relatively easily rigged and, in any case, the LDP could always amend the law to allow it to fire senior bureaucrats if more lax standards were politically expedient.

8. Political Structure and Judicial Incentives

1. In talking about "judicial independence" we refer only to one aspect of the question: the extent to which courts decide cases independently of the policy preferences of the people controlling the central government. We do not address several related, but at least equally important, issues: whether judges are independent of the parties to the dispute (except when the government is a party), or whether national courts are independent of the local political elites. See generally Shapiro (1981, ch. 1).

2. For a summary of the comparative statics of judicial independence, see the appendix to Chapter 9. Some scholars have argued that rational politicians will prefer independent judges because voters will give politicians credit for successful policies and blame judges for unsuccessful ones. They offer no justification for this hypothesis and we know of none.

3. Voters may well prefer politicians who can commit themselves to refusing graft. If that proves to be so, then a rational politician might offer judicial (and prosecutorial) independence in political corruption

cases. The same considerations explain such phenomena as the increased independence of the JAG Corps and the Court of Military Appeals.

4. For a historical application of a closely related argument, see North and Weingast (1989); North (1990, pp. 138–39).

5. For a contrary view, see Macey (1986).

6. McCubbins, Noll, and Weingast (1987; 1989) argue that administrative procedure can stack the decks at the agency and thereby force a court to replicate the outcome that the enacting coalition would have produced. Robinson (1989), however, denies this occurs.

7. A similar argument on the relation between judicial independence and parliamentary versus presidential structures is made by Ladha (1990). Britain, where a parliamentary system is combined with an apparent tradition of judicial independence, appears to be an exception. Shapiro (1981, pp. 66, 33) argues, however, that British judges have always been subordinate to the King or Parliament, and that the modern Parliament has withdrawn bureaucratic oversight from the courts on a wide scale.

8. In addition, courts impose two other costs. First, the state subsidizes the courts. Litigation thus imposes large budgetary expenses. Second, plaintiffs can use the threat of litigation to manipulate policy. In circumstances of uncertainty and asymmetric information, plaintiffs can profitably bring meritless strike suits (Bebchuk, 1988; Png, 1983; Rosenberg and Shavell, 1985). In private disputes, they extract settlements from defendants who wish to avoid the cost of defense. In public disputes, they negotiate policy shifts toward points more advantageous to themselves.

9. *Aizawa v. Kuni*, 27 Saihan keishū 265 (S. Ct. Apr. 4, 1973); *K.K. Kakukichi v. Hiroshima kenchiji*, 29 Saihan minshū 572 (S. Ct. Apr. 30, 1975); *Kurokawa v. Chiba senkyo kanri iinkai*, 30 Saihan minshū 223 (S. Ct. Apr. 14, 1976); *Kanao v. Hiroshima senkyo kanri iinkai*, 39 Saihan minshū 1100 (S. Ct. July 17, 1985); *Hiraguchi v. Hiraguchi*, 41 Saihan minshū 408 (S. Ct. Apr. 22, 1987). See Matsui (1991); Okudaira (1990, p. 37); Urabe (1990, p. 69).

10. Discussions of judicial review of administrative actions, besides those mentioned in the text, include Dziubla (1985); Haley (1986b); Matsui (1991); Narita (1968); Rosenbluth (1989a, pp. 21–23); Sanekata (1977); Tanakadate (1986); Upham (1979); Yamanouchi (1974).

11. For the game-theoretic argument that a judicial willingness to follow precedent can be self-reinforcing, see Rasmusen (1991).

12. See *Kempō* (Constitution) of 1947, arts. 76, 79, 80. For the American rule against pay decreases, see *U.S. Constitution*, Art. III, §1.

13. *Kempō*, art. 79; *Saibansho hō* (Judiciary Act), Law No. 59 of 1947, §39.

14. Justice Takejirō Sawada received the 4.00% negative vote in 1949. Before joining the Supreme Court in 1947, he had been an administrative judge. Justice Takezō Shimoda received the 15.17% vote in 1972. He had been ambassador to the United States before joining the Supreme Court, and was known as an outspoken conservative. *ZSKS* (1990, pp. 468–74); Nomura (1986, pp. 166–69).

15. *ZSKS* (1990, pp. 468–70). From the first U.S. Supreme Court nominee to Justice Rehnquist, the mean age of appointment in the United States was 53.4 (*Nihon bengoshi* 1986, p. 128).

16. See Damaska (1986, ch. 1); Merryman (1985, p. 35); Shapiro (1981, p. 150).

17. To be sure, a judge assigned to a rural branch office by the Secretariat could always quit the courts and open a private practice in Tokyo. The leeway a judge has to do so reduces—but does not eliminate—the Secretariat's power. Because a judge's reputation for excellence influences his or her outside options, the higher it is the more lucrative a practice he or she will be able to build. Furthermore, LRTI graduates who become judges do so because they place a high value on that position—or they would not have forsaken a higher paying job in private practice in the first place. Having chosen a career as a judge, their first choice position will be a high-ranking, high-paying job in Tokyo *as a judge*. Critically, the Secretariat controls the access to that job.

18. *Saibansho hō*, §50. Summary Court judges are subject to retirement at age 70. Hence, some judges join the Summary Court bench after retiring from the District or High Court bench.

19. Hattori and Henderson (1983, §3.01[3]); *Nihon bengoshi* (1980, pp. 105–106); *Kakyū saiban sho jimu shori kisoku* (Rules for Disposition of Administrative Matters Relating to Lower Courts), Supreme Court Rule No. 16 of Aug. 18, 1948, §§3–7.

20. The Supreme Court also has rule-making authority over the judiciary, which it traditionally delegates to the Secretariat. The LDP effectively controls this rule-making in two ways. First, as noted in the text, it indirectly controls Secretariat membership. Second, the rules (except where they concern constitutionally mandated matters) can be revoked by statute.

21. Because most lawyers work in very small law firms, it is hard to determine their income reliably. Tan and Alexander (1987, p. 14) estimate the 1982 annual income of lawyers in Tokyo engaged in a domestic practice as ¥4,430,000 and of those in international practice as ¥11,941,000. One should not directly compare these figures with Table 8.2. For one thing, Tan and Alexander base their study on tax

data, and lawyers are widely reputed to underreport their income. Moreover, Tan and Alexander's data are from 1982, whereas Table 8.2 is from 1989. All conversations we have had with Japanese legal practitioners suggest that a good judge could increase his or her income by quitting and joining the bar.

22. *Nihon bengoshi* (1980, p. 105); Miyamoto and Shioya (1984, pp. 297–99); Miyazawa (1991, p. 3); Tsukahara (1990, p. 27).

23. This is more extreme than during at least some of the prewar period. In 1881, for example, the comparable multiple was 8.33 (Kusunoki, 1989, p. 69 tab. 1). In the United States in recent years the salary of the chief justice of the Supreme Court was $160,600, while a federal district judge earned $125,100. Exec. Ord. 12736 of Dec. 12, 1990, 55 Fed. Reg. 51385 Sched. 7 (effective Jan. 1, 1991). Salary ranges for state court judges were: $84,765 to $130,469 (California); $75,113 to $93,266 (Illinois); $71,520 to $80,500 (Massachusetts); and $95,000 to $115,000 (New York). See Wright and Dwyer (1990, pp. 51–86).

24. From 1971 to 1990, one career judge was appointed to the Supreme Court every 1.05 years (*ZSKS* 1990, pp. 468–70). At any given time, there are only eight High Court presidents. From 1971 to 1990, the number of judges hired each year has ranged from 52 (in 1985) to 88 (in 1974), with an annual mean of 69.5 (*ZSKS* 1990, pp. 156–212).

25. *ZSKS* (1990, pp. 9, 26–27). The transfer had been a promotion to the Fukuoka High Court. Hasegawa (1969, p. 12); Ushiomi (1969). By all odds, Hasegawa was (as Japanese judges go) a mildly liberal judge without a particularly distinguished background (Ushiomi, 1969, pp. 5–6).

26. On judicial monitoring, see Kansai (1983, p. 170); Saitō (1985, p. 308); Wagatsuma (1983, p. 33). On prewar tenure, see *Choku rei* (Imperial Order) No. 40 of May 4, 1886, §12; *Dainihon teikoku kempō* (Imperial Constitution of Great Japan) of 1889, art. 58(b); Kusunoki (1989, p. 3); Saitō (1971, p. 69).

27. *ZSKS* (1990, pp. 38–45). To check these results, we calculated the failure rates for the class of 1950: the University of Tokyo—7.1%, Kyoto University—10.5%, Chuo University—20.0%, other universities—20.0%, and apparent nongraduates—23.1% (*ZSKS* 1990, pp. 30–36).

28. *ZSKS* (1990, pp. 38–45). The class of 1950 had 12 cases of career failure in the oldest quartile (those born before April 1920), 3 in the middle two quartiles, and 3 in the youngest quartile (those born after May 20, 1924). This yields a failure rate of 42.9% for the oldest quartile and 10.7% for the youngest (*ZSKS*, 1990, pp. 30–36).

29. Ibid., pp. 38–45. For the class of 1950, the comparable figure was 70.6% (pp. 30–36).

9. Judicial Manipulation

1. We note three caveats. First, most cases in most courts have little political importance. Most cases—whether traffic accidents, divorces, or debt collections—involve issues on which the various parties have no particular stand. Second, we make only a tentative argument. In view of the difficulty of coding opinions by their political "controversialness," our evidence is inherently arbitrary and anecdotal. Last, as in the rest of this book our argument is more positive than normative. Whether in Japan or in the United States, most scholars writing on the subject use the euphemism "judicial independence" for agency slack and extoll its putative virtues. By contrast, we make no normative judgments about the issue.

2. Note that the famous Supreme Court cases holding the Japanese electoral apportionment system unconstitutional did *not* harm the LDP. Instead, when the government finally redistricted the country pursuant to these cases, the Socialists suffered; the LDP had already moved away from its earlier reliance on the rural vote. The Court actions should thus be understood as enabling the LDP leadership to force reluctant backbenchers (with heavy constituency-specific investments) to acquiesce to a change that favored the party as a whole (see Chapter 5).

3. Becker (1968); McMillan (1991, p. 13); Polinsky and Shavell (1979).

4. English-language discussions of this incident include Hayakawa (1971); Itoh (1989, pp. 261–69); Luney (1990, pp. 153–60). Japanese sources include Watanabe, Miyazawa, Kisa, Yoshino, and Satō (1992, ch. 1), Ikeda and Moriya (1972), the special Feb. 1971 issue of *Hōgaku seminaa*, the special Feb. and June 1971 issues of *Hōritsu jihō*, and the materials cited in the massive bibliography, *Hōgaku seminaa* (1971).

5. ZSKS (1990, pp. 86–87). The courts probably maintain largely randomized docket assignments to minimize the potential for bribery and favoritism. As this case shows, the system does make it harder (though not impossible) for the Secretariat to control controversial cases.

6. Article 9 provides, *inter alia:* "the Japanese people forever renounce war as a sovereign right of the nation . . . In order to accomplish the aim of the preceding paragraph, land, sea, and air forces, as well as other war potential, will never be maintained."

7. *Itō v. Hasegawa*, 565 *Hanrei jihō* 23 (Sapporo D.C. Aug. 22, 1969), *rev'd sub nom. Kuraishi v. Itō*, 581 *Hanrei jihō* 5 (Sapporo High Ct. Jan. 23, 1970). Hiraga's letter is reproduced in Fukase (1971, pp. 59–60).

8. The report is reproduced in the February 1971 issue of *Hōgaku seminaa*, pp. 162–64.
9. It suspended punishment pending his good behavior. The report is reproduced in the February 1971 issue of *Hōgaku seminaa*, pp. 164–68.
10. Compare Fukushima's opinion, *Itō v. Sakurauchi*, 712 *Hanrei jihō* 24 (Sapporo D.C. Sept. 7, 1973), rev'd, 821 *Hanrei jihō* 23 (Sapporo High Ct. Aug. 5, 1976), aff'd, 36 *Saihan minshū* 1679 (S. Ct. Sept. 9, 1982), with Supreme Court precedent, *Tokyo chihō kensatsu chō v. Sakada*, 13 *Saihan keishū* 3225 (S. Ct. Dec. 16, 1959) (presence of American military bases not unconstitutional).
11. An excellent summary of empirical evidence on this point appears in Miyazawa (1991, p. 22).
12. *Nihon bengoshi* (1980, p. 109). For a report on what the Young Jurists League members at the LRTI were told about their prospects in the judiciary, see *Tokyo bengoshi kai* (1970). There was a shortage of judges during this time (*Zadankai*, 1970c, pp. 20–22; Nose, 1971).
13. For example, *Japan v. Shimana*, 491 *Hanrei jihō* 25 (Niigata D.C., Nagaoka branch office, Aug. 7, 1967) (exonerating picket line members who prevented other employees from working); [no names given], 529 *Hanrei jihō* 89 (Tokyo D.C. Aug. 3, 1968) (rejecting general prosecutorial rules governing contacts between defendant and counsel); [no names given], 555 *Hanrei jihō* 29 (Tokyo D.C. Apr. 30, 1969) (arguably violating Supreme Court precedent in ordering police to disclose evidence in case against students who occupied Tokyo University buildings); [no names given], 598 *Hanrei jihō* 45 (Tokyo D.C. May 14, 1970) (dicta sympathetic to striking students in case over Tokyo University riots).
14. Odanaka (1972, p. 98); Luney (1990, p. 158 n114). Konno had published an opinion in which he held, contrary to Supreme Court precedent, that it was unconstitutional to require drivers involved in traffic accidents to report their accidents to the police (Ebato, 1990, pp. 106–107).
15. Note that there is little evidence that League members had unusually strong educational backgrounds (see Appendix to Chapter 8). Of the entire class of 1960, 29.5% were from the University of Tokyo; of the League members, 19.4% were from the University of Tokyo. Of the entire class of 1961, 12.5% were from the University of Tokyo; of the League members, 15.0% were from the University of Tokyo (*ZSKS*, 1990, pp. 90–101).
16. The protests appear in Ikeda and Moriya (1972, pp. 363–64); Shihō (1971, p. 104). Note Hanada's defense of the YJL in Hanada (1970a; 1970b).
17. For example, most of the judges who held against the Ministry of

Education in the controversial proficiency test cases, *Japan v. Komaki,* 453 *Hanrei jihō* 6 (Osaka D.C. Apr. 13, 1966) (Kiyoshi Yoshimasa, Masao Ishikawa, Keiji Kawabata, JJ.); *Japan v. Satō,* 453 *Hanrei jihō* 16 (Asahikawa D.C. May 25, 1966) (Takashi Kon, Makoto Yoshimaru, Yoshio Okada, JJ.); *Japan v. Satō,* 524 *Hanrei jihō* 24 (Sapporo High Ct. June 26, 1968) (Katsuo Saitō, Masaaki Kurokawa, Mitsuru Kobayashi, JJ.) had very successful careers.

18. Usaki (1990, p. 141). The statute is the *Kōshoku senkyo hō* (Public Offices Election Act), Law no. 100 of Apr. 15, 1950. On the political effects of the statute, see Abe et al. (1990, p. 114); Beer (1984, p. 374); Curtis (1971, pp. 219–20).

19. *Japan v. Masako,* 4 Saihan keishū 1799 (S. Ct. Sept. 27, 1950).

20. [No names given], 493 *Hanrei jihō* 72 (Tokyo D.C. Mar. 27, 1967) (Naohisa Tamaki, J.).

21. *Japan v. Taniguchi,* 21 Saihan keishū 1245 (S. Ct. Nov. 21, 1967).

22. [No names given], 512 *Hanrei jihō* 76 (Myōji Summary Ct. Mar. 12, 1968).

23. *Japan v. Sugimoto,* 23 Saihan keishū 235 (S. Ct. Apr. 23, 1969); [no names given], 933 *Hanrei jihō* 147 (July 5, 1979); [No names given], 964 *Hanrei jihō* 129 (S. Ct. June 6, 1980); *Japan v. Yada,* 35 Saihan keishū 205 (S. Ct. June 15, 1981); *Japan v. Takatsu,* 35 Saihan keishū 568 (S. Ct. July 21, 1981); *Japan v. Matsuishi,* 1099 *Hanrei jihō* 39 (S. Ct. Nov. 10, 1983); *Japan v. Yada,* 38 Saihan keishū 387 (S. Ct. Feb. 21, 1984). See also *Japan v. Yamashita,* 22 Saihan keishū 1319 (Nov. 1, 1968) (electioneering practice at bar held not to violate §138(a); constitutional issues not reached).

24. [No names given], 915 *Hanrei jihō* 135 (Matsuyama D.C. Saijō branch office, Mar. 30, 1978).

25. *Japan v. Yada,* 923 *Hanrei jihō* 141 (Matsue D.C. Unzen branch office, Jan. 24, 1979), *aff'd,* 964 *Hanrei jihō* 134 (Hiroshima High Ct. Matsue branch office, Apr. 28, 1980), *rev'd,* 35 Saihan keishū 205 (S. Ct. June 15, 1981), *on remand,* (Hiroshima High Ct. Oct. 26, 1982), *aff'd,* 38 Saihan keishū 387 (S. Ct. Feb. 21, 1984).

26. [No names given], 962 *Hanrei jihō* 130 (Morioka D.C. Tōno branch office, Mar. 25, 1980), *rev'd,* 1069 *Hanrei jihō* 149 (Sendai High Ct. May 25, 1982).

27. *Japan v. Matsuishi,* 944 *Hanrei jihō* 133 (Fukuoka D.C. Yanagawa branch office, Sept. 7, 1979), *rev'd,* (Fukuoka High Ct. Mar. 25, 1982), *aff'd,* 1099 *Hanrei jihō* 39 (S. Ct. Nov. 10, 1983).

28. *Hoshino v. Tokyo kōan iinkai,* 483 *Hanrei jihō* 3 (Tokyo D.C. June 9, 1967).

29. He justified his intervention on the basis of *Gyōsei jiken soshō hō* (Ad-

ministrative Case Procedure Act), Law no. 139 of 1962, §27. See 483 *Hanrei jihō* 11 (the Satō petition).

30. [No names given], 483 *Hanrei jihō* 12 (Tokyo D.C. June 10, 1967) (Ryōkichi Sugimoto, Fujio Senda, Keiichi Murakami, JJ.), revoking June 9 order.

31. *Horii v. Tokyo kōan iinkai,* 487 *Hanrei jihō* 19 (Tokyo D.C. July 10, 1967) (Sugimoto, Nakahira, Senda, JJ.).

32. See 487 *Hanrei jihō* 19 (the Satō petition); *Horii v. Tokyo kōan iinkai,* 487 *Hanrei jihō* 18 (Tokyo D.C. July 11, 1967), retraction of earlier order.

33. *Hoshino v. Tokyo to,* 575 *Hanrei jihō* 10 (Tokyo D.C. Dec. 2, 1969) (Sugimoto, Nakahira, Iwai, JJ.).

34. *Kō v. Tokyo kōan iinkai,* 501 *Hanrei jihō* 52 (Tokyo D.C. Nov. 23, 1967) (Sugimoto, Nakahira, Iwai, JJ.); [no names given], 517 *Hanrei jihō* 23 (Tokyo D.C. May 20, 1968) (Sugimoto, Iwai, Akira Watanabe, JJ.). These judges did sometimes rule in favor of the TPSC: for example [no names given], 514 *Hanrei jihō* 38 (Tokyo D.C. Apr. 8, 1968) (Sugimoto, Nakahira, Iwai, JJ.); *Tachikawa kara kichi wo nakusu shimin no kai v. Tokyo kōan iinkai,* 571 *Hanrei jihō* 35 (Tokyo D.C. Apr. 26, 1969) (Sugimoto, Watanabe, Iwai, JJ.).

35. *Ienaga v. Monbu shō,* 530 *Hanrei jihō* 12 (Tokyo D.C. Sept. 27, 1968) (Sugimoto, Nakahira, Iwai, JJ.); *Ienaga v. Monbu shō,* 597 *Hanrei jihō* 3 (Tokyo D.C. July 17, 1970) (same judges) (holding Ministry of Education action unconstitutional), *aff'd without reaching constitutional issues,* 800 *Hanrei jihō* 19 (Tokyo High Ct. Dec. 19, 1975).

36. *1969 nen hokkyō jōkai nippon kōgyō tenrankai v. Kuni,* 560 *Hanrei jihō* 6, 21 (Tokyo D.C. July 8, 1969) (Sugimoto, Watanabe, Iwai, JJ.).

37. *Saka v. Kuni,* 1063 *Hanrei jihō* 30 (Gifu D.C. Dec. 10, 1982) (decision of Matsunaga, Ikadatsu and Akimoto, JJ.), *rev'd sub nom., Kuni v. Takahashi,* 1346 *Hanrei jihō* 9 (Nagoya High Ct. Feb. 20, 1990).

38. *Shimizu v. Kuni,* 1117 *Hanrei jihō* 13 (Gifu D.C. May 29, 1984) (decision of Watanabe, Matsunaga and Ikadatsu, JJ.), *aff'd sub nom. Muraoka v. Kuni,* 1346 *Hanrei jihō* 58 (Nagoya High Ct. Feb. 20, 1990).

39. *Asano v. Japan,* 1104 *Hanrei jihō* 26 (S. Ct. Jan. 26, 1984). The Supreme Court has since switched to a position more favorable to plaintiffs in river-damage cases. *Takeda v. Japan,* 1369 *Hanrei jihō* 24 (S. Ct. Dec. 13, 1990); see generally articles collected in the March 1991 issues of *Hōritsu jihō* and *Hōritsu no hiroba.*

40. According to Case Comment (1984, p. 15). Shiomi (1987, p. 21) lists 18 cases from 1975 through March 1984, of which the government lost all but 5.

41. *Noguchi v. Katō,* 1109 *Hanrei jihō* 44 (Fukuoka High Ct. Mar. 16, 1984).

42. *Yokochi v. Kanemi sōko, K.K.*, 1191 *Hanrei jihō* 28 (Fukuoka High Ct. May 15, 1986); see Abe (1986).

10. Conclusion

1. One LDP politician we know advertises his ability to "bring home the bacon" with a mnemonic device in his telephone number. The last four digits of his number are 8438, which can be read in Japanese as *yappari yosan ha da*, or "He's in the budget crowd, all right."
2. Carol Gluck, at the third of three Japan Political Economy Research Conference (JPERC) meetings, this one on Japanese culture; International House of Japan, January 1988.
3. *Kanao v Hiroshima senkyo kanri iinkai*, 39 Saihan minshū 1100 (S. Ct. July 17, 1985).
4. We do not claim this characterized *all* prewar legislation. The prewar government also enacted a variety of laws (like tenant-protection statutes) that inefficiently redistributed some wealth *to* those outside the large business community.
5. Ishikawa (1991, p. 34). Prime Minister Sōsuke Uno convened the Eighth Electoral System Advisory Council in June 1989, appointing as members 25 private citizens including scholars, members of the media, and businessmen. The council was chaired by Yōzō Kobayashi, chairman of the Japan Newspaper Association and president of Yomiuri Newspaper. Tsutomu Satō, dean of the law faculty of Tōkai University, was selected to be vice-chairman. The first subcommittee of the advisory council, whose primary responsibility was to study redistricting, was chaired by F. Horie, dean of the law faculty of Keiō University. The second subcommittee, charged with examining political campaign contributions, was chaired by Y. Kōno, former head of the Upper House Secretariat and former director of the National Diet Library.
6. Most of this information is drawn from interviews with LDP leaders and backbenchers on February 19–27 and August 19–23, 1991.
7. A few senior backbenchers known as the YKK Group (for the initials of the leaders) worked behind the scenes to have the decision of the party's Executive Committee overturned: Taku Yamaguchi (a ranking member of the Watanabe faction whose job it is to prevent this issue from blocking Watanabe's chances of becoming party president in October); Kōichi Katō, a leader in the Miyazawa faction (who is to do the same for his faction); and Junichirō Koizumi of the Mitsuzuka faction. When the YKK Group charged Executive Committee Chairman Nishioka with heavy-handedness in calling a voice ballot over

the objections of a number of Committee members, it had hoped to hurt the Kaifu administration enough to ruin his chances for a third term. The Committee reopened the issue on July 9 and voted once again in favor of the reform bills, though Koizumi continued to challenge the decision openly.

References

Abe, Haruhiko. 1971. "Saibankan ron" [A Theory of Judges]. *Jurisuto*, 469: 194–98.

Abe, Yasutaka. 1986. "Kanemi yushō kokubai hitei hanketsu" [Decision Denying National Responsibility for the Kanemi Oil Illness]. *Jurisuto*, 869: 57–64.

Abe, Hitoshi, Muneyuki Shindō, and Sadafumi Kawato. 1990. *Gaisetsu: Gendai Nihon no seiji* [*Outline: Modern Japanese Politics*]. Tokyo: Tokyo daigaku shuppankai.

Aiba, Juichi, Tadashi Iyasu, and Shōji Takashima. 1987. *Nihon no seiji o yomu* [*Reading Japanese Politics*]. Tokyo: Yūhikaku.

Aivazian, Varouj A., and Jeffrey L. Callen. 1981. "The Coase Theorem and the Empty Core." *Journal of Law and Economics*, 24: 175–81.

Alt, James E., and Kenneth A. Shepsle. 1990. *Perspectives on Positive Political Economy*. Cambridge: Cambridge University Press.

Anderson, Gary M., William F. Shughart II, and Robert D. Tollison. 1989. "On the Incentives of Judges to Enforce Legislative Wealth Transfers." *Journal of Law and Economics*, 32: 215–28.

Anderson, Stephen. 1987. "The Politics of the Welfare State in Japan." Ph.D. diss., M.I.T.

Arai, Kunio. 1988. *Senkyo, jōhō, yoron* [*Elections, Information, and Public Opinion*]. Tokyo: Nihon hōsō kyōkai.

Arrow, Kenneth J. 1950. "A Difficulty in the Concept of Social Welfare." *Journal of Political Economy*, 58: 328–46.

Asahi senkyo taikan: dai 38-kai shūgiin sōsenkyo, dai 14-kai sangiin tsūjō senkyo [*Asahi Election Survey: The 38th House of Representatives General Election, and 14th House of Councillors Regular Election*]. 1986. Tokyo: Asahi shimbun senkyo honbu.

Asahi shimbun keizaibu. 1989. *Gohyakuchō en no ogori* [*The 500 Trillion Yen Extravagance*]. Tokyo: Asahi shimbunsha.

Asahi shimbun seijibu. 1968. *Seitō to habatsu* [*Political Parties and Factions*]. Tokyo: Asahi shimbunsha.

Austen-Smith, David, and Jeffrey Banks. 1989. "Electoral Accountability and Incumbency." In Peter Ordeshook, ed. *Models of Strategic Choice in Politics*. Ann Arbor: University of Michigan Press.

Baerwald, Hans H. 1986. *Party Politics in Japan*. Boston: Allen & Unwin.

———— 1979. "Committees in the Japanese Diet." In J. D. Lees and

M. Shaw, eds. *Committees in Legislatures*. Durham: Duke University Press, pp. 327–60.

Bagnoli, Mark and Michael McKee. 1991. "Controlling the Game: Political Sponsors and Bureaus." *Journal of Law, Economics and Organization*, 7: 229–47.

Banks, Jeffrey S. 1990. "A Model of Electoral Competition with Incomplete Information." *Journal of Economic Theory*, 50: 309–25.

Baron, David P. 1989. "Service-Induced Campaign Contributions and the Electoral Equilibrium." *The Quarterly Journal of Economics*, 54: 45–72.

Bates, Robert H. 1981. *Markets and States in Tropical Africa: The Political Basis of Agricultural Policies*. Berkeley: University of California Press.

——— 1987. *Essays on the Political Economy of Rural Africa*. Berkeley: University of California Press.

——— 1989. *Beyond the Miracle of the Market: The Political Economy of Agrarian Development in Kenya*. Cambridge: Cambridge University Press.

Bebchuk, Lucian Arye. 1988. "Suing Solely to Extract a Settlement Offer." *Journal of Legal Studies*, 17: 437–50.

Becker, Gary S. 1968. "Crime and Punishment: An Economic Approach." *Journal of Political Economy*, 76: 169–217.

——— 1983. "A Theory of Competition among Pressure Groups for Political Influence." *Quarterly Journal of Economics*, 98: 377.

Becker, Gary, and George Stigler. 1974. "Law Enforcement, Malfeasance and the Compensation of Enforcers." *Journal of Legal Studies*, 3: 1–18.

Beer, Lawrence Ward. 1984. *Freedom of Expression in Japan: A Study in Comparative Law, Politics, and Society*. Tokyo: Kodansha International.

Bernstein, Robert. 1977. "Divisive Primaries: U.S. Senate Races, 1956–1962." *American Political Science Review*, 71: 540–45.

Bishop, William. 1990. "A Theory of Administrative Law." *Journal of Legal Studies*, 19: 489–530.

Blumenthal, Tuvia. 1985. "The Practice of Amakudari within the Japanese Employment System." *Asian Survey*, 25: 310–21.

Buchanan, James M. 1965. "An Economic Theory of Clubs." *Economica*, 32: 1–14.

Cain, Bruce, John Ferejohn, and Morris Fiorina. 1987. *The Personal Vote: Constituency Service and Electoral Independence*. Cambridge, Mass.: Harvard University Press.

Calder, Kent E. 1982. "Kanryō vs. Shomin: Contrasting Dynamics of Conservative Leadership in Postwar Japan." In Terry Edward MacDougall, ed. *Political Leadership in Contemporary Japan*. Ann Arbor: Center for Japanese Studies, University of Michigan, pp. 1–28.

——— 1988. *Crisis and Compensation: Public Policy and Political Stability in Japan, 1949–1986*. Princeton: Princeton University Press.

Calvert, Randall L. 1987. "Coordination and Power: The Foundation of

Leadership among Rational Legislators." Paper prepared for American Political Science Association annual meeting.

Calvert, Randall L., Mathew D. McCubbins, and Barry R. Weingast. 1989. "A Theory of Political Control and Agency Discretion." *American Journal of Political Science*, 33: 588–611.

Calvert, Randall L., Mark J. Moran, and Barry R. Weingast. 1987. "Congressional Influence over Policy Making: The Case of the FTC." In McCubbins and Sullivan (1987), pp. 493–522.

Campbell, John Creighton. 1977. *Contemporary Japanese Budget Politics.* Berkeley: University of California Press.

———— ed. 1981. *Parties, Candidates, and Voters in Japan: Six Quantitative Studies.* Ann Arbor: University of Michigan Center for Japanese Studies.

———— 1989. "Democracy and Bureaucracy in Japan." In Ishida and Krauss (1989), pp. 113–37.

———— 1991. *Policy Change: The Japanese Government and the Elderly.* Princeton: Princeton University Press.

Cargill, Thomas F., and Michael M. Hutchison. 1991. "The Bank of Japan's Response to Elections." *Journal of Japanese and International Economies,* 5: 120–39.

(Case comment.) 1984. *Hanrei jihō,* 1117: 14–15.

Che, Yeon Koo. 1990. "'Revolving Doors' and Optimal Tolerance for Agency Collusion." Stanford University Department of Economics, unpublished.

Chūshō kigyō chō, ed. 1979. *Chūshō kigyō hakusho [Small- and Medium-Sized Industries White Paper].* Tokyo: Ōkura shō insatsu kyoku.

———— ed. 1990. "Nissenren, nisshōren kankei shiryō" [Materials on Nissenren and Nisshōren]. Unpublished document on file with authors.

———— ed. 1991. *Chūshō kigyō yōran [Survey of Small- and Medium-Sized Industries].* Tokyo: Chūshō kigyō chōsa kyōkai.

Coase, R. H. 1937. "The Nature of the Firm." *Economica* (n.s.), 4: 386.

———— 1960. "The Problem of Social Cost." *Journal of Law and Economics,* 3: 1–44.

Coate, Malcolm B., Richard S. Higgins, and Fred S. McChesney. 1990. "Bureaucracy and Politics in FTC Merger Challenges." *Journal of Law and Economics,* 33: 463–82.

Cohen, Mark A. 1991. "Explaining Judicial Behavior or What's 'Unconstitutional' about the Sentencing Commission." *Journal of Law, Economics and Organization,* 7: 183–99.

Congleton, Roger. 1989. "Campaign Finances and Political Platforms: The Economics of Political Controversy." *Public Choice,* 62: 101–18.

Cox, Gary. 1989. *The Efficient Secret.* Cambridge: Cambridge University Press.

——— 1990. "Centripetal and Centrifugal Incentives in Electoral Systems." *American Journal of Political Science,* 34: 903–35.

Curtis, Gerald L. 1971. *Campaigning, Japanese Style.* New York: Columbia University Press.

——— 1979. "The Opposition." In H. Passin, ed. *A Season of Voting.* Washington D.C.: American Enterprise Institute.

——— 1988. *The Japanese Way of Politics.* New York: Columbia University Press.

Cusumano, Michael A. 1985. *The Japanese Automobile Industry.* Cambridge, Mass.: Harvard University Press.

Damaska, Mirjan R. 1986. *The Faces of Justice and State Authority: A Comparative Approach to the Legal Process.* New Haven: Yale University Press.

David, Paul A. 1985. "Clio and the Economics of QWERTY." *American Economic Review,* 75: 332–37.

Demsetz, Harold. 1990. "Amenity Potential, Indivisibilities, and Political Competition." In Alt and Shepsle (1990).

Denzau, Arthur T., and Michael C. Munger. 1986. "Legislators and Interest Groups: How Unorganized Interests Get Represented." *American Political Science Review,* 80: 89–106.

Dick, Andrew R. 1991. "The Competitive Consequences of Japan's Export Cartel Association." Unpublished manuscript on file with authors.

——— 1991. "Japanese Antitrust Law and Competitive Mix." Unpublished manuscript on file with authors.

Doi, Takeo. 1973. *The Anatomy of Dependence.* Tokyo: Kodansha International.

Dore, Ronald. 1986. *Flexible Rigidities: Industrial Policy and Structural Adjustment in the Japanese Economy, 1970–80.* Stanford: Stanford University Press.

Downs, Anthony. 1957. *An Economic Theory of Democracy.* New York: Harper and Row.

Duverger, Maurice. 1963. *Political Parties.* New York: Wiley.

Dziubla, Robert W. 1985. "The Impotent Sword of Japanese Justice: The Doctrine of Shobunsei as a Barrier to Administrative Litigation." *Cornell International Law Journal,* 18: 37.

Easterbrook, Frank H. 1984. "The Supreme Court, 1983 Term—Foreword: The Court and the Economic System." *Harvard Law Review,* 98: 4–60.

——— 1992. "Some Tasks in Understanding Law through the Lens of Public Choice." *International Review of Law and Economics,* forthcoming.

Ebato, Tetsuo. 1990. *Kanryō dai kenkyū* [*A Major Study of Bureaucrats*]. Tokyo: Chikuma shobō.

Edinger, Lewis J. 1986. *West German Politics.* New York: Columbia University Press.

Eggertsson, Thráin. 1990. *Economic Behavior and Institutions*. Cambridge: Cambridge University Press.

Enelow, James M., and Melvin J. Hinich. 1984. *The Spatial Theory of Voting*. Cambridge: Cambridge University Press.

Epstein, Richard A. 1990. "The Independence of Judges: The Uses and Limitations of Public Choice Theory." *Brigham Young Law Review*, 827–55.

Faith, Roger L., Donald R. Leavens, and Robert D. Tollison. 1982. "Antitrust Pork Barrel." *Journal of Law and Economics*, 25: 329–42.

Fenno, Richard. 1978. *Home Style: House Members and Their Districts*. Boston: Little, Brown.

Ferejohn, John, and Charles Shipan. 1990. "Congressional Influence on Bureaucracy." *Journal of Law, Economics and Organization*, 6 (spec. issue): 1–20.

Fiorina, Morris. 1977. "The Case of the Vanishing Marginals: The Bureaucracy Did It." *American Political Science Review*, 71: 177–81.

Flanagan, Scott, 1984. "Electoral Change in Japan: A Study of Secular Realignment." In Russell Dalton, Scott Flanagan, and Paul Beck, eds. *Electoral Change in Advanced Industrial Democracies*. Princeton: Princeton University Press.

————. 1980. "Electoral Change in Japan: An Overview." In Kurt Steiner, Ellis Krauss, and Scott Flanagan, eds. *Political Opposition and Local Politics in Japan*. Princeton: Princeton University Press.

Fujimoto, Kasumi. 1990. *Kokkai kinō riron* [*Theory of the Diet's Function*]. Tokyo: Hōgaku shoin.

Fujimoto, Takashi, ed. 1991. *Sōkagakkai ni nani ga okiteiru no ka* [*What is Happening in the Sōkagakkai*]. Tokyo: IPEC Press.

Fujita, Hiroaki. 1980. *Nihon no seiji to kane* [*Japanese Politics and Money*]. Tokyo: Chinsō shobō.

Fukase, Chūichi. 1971. "Tenkaiten ni tatsu mugunbi-hikaku heiwa shugi: 7" [Turning Point in Non-Military, Non-Nuclear Peace Principle: 7]. *Hōritsu jihō* (Aug.): 48–61.

Fukui, Haruhiro. 1978. "Japan: Factionalism in a Dominant Party System." In Frank P. Belloni and Dennis C. Beller. *Faction Politics: Political Parties and Factionalism in Comparative Perspective*. Santa Barbara: ABC-Clio.

———— 1984. "The Liberal Democratic Party Revisited: Continuity and Change in the Party's Structure and Performance." *Journal of Japanese Studies*, 10: 385–435.

———— 1987. "The Policy Research Council of Japan's Liberal Democratic Party: Policy Making Role and Practice." *Asian Thought and Society*, 12: 3–31.

———— 1988. "Electoral Laws and the Japanese Party System." In Gail Lee Bernstein and Haruhiro Fukui, eds. *Japan and the World*. London: Macmillan.

Fukunaga, Fumio. 1986. "Sengo ni okeru chusenkyokusei no keisei katei" [The Process of Reintroducing the Medium-Sized District Electoral System in Postwar Japan]. *Kōbe hōgagku zasshi*, 36: 403–57.

Fukuoka, Masayuki. 1986. *Gendai nihon no seito seiji* [*Party Politics in Contemporary Japan*]. Tokyo: Tōyō keizai shimpōsha.

Fukushima, Shigeo. 1971. "Chūi shobun ni taisuru hanron" [Rebuttal to Reprimand]. *Hōritsu jihō* (Jan.): 69–74.

Geertz, Clifford. 1973. *The Interpretation of Cultures*. New York: Basic Books.

Gely, Rafael and Pablo T. Spiller. 1990. "A Rational Choice Theory of Supreme Court Statutory Decisions with Applications to the State Farm and Grove City Cases." *Journal of Law, Economics, and Organization*, 6: 263–300.

Gendai, ed. 1991. "Ōmori Minoru to nettō! Miyazawa Kiichi 'kekki sengen' " [A Heated Debate with Minoru Ōmori: Kiichi Miyazawa's Proclamation of Dissent]. *Gendai* (Aug.): 40–73.

Gendai seiji mondai kenkyūkai, ed. 1976. *Jimintō gigokushi* [*A History of LDP Scandals*]. Tokyo: Gendai hyōronsha.

Gilligan, Thomas W., and Keith Krehbiel. 1987. "Collective Decision-making and Standing Committees: An Informational Rationale for Restrictive Amendment Procedures." *Journal of Law, Economics, and Organization*, 3: 287–335.

Gotōda, Masaharu. 1989. *Naikaku Kanbōchōkan* [*Cabinet Secretary*]. Tokyo: Kōdansha.

Grofman, Bernard, and Arend Lijphart, eds. 1987. *Electoral Laws and Their Political Consequences*. New York: Agathon Press.

Haley, John O. 1978. "The Myth of the Reluctant Litigant." *Journal of Japanese Studies*, 4: 359–90.

———— 1982. "The Oil Cartel Cases: The End of An Era." *Law in Japan*, 15: 1–11.

———— 1986a. "Administrative Guidance versus Formal Regulation: Resolving the Paradox of Industrial Policy." In Gary R. Saxonhouse and Kozo Yamamura, eds. *Law and Trade Issues of the Japanese Economy*. Seattle: University of Washington Press, pp. 107–28.

———— 1986b. "Introduction" [To Japanese Administrative Law]. *Law in Japan*, 19: 1–14.

———— 1988a. "Introduction: Legal vs. Social Controls." In Haley (1988c), pp. 1–6.

———— 1988b. "Japanese Administrative Law: An Introduction." In Haley (1988c), pp. 37–48.

————, ed. 1988c. *Law and Society in Contemporary Japan: American Perspectives*. Dubuque: Kendall/Hunt.

———— 1991. *Authority without Power: Law and the Japanese Paradox*. New York: Oxford University Press.

Hanada, Masamichi. 1970a. "Saibankan no 'seijiteki chūritsusei'" [The "Political Neutrality" of Judges]. *Hōgaku seminaa* (June): 2–6.

———— 1970b. "Seihōkyō saibankanbukai: sono jittai to seika" [The Reality and Results of the Judicial Section of the Young Jurists League]. *Hōritsu jihō* (June): 139–43.

Hasegawa, Shigeharu. 1969. "Wakaki saibankan ni" [To Young Judges]. *Hōritsu seminaa* (Aug.): 9–12.

Hattori, Takaaki, and Dan Fenno Henderson. 1983. *Civil Procedure in Japan*. New York: Matthew Bender.

Hayakawa, Takeo. 1971. "The Japanese Judiciary in the Whirlwind of Politics." *Kobe University Law Review*, 7: 17.

Hayashi, Shigeru, ed. 1975. *Dokyumento Shōwashi* [*Documents from the Shōwa Period*]. Tokyo: Heibonsha.

Hazama, Otohiko. 1982. *Shōwa kyōko no seiji keizaigaku* [*The Political Economy of the Great Depression*]. Tokyo: Sōgō keizai senta.

Henderson, Dan Fenno. 1990. "Comment." *Law and Contemporary Problems*, 53(1): 89–96.

Hillman, Arye L., and John G. Riley. 1989. "Politically Contestable Rents and Transfers." *Economics and Politics*, 1: 17–39.

Hirata, Takujirō. 1981. *Dare no tame no ginkō* [*Banks for Whom?*]. Tokyo: Otsuki shoten.

Hirose, Michisada. 1989. *Seiji to kane* [*Politics and Money*]. Tokyo: Iwanami shoten.

Hōgaku seminaa henshū kai, ed. 1971. "Bunken kaidai: shihōken no dokuritsu" [A Bibliographic Synopsis: Judicial Independence]. *Hōgaku seminaa* (spec. Feb. issue): 228–31.

Holmes, Oliver Wendell. 1953. *Holmes-Laski Letters* (vol. I). Mark DeWolfe Howe, ed. Cambridge, Mass.: Harvard University Press.

Holmstrom, Bengt. 1979. "Moral Hazard and Observability." *Bell Journal of Economics*, 10: 74–91.

Holmstrom, Bengt, and Jean Tirole. 1989. "The Theory of the Firm." In Richard L. Schmalensee and Robert D. Willig, eds. *Handbook of Industrial Organization*, Vol. I. New York: Elsevier Science Publishers.

Honsho, Jirō. 1985. *Keidanren*. Tokyo: Tōyō keizai shimpōsha.

Honzawa, Jirō. 1989. *Shakaitō daikenkyū* [*An Investigation of the Socialist Party*]. Tokyo: Piipuru sha.

———— 1990. *Jimintō habatsu* [*LDP Factions*]. Tokyo: Piipuru sha.

Horie, Fukashi, and Mitsuhiro Umemura, eds. 1986. *Tōhyō kōdō to seiji ishiki* [*Voting Behavior and Political Awareness*]. Tokyo: Keiō tsūshin.

Horne, James. 1985. *Japan's Financial Markets.* London: Allen & Unwin.

Hosono, Sukehiro. 1991. *Posuto Daitenhō [Post-Large Stores Act].* Tokyo: Nihon jitsugyō shuppansha.

Hrebenar, Ronald J. 1986. *The Japanese Party System: From One-Party Rule to Coalition Government.* Boulder: Westview Press.

Ichikawa, Taichi. 1990. *Seshū daigishi no kenkyū [Research on Second-Generation Diet Members].* Tokyo: Nihon keizai shimbunsha.

Ike, Brian. 1980. "The Japanese Textile Industry: Structural Adjustment and Government Policy." *Asian Survey,* 20: 532–51.

Ikeda, Masaaki, and Katsuhiko Moriya, eds. 1972. *Saibankan no mibun hoshō [Security of Status for Judges].* Tokyo: Keisō shobō.

Inō, Takashi. 1984. *Giinsan wo tetteiteki ni riyō suru hō [How to Make Complete Use of Your Representative].* Tokyo: Kigensha.

Inoguchi, Takashi. 1989. "Seisaku kettei e no 'ishiki kōzō' o miru" [Looking at the "Structure of Preferences" in Policymaking]. *Ekonomisuto* (July) 3: 84–91.

——— 1990. "The Political Economy of Conservative Resurgence under Recession: Public Policies and Political Support in Japan, 1977–1983." In Pempel (1990).

Inoguchi, Takashi, and Tomoaki Iwai. 1987. *Zoku giin no kenkyū: Jimintō o gyūjiru shuyakutachi [Research on Diet Policy Tribes: The Actors Who Control the LDP].* Tokyo: Nihon keizai shimbunsha.

Inoue, Kyōko. 1991. *MacArthur's Japanese Constitution.* Chicago: University of Chicago Press.

Ishida, Takeshi, and Ellis Krauss, eds. 1989. *Democracy in Japan.* Pittsburgh: University of Pittsburgh Press.

Ishikawa, Masumi. 1991. *Senkyo seido [The Electoral System].* Tokyo: Iwanami shoten.

Ishikawa, Masumi, and Michisada Hirose. 1989. *Jimintō: chōki shihai no kōzō [The LDP: The Structure of Longterm Dominance].* Tokyo: Iwanami shoten.

Itō, Tatsumi. 1991. "Shimbun ga kakanai Jimin kaikakuan no honshitsu o tsuku" [The Essence of the LDP Reform Plan Not Written About in the Newspapers]. *Chūō kōron* (Aug.): 76–85.

Itoh, Hiroshi. 1989. *The Japanese Supreme Court: Constitutional Policies.* New York: Markus Wiener Publishing.

Itoh, Takatoshi. 1990. "Election Timing and Business Cycles." *Journal of Asian Economics.*

Iwai, Tomoaki. 1990. *Seiji shikin no kenkyū [Research on Political Campaign Financing].* Tokyo: Nihon keizai shimbunsha.

Jacobson, Gary. 1987a. *The Politics of Congressional Elections.* Boston: Scott, Foresman.

——— 1987b. "The Marginals Never Vanished: Incumbency and Competition in Elections to the U.S. House of Representatives, 1952–1982." *American Journal of Political Science*, 31: 126–41.

Jensen, Michael C. 1983. "Organization Theory and Methodology." *Accounting Review*, 58: 319–39.

Jichi shō gyōsei kyoku, ed. 1988. *Zenkoku shichōson yōran* [*National Survey of Cities, Towns and Villages*]. Tokyo: Daiichi hōki shuppan.

Jichi shō senkyo bu, ed. 1991. *Seiji katsudō no tebiki* [*A Dictionary of Political Activities*]. Tokyo: Daiichi hōki shuppan.

Jinji in, ed. 1986. *Nenji hōkoku sho* [*Annual Report of the Government Personnel Office*]. Tokyo: Jinji in.

—— 1967–87. *Eiri kigyō e no shūshoku no shōnin ni kansuru nenji hōkoku* [*Annual Report on the Approval of Employment in For-Profit Firms*]. Tokyo: Jinjiin geppō.

—— 1986. *Nenji hōkoku sho* [*Annual Report*]. Tokyo: Ōkurashō insatsu kyoku.

—— 1988–90. *Kōmuin hakusho* [*Public Servant White Paper*]. Tokyo: Ōkurashō insatsu kyoku.

Jiyū minshu tō, ed. 1986. "Zeisei no bapponteki kaikaku to Shōwa 60-nendo kaisei taikō" [Restructuring the Tax System and the Tax Reform Plan for 1987]. Unpublished manuscript on file with authors.

—— 1989. "Heisei 2-nendo zeisei taikō" [1990 Tax Reform Outline]. Unpublished manuscript on file with authors.

—— 1990. "Heisei 2-nendo zeisei kaisei no yōkō: kakugi kettei" [1990 Cabinet Decision on Tax Reform]. Unpublished manuscript on file with authors.

Johnson, Chalmers. 1974. "The Reemployment of Retired Government Bureaucrats in Japanese Big Business." *Asian Survey*, 14: 953–65.

—— 1975. "Who Governs? An Essay on Official Bureaucracy." *Journal of Japanese Studies*, 2: 1–28.

—— 1982. *MITI and the Japanese Miracle*. Stanford: Stanford University Press.

—— 1985. "The Institutional Foundations of Japanese Industrial Policy." *California Management Review*, 27: 59.

—— 1986. "Tanaka Kakuei, Structural Corruption, and the Advent of Machine Politics in Japan." *Journal of Japanese Studies*, 12: 1–28.

—— 1989. "MITI, MPT, and the Telecom Wars: How Japan Makes Policy for High Technology." In Chalmers Johnson, Laura D'Andrea Tyson, and John Zysman, eds. *Politics and Productivity: The Real Story of Why Japan Works*. New York: Harper Business, pp. 177–244.

—— 1990. "The People Who Invented the Mechanical Nightingale." *Daedalus* (Summer): 71–90.

Kamishima, Jirō. 1982. *Nichijōsei no seijigaku* [*Everyday Politics*]. Tokyo: Chikuma shobō.

Kaneko, Hiroshi. 1988. *Sozei hō* [*Tax Law*]. Rev. ed. Tokyo: Kōbundō.

Kansai, Ariyuki. 1983. "Kansai Ariyuki saibankan ni yoru gōdō hōkoku yōshi" [Summary of Plenary Report of Judge Ariyuki Kansai]. In Kondan kai (1983), pp. 169–86.

Katō, Ichirō. 1984. "Daitō suigai soshō hanketsu wo megutte" [Regarding the Daitō Water Damage Decision]. *Jurisuto*, 811: 23–29.

Katō, Junko. 1991. "Public Pension Reforms in the United States and Japan: A Study of Comparative Public Policy." *Comparative Political Studies*, 24: 100–126.

Kawamura, Yasuo, and Shigeaki Matsui. 1990. *Shōsenkyokusei-seitō hō no kiken na nerai* [*The Dangerous Goal of the Small District System and Political Party Act*]. Tokyo: Gakushū no yūsha.

Kawato, Sadafumi. 1987. "The Distribution of the Vote in Multimember District System." *Hokkaido Law Review*, 38: 341–407.

———— 1990. "Kyūjūnen sōsenkyo to nashionaru suingu" [The 1990 Elections and National Swing]. *Sekai*, 5: 216–25.

Keehn, Edward B. 1990. "Managing Interests in the Japanese Bureaucracy." *Asian Survey*, 30: 1021–37.

Kiewiet, Roderick, and Mathew McCubbins. 1991. *The Logic of Delegation: Congressional Parties and the Appropriations Process.* Chicago: University of Chicago Press.

King, Gary. 1991. "Constituency Service and Incumbency Advantage." *British Journal of Political Science*, 21: 119–28.

Kinoshita, Atsushi. 1991. "Dare ga Jimintō o 'okiya' ni shita!" [Who has Turned the LDP into a Geisha House?] *Gendai* (Aug.): 62–73.

Kiseki, Ikusaburō. 1965. *Seikai gojūnen no butai ura.* [*Behind the Scenes of Fifty Years of Politics*]. Tokyo: Seikai jūraisha.

Kishiro, Yasuyuki. 1985. *Jimintō zeisei chōsakai* [*The LDP Tax Committee*]. Tokyo: Tōyō keizai shimpōsha.

Kitahara, Michiyuki. 1985. *Nihon no kin'yū* [*Japanese Finance*]. Tokyo: Zaikei shōhōsha.

Kitaoka, Shinichi, 1985. "Jiyū minshutō: hōkatsu seitō no gōrika" [The LDP: The Rationalization of a Catch-All Party]. In Ichirō Kamishima, ed. *Gendai nihon no seiji kōzō* [*The Political Structure of Contemporary Japan*]. Tokyo: Hōritsu bunkasha.

———— 1990. *Kokusaika jidai no seiji shidō* [*Political Leadership in an Age of Internationalization*]. Tokyo: Chūō Kōronsha.

Klein, Benjamin R., Robert G. Crawford, and Armen A. Alchian. 1978. "Vertical Integration, Appropriable Rents, and the Competitive Contracting Process." *Journal of Law and Economics*, 21: 297–326.

Klein, Benjamin R., and Keith B. Leffler. 1981. "The Role of Market Forces in Assuring Contractual Performance." *Journal of Political Economy*, 89: 615–41.

Klein, William A., and John C. Coffee, Jr. 1990. *Business Organization and Finance: Legal and Economic Principles*. 4th ed. Mineola, N.Y.: Foundation Press.

Kobayashi, Kichiya. 1989. *Kakuei ichidai* [*Kakuei—A Life*]. Tokyo: Nesco.

Kobayashi, Yoshiaki. 1990. *Gendai nihon no senkyo* [*Contemporary Japanese Elections*]. Tokyo: University of Tokyo Press.

Koh, B. C. 1989. *Japan's Administrative Elite*. Berkeley: University of California Press.

Kohama, Taiji. 1991. *Daitenhō no kaisei to chūshōten ikinokori senryaku* [*The Revisions to the Large Stores Act and Survival Strategies for Small- and Medium-Sized Stores*]. Tokyo: Gyōsei.

Kohno, Masaru. 1991. "Jimintō—soshiki riron kara no kentō" [The LDP—Lessons from Organizational Theory]. *Ribaiasan* (Spring): 32–54.

———— 1992. "Rational Foundations for the Organization of the Liberal Democratic Party in Japan." *World Politics*, 44: 369–97.

Kokkai binran [*National Diet Roster*]. Various years. Tokyo: Nihon seikei shimbunsha.

Kokumin seiji nenkan henshū iinkai, ed. 1990. *Kokumin seiji nenkan 90 nen ban* [*1990 Annual of National Citizenry Politics*]. Tokyo: Nihon shakai tō.

Komaki, Hiroshi. 1983. *Daigishi wa mainichi nani o shiteiru no ka* [*What Do Diet Members Do Every Day?*] Tokyo: Sōshisha.

Kondan kai, ed. 1983. *Saibankan no dokuritsu no tame ni* [*For the Independence of Judges*]. Tokyo: Hanrei jihō sha.

Kōsei torihiki iinkai, ed. Various years. *Kōsei torihiki iinkai nenji hōkoku* [*Fair Trade Commission Annual Report*]. Tokyo: Kōsei torihiki iinkai.

Krauss, Ellis, and Michio Muramatsu, 1987. "The Conservative Policy Line and the Development of Patterned Pluralism." In Kozo Yamamura and Yasuki Yasuba, eds. *The Political Economy of Japan*. Vol. 1: *The Domestic Transformation*. Stanford: Stanford University Press, pp. 516–54.

Krauss, Ellis, and Bradford Simcock. 1980. "Citizens' Movements: The Growth and Impact of Environmental Protest in Japan." In Steiner, Krauss, and Flanagan (1980).

Krehbiel, Keith. 1990a. "Are Congressional Committees Composed of Preference Outliers?" *American Political Science Review*, 84: 149–63.

———— 1990b. "Seniority, Commitment, and Self-Governing Groups." *Journal of Law, Economics, and Organization*, 6: 73–77.

———— 1991. "Where's the Party?" Unpublished manuscript on file with authors.

Kreps, David M. 1990. "Corporate Culture and Economic Theory." In Alt and Shepsle (1990), pp. 90–143.

Krueger, Anne O. 1974. "The Political Economy of the Rent-Seeking Society." *American Economic Review*, 64: 291–303.

Krugman, Paul. 1991. "History versus Expectations." *Quarterly Journal of Economics*, 106: 651–67.

Kuhn, Thomas S. 1970. *The Structure of Scientific Revolutions*. 2d ed. Chicago: University of Chicago Press.

Kumon, Shumpei. 1984. "Japan Faces Its Future: The Political Economics of Administrative Reform." *Journal of Japanese Studies*, 10: 143–65.

Kuni no yosan. See Ōkura shō.

Kusunoki, Ichirō. 1989. *Meiji rikken sei to shihōkan* [*The Meiji Constitutional System and Judicial Officers*]. Tokyo: Keiō tsūshin.

Ladha, Krishna. 1990. "The Pivotal Role of the Judiciary in the Deregulation Battle between the Executive and the Legislature." Washington University Political Economy Working Paper 147.

Laitin, David D. 1986. *Hegemony and Culture: Politics and Religious Change among the Yoruba*. Chicago: University of Chicago Press.

Landes, William M., and Richard A. Posner. 1975. "The Independent Judiciary in an Interest-Group Perspective." *Journal of Law and Economics*, 18: 875–901.

Laver, Michael and Kenneth Shepsle. 1990. "Coalitions and Cabinet Government." *American Political Science Review*, 84: 873–90.

Lazear, Edward P. 1979. "Why Is there Mandatory Retirement?" *Journal of Political Economy*, 87: 1261–84.

———— 1981. "Agency, Earnings Profiles, Productivity, and Hours Restrictions." *American Economic Review*, 71: 606–20.

———— 1991. "Labor Economics and the Psychology of Organizations." *Journal of Economic Perspectives*, 5: 89–110.

Lazear, Edward P., and Sherwin Rosen. 1981. "Rank-Order Tournaments as Optimum Labor Contracts." *Journal of Political Economy*, 89: 841–64.

Leiserson, Michael. 1968. "Factions and Coalitions in One-Party Japan: An Interpretation Based on the Theory of Games." *American Political Science Review*, 66: 770–87.

Liebowitz, S. J., and Stephen E. Margolis. 1990. "The Fable of the Keys." *Journal of Law and Economics*, 33: 1–25.

Lijphart, Arend, Rafael Pintor, and Yasunori Sone. 1987. "The Limited Vote and the Single Nontransferable Vote: Lessons from the Japanese and Spanish Examples." In Grofman and Lijphart (1987), pp. 154–79.

Luney, Percy R., Jr. 1990. "The Judiciary: Its Organizational Status in the Parliamentary System." *Law and Contemporary Problems*, 53(1): 135–67.

Mabuchi, Katsu. 1989. "Ōkurashō shuzeikyoku no kikan tetsugaku" [The Organizational Ideology of the Ministry of Finance Tax Bureau]. *Rebaiasan*, 4: 41–58.

Matsui, Shigenori. 1991. "Lochner v. New York in Japan—or How Economic Liberties are Protected in a Country Governed by Bureaucrats." Unpublished manuscript on file with authors.

McAfee, R. Preston, and John McMillan. 1991. "Organizational Diseconomies of Scale." Unpublished manuscript on file with authors.

McChesney, Fred S. 1991. "Rent Extraction and Interest-Group Organization in a Coasian Model of Regulation." *Journal of Legal Studies*, 20: 73–90.

McCubbins, Mathew D., and Gregory W. Noble. 1991. Untitled manuscript on file with authors.

McCubbins, Mathew D., Roger G. Noll, and Barry R. Weingast. 1987. "Administrative Procedure as Instruments of Political Control." *Journal of Law, Economics and Organization*, 3: 243–77.

———— 1989. "Structure and Process, Politics and Policy: Administrative Arrangements and the Political Control of Agencies." *Virginia Law Review*, 75: 431–82.

———— 1990. "Positive and Normative Models of Procedural Rights: An Integrative Approach to Administrative Procedure." *Journal of Law, Economics and Organization*, 6 (Spec. issue): 307–32.

McCubbins, Mathew D., and Frances M. Rosenbluth. 1991. "Electoral Structure and the Organization of Policymaking in Japan." Unpublished manuscript on file with authors.

McCubbins, Mathew D., and Thomas Schwartz. 1984. "Congressional Oversight Overlooked: Police Patrols versus Fire Alarms." *American Journal of Political Science*, 28: 165–79.

McCubbins, Mathew D., and Terry Sullivan. 1987. *Congress: Structure and Policy*. Cambridge: Cambridge University Press.

MacDougall, Terry Edward. 1989. "Democracy and Local Government in Postwar Japan." In Ishida and Krauss, eds.

Macey, Jonathan R. 1986. "Promoting Public-Regarding Legislation through Statutory Interpretation: An Interest Group Model." *Columbia Law Review*, 86: 223.

McKean, Margaret. 1981. *Environmental Protest and Citizen Politics in Japan.* Berkeley: University of California Press.

———— 1980. "Political Socialization through Citizen's Movements." In Steiner, Krauss, and Flanagan (1980).

McKelvey, Richard. 1976. "Intransitivities in Multi-Dimensional Voting Models, and Some Implications for Agenda Control." *Journal of Economic Theory*, 2: 472–82.

McKenzie, R. T. 1963. *British Political Parties.* New York: St. Martin's Press.

McManus, John C. 1975. "The Costs of Alternative Economic Organizations." *Canadian Journal of Economics*, 8: 334–50.

McMillan, John. 1992. *Games, Strategy, and Managers*. Oxford: Oxford University Press.

McNelly, Theodore. 1982. "Limited Voting in Japanese Parliamentary Elections." Paper delivered at the annual meetings of the American Political Science Association.

Magee, Stephen P., William A. Brock and Leslie Young. 1989. *Black Hole Tariffs and Endogenous Policy Theory: Political Economy in General Equilibrium*. Cambridge: Cambridge University Press.

Mainichi shimbunsha, ed. 1990a. *Kyūjūnen sōsenkyo* [*The 1990 General Election*]. Tokyo: Mainichi shimbunsha.

———— 1990b. *Seijika to kane* [*Politicians and Money*]. Tokyo: Mainichi shimbunsha.

———— 1990c. *Mainichi senkyo zenkiroku: '90 sōsenkyo* [*The Mainichi Election Documentary: The 1990 Election*]. Tokyo: Mainichi shimbunsha.

Marks, Brian Andrew. 1989. "A Model of Judicial Influence on Congressional Policymaking: Grove City College v. Bell (1984)." Ph.D. diss. Washington University Department of Economics.

Maruyama chōsakai, ed. 1985. "Zeisei kaikaku ni mukete" [Towards Tax Reform]. Unpublished manuscript on file with authors.

Masumi, Junnosuke. 1983. *Sengo seiji: 1945–1955 nen, jō* [*Postwar Politics: 1945–1955* (vol. I). Tokyo: University of Tokyo Press.

———— 1985a. *Gendai seiji: 1955 nen igo, jō* [*Contemporary Politics: 1955 and After* (vol. I). Tokyo: University of Tokyo Press.

———— 1985b. *Gendai seiji: 1955 nen igo, ge* [*Contemporary Politics: 1955 and After* (vol. II). Tokyo: University of Tokyo Press.

Matsubara, Nozomu, and Ikuo Kabashima. 1983. "Tanaka ha asshō Jimintō taihai no kōzu" [The Tanaka Faction Victory amidst an LDP Defeat]. *Chūō kōron* (Mar.): 74–85.

Matsui, Akira. 1984. "Kōmuin chingin no suijun to taikei" [The Level and Organization of Wages of Public Servants]. In Satō Hayakawa and Uchiyama (1984), pp. 174–207.

Matsui, Shegenori. 1991. "Lochner v. New York in Japan." Unpublished manuscript on file with authors.

Matsuo, Takayoshi. 1989. *Futsū senkyo seido seiritsushi no kenkyū* [*Research on the Introduction of Universal Suffrage*]. Tokyo: Iwanami shoten.

Matsushita, Mitsuo. 1986. "The Legal Framework of Trade and Investment in Japan." *Harvard International Law Journal*, 27: 361–88.

Matsuzawa, Takuji. 1985. *Watakushi no ginkō Shōwashi* [*My History of Banking in the Showa Era*]. Tokyo: Tōyō keizai shimpō sha.

Mayhew, David R. 1974. *Congress: The Electoral Connection*. New Haven: Yale University Press.

Merryman, John Henry. 1985. *The Civil Law Tradition: An Introduction to the Legal Systems of Western Europe and Latin America*. 2d ed. Stanford: Stanford University Press.

Milgrom, Paul, and John Roberts. 1986. "Relying on the Information of Interested Parties." *Rand Journal of Economics,* 17: 18–32.

Mitarai, Tatsuo. 1958. *Yamagata Aritomo* [*Aritomo Yamagata*]. Tokyo: Jiji tsūshinsha.

Miwa, Yoshirō, and Kiyohiko Nishimura, eds. 1991. *Nihon no ryūtsū* [*Japanese Distribution*]. Tokyo: Tokyo daigaku shuppankai.

Miyake, Hisayuki. 1982. *Sōsai o arasou otokotachi* [*The Men Who Compete for the Prime Ministership*]. Tokyo: Jiji tsūshinsha.

Miyake, Ichirō. 1989. *Tōhyō kōdō* [*Voting Behavior*]. Tokyo: Tokyo daigaku shuppan kai.

Miyamoto, Yasuaki, and Kuniaki Shioya. 1984. "Saibankan no shogū ni tsuite no kenkyū" [Research into the Treatment of Judges]. *Hōgaku seminaa zōkan,* 27: 292–302.

Miyazawa, Setsuo. 1991. "Administrative Control of Japanese Judges." Unpublished manuscript on file with authors.

Mizuno, Kunio. 1988. "Saibansho to hōmushō no jinji kōryū" [Personnel Exchange between the Courts and the Ministry of Justice]. *Hōgaku seminaa* (Apr.): 32–36.

Mizuno, Tadatsune. 1989. *Shōhizei no seido to riron* [*The Structure and Theory of the Consumption Tax*]. Tokyo: Kōbundō.

Mochizuki, Mike M. 1982. "Managing and Influencing the Japanese Legislative Process: The Roles of Parties and the National Diet." Ph.D. diss., Harvard University.

Moe, Terry M. 1982. "Regulatory Performance and Presidential Administration." *American Journal of Political Science,* 26: 197–224.

——— 1984. "The New Economics of Organization." *American Journal of Political Science,* 28: 739–77.

——— 1990. "Political Institutions: The Neglected Side of the Story." *Journal of Law, Economics, and Organization,* 6 (Spec. issue): 213–53.

Mondo, Okura. 1985. *Ōkurashō ginkō kyoku* [*The Ministry of Finance Banking Bureau*]. Tokyo: Paaru Books.

Mori, Kishio. 1982. *Shushō kantei no himitsu* [*Secrets of the Prime Minister's Residence*]. Tokyo: Chōbunsha.

Murakawa, Ichirō. 1979. *Seisaku kettei katei* [*The Policymaking Process*]. Tokyo: Kyōikusha.

——— 1985. *'Zei' no butai ura* [*Behind the Scenes in Tax Policy*]. Tokyo: Kyōikusha.

——— 1989. *Jimintō no seisaku kettei shisutemu* [*The LDP's Policymaking System*]. Tokyo: Kyōikusha.

Muramatsu, Michio. 1981. *Sengo Nihon no kanryōsei* [*The Bureaucratic System of Post-War Japan*]. Tokyo: Tōyō keizai shimpōsha.

——— 1990. "Bringing Politics Back into Japan." *Daedalus* (Summer): 141–54.

Muramatsu, Michio, and Ellis S. Krauss. 1984. "Bureaucrats and Politicians in Policymaking: The Case of Japan." *American Political Science Review*, 78: 126–46.

Muramatsu, Michio, Mitsutoshi Itō, and Yutaka Tsujinaka. 1986. *Sengo nihon no atsuryoku dantai* [*Pressure Groups in Postwar Japan*]. Tokyo: Tōyō keizai shimpōsha.

———— 1990. "The Dominant Party and Social Coalitions in Japan." In Pempel (1990), pp. 282–305.

Murase, Shinichi. 1988. "Kokuritsu ginkō shobun mondai to jiyūtō" [The Problem of the National Banks Ordinance and the Liberal Party]. *Nihon no rekishi*, 11: 71–84.

Murayama, Hiroshi. 1990. *Senkyo kōdō to taishū seiji bunka no riron* [*The Theory of Electoral Behavior and Mass Political Culture*]. Tokyo: Sagaya shoin.

Murobashi, Tetsurō. 1983. *Kōkyū kanryō* [*Elite Bureaucrats*]. Tokyo: Sekai shoin.

"Naikaku hōsei kyoku" [Cabinet Legislative Bureau]. 1991. *Sentaku* (Apr.): 126–29.

Naka, Kura, ed. 1980. *Kokkai giin no kōsei to henka* [*The Change and Structure of Diet Membership*]. Tokyo: K. K. Seiji jōhō Sentaa.

Nakajima, Toshihiro. 1979. *Aru ginkō gappei no zasetsu* [*The Failure of One Bank's Merger*]. Tokyo: Tōyō keizai shimpō sha.

Nakane, Chie. 1967. *Tate shakai no ningen kankei* [*Interpersonal Relations in a Vertical Society*]. Tokyo: Kōdansha.

———— 1978. *Tate shakai no riki gaku* [*The Power Politics of Hierarchical Society*]. Tokyo: Kodansha.

Narita, Yoriaki. 1968. "Administrative Guidance." *Law in Japan*, 2: 45–79.

Nihon bengoshi rengō kai, ed. 1980. *Saikō saiban sho* [*The Supreme Court*]. Tokyo: Nihon hyōron sha.

Nihon keizai shimbunsha, ed. 1984. *Jimintō seichōkai* [*The LDP Policy Affairs Research Council*]. Tokyo: Nihon keizai shimbunsha.

Nihon minshu hōritsuka kyōkai, ed. 1990. *Zen saibankan keireki sōran: kaitei shinban (ZSKS)* [*Biographical Information on All Judges: New Revised Edition*]. Tokyo: Kōnin sha.

Nihon seikei shimbun, ed. 1978. *Kokkai binran* [*Diet Survey*]. Tokyo: Nippon seikei shimbun.

Nihon tōkei nenkan [*Japan Statistical Yearbook*]. Various years. Tokyo: Sōrifu tōkei kyoku.

Nishioka, Takeo, and Shūsei Tanaka. 1979. *Shin jiyū kurabu no tenkai* [*The Development of the New Liberal Club*]. Tokyo: Keiei bijyon sentaa.

Noble, Gregory W. 1989. "The Japanese Industrial Policy Debate." In Stephan Haggard and Chung-In Moon, eds. *Pacific Dynamics*. Boulder: Westview Press, pp. 53–95.

Noll, Roger. 1988. "Economic Perspectives on the Politics of Regulation." In Richard L. Schmalensee and Robert D. Willig, eds. *Handbook on Industrial Organization*, vol. 2. New York: Elsevier Science Publishers.

Nomura, Jirō. 1986. *Saikōsai zen saibankan—hito to hanketsu* [*The Justices of the Supreme Court: The People and the Decisions*]. Tokyo: Sanshōdō.

North, Douglass C. 1981. *Structure and Change in Economic History*. New York: W. W. Norton.

———— 1990. *Institutions, Institutional Change and Economic Performance*. New York: Cambridge University Press.

North, Douglass C., and Barry R. Weingast. 1989. "Constitutions and Commitment: The Evolution of Institutions Governing Public Choice in Seventeenth-Century England." *Journal of Economic History*, 49: 803–32.

Nose, Takao. 1971. "Saibankan fuzoku to sono taisaku" [The Judge Shortage and Policies against It]. *Hōritsu jihō* (Jan.): 75–82.

Odanaka, Toshiki, and Hidenori Sasaki. 1970. "Shihō no kiki to so no yukue" [The Crisis in the Judiciary and Its Whereabouts]. *Hōgaku seminaa* (June): 2–6.

O'Flaherty, Brendan, and Aloysius Siow. 1991. "Promotion Lotteries." *Journal of Law, Economics and Organization*, 7: 401–409.

Ogawa, Kunihiko. 1984. "Taishokukin mamire no 'amakudari shokuminchi' [Government Retirement Colonies Full of Retirement Benefits]. *Bungei shunju* (Mar.): 154–65.

Ohkawa, Masazō. 1985. "The Role of Political Parties and Executive Bureaucrats in Governmental Budget-Making: The Case of Japan." In Horst Hanusch, Karl Roskamp, and Jack Wiseman, eds. *Public Sector and Political Economy Today*. New York: Gustav Fischer Verlag, pp. 123–34.

Ohyama, Kohsuke. 1989. "Gendai Nihon ni okeru gyōsei shido no seiji kōzō" [The Political Structure of Administrative Guidance in Modern Japan]. *Shakai kagaku kenkyū*, 40: 1–134.

Okimoto, Daniel I. 1989. *Between MITI and the Market: Japanese Industrial Policy for High Technology*. Stanford: Stanford University Press.

Okudaira, Yasuhiro. 1990. "Forty Years of the Constitution and Its Various Influences: Japanese, American, and European." *Law and Contemporary Problems*, 53(1): 17–49.

Ōkura shō insatsu kyoku, ed. 1951–90. *Hōrei zensho* [*Complete Statutes and Regulations*]. Tokyo: Ōkura shō insatsu kyoku.

Ōkura sho, ed. Various years. *Kuni no yosan* [*The National Budget*]. Tokyo: Ōkura shō insatsu kyoku.

Olson, Mancur. 1965. *The Logic of Collective Action: Public Goods and the Theory of Groups*. Cambridge: Harvard University Press.

Osadake, Takeki. 1943. *Meiji taishō seijishi kōwa* [*Lectures on Meiji and Taisho Political History*]. Tokyo: Ichigensha.

Ostrom, Elinor. 1990. *Governing the Commons: The Evolution of Institutions for Collective Action.* Cambridge: Cambridge University Press.

Park, Yung Chul. 1986. *Bureaucrats and Ministers: Contemporary Japanese Government.* Berkeley: University of California Institute of East Asian Studies.

Peltzman, Sam. 1990. "How Efficient Is the Voting Market?" *Journal of Law and Economics,* 33: 27–63.

——— 1991. "Voters as Fiscal Conservatives." Paper presented at USC/UCLA Applied Microeconomics Seminar.

Pempel, T. J. 1974. "The Bureaucratization of Policymaking in Postwar Japan." *American Journal of Political Science,* 18: 647–64.

——— 1978. "Japanese Economic Policy: The Domestic Bases for International Behavior." In Peter J. Katzenstein, ed. *Between Power and Plenty: Foreign Economic Policies of Advanced Industrial States.* Madison: University of Wisconsin Press, pp. 139–90.

——— 1982. *Policy and Politics in Japan: Creative Conservatism.* Philadelphia: Temple University Press.

——— 1987. "The Tar Baby Target: 'Reform' of the Japanese Bureaucracy." In Ward and Sakamoto (1987), pp. 157–87.

———, ed. 1990. *Uncommon Democracies: The One-Party Dominant Regimes.* Ithaca: Cornell University Press.

——— 1992a. "Japanese Democracy and Political Culture." *PS: Political Science & Politics,* 25: 5–12.

——— 1992b. "Bureaucracy in Japan." *PS: Political Science & Politics,* 25: 19–24.

Pinto-Duchinsky, M. 1981. *British Political Finance.* Washington, D.C.: American Enterprise Institute.

P'ng, I. P. L. 1983. "Strategic Behavior in Suit, Settlement, and Trial." *Bell Journal of Economics,* 14: 539.

Polinsky, A. Mitchell, and Steven Shavell. 1979. "The Optimal Tradeoff between the Probability and Magnitude of Fines." *American Economic Review,* 69: 880–91.

Poole, Keith, and Thomas Romer. "Patterns of Political Action Committee Contributions to the 1980 Campaigns for the United States House of Representatives." *Public Choice,* 47: 63–111.

Posner, Richard A. 1975. "The Social Costs of Monopoly and Regulation." *Journal of Political Economy,* 83: 807–27.

——— 1985. *The Federal Courts: Crisis and Reform.* Cambridge, Mass.: Harvard University Press.

Ramseyer, J. Mark. 1981a. "Trustbusting in Japan: Cartels and Government-Business Cooperation." *Harvard Law Review,* 94: 1064–84.

—— 1981b. "Letting Obsolete Firms Die: Trade Adjustment Assistance in the United States and Japan." *Harvard International Law Journal,* 22: 595–619.

—— 1983. "Japanese Antitrust Enforcement after the Oil Embargo." *American Journal of Comparative Law,* 31: 395–430.

—— 1985. "The Costs of the Consensual Myth: Antitrust Enforcement and Institutional Barriers to Litigation in Japan." *Yale Law Journal,* 94: 604–45.

—— 1986. "Lawyers, Foreign Lawyers, and Lawyer-Substitutes: The Market for Regulation in Japan." *Harvard International Law Journal,* 27: 499–539.

—— 1991. "Legal Rules in Repeated Deals: Banking in the Shadow of Defection in Japan." *Journal of Legal Studies,* 20: 91–117.

—— 1992. "The Antitrust Pork Barrel in Japan." *Antitrust Magazine,* Summer.

Ramseyer, J. Mark, and Minoru Nakazato. 1989. "The Rational Litigant: Settlement Amounts and Verdict Rates in Japan." *Journal of Legal Studies,* 18: 263–90.

Ramseyer, Robert L. 1974. "Takachiho: A Century of Continuity in Change." Unpublished manuscript on file with authors.

Rasmusen, Eric. 1989. *Games and Information: An Introduction to Game Theory.* New York: Blackwell.

—— 1990. "A One-Period, Income-Satiation Model of Efficiency Wages." Working Paper, Center for the Study of the Economy and the State, University of Chicago.

—— 1991. "Judicial Legitimacy: An Interpretation as a Repeated Game." Unpublished manuscript on file with authors.

Rasmusen, Eric, and J. Mark Ramseyer. 1992. "Trivial Bribes and the Corruption Ban: A Coordination Game Among Rational Legislators." Unpublished manuscript on file with authors.

Reed, Steven R. 1981. "Gubernatorial Elections in Japan." In Campbell (1981), pp. 139–67.

—— 1986. *Japanese Prefectures and Policymaking.* Pittsburgh: University of Pittsburgh Press.

—— 1988. "The People Spoke: The Influence of Elections on Japanese Politics, 1949–1955." *Journal of Japanese Studies,* 14: 309–39.

—— 1990. "Structure and Behaviour: Extending Duverger's Law to the Japanese Case." *British Journal of Politics,* 29: 337–56.

Rhode, David. 1990. *Parties and Leaders in the Postreform House.* Chicago: University of Chicago Press.

Richardson, Bradley M. 1974. *The Political Culture of Japan.* Berkeley: University of California Press.

Richardson, Bradley M., and Scott C. Flanagan. 1984. *Politics in Japan.* Boston: Little, Brown.

Robinson, Glen O. "Commentary on 'Administrative Arrangements and the Political Control of Agencies': Political Uses of Structure and Process." *Virginia Law Review,* 75: 483–98.

Rōdōshō, ed. 1989. *Chingin tōkei sōran: '90 nendo ban [Wage Census: 1990 Edition].* Tokyo: Sōgō rōdō kenkyū sha.

———— 1990. *Rōdō hakusho [Labor White Paper].* Tokyo: Nihon rōdō kenkyū kiko.

Rogowski, Ronald. 1990. "The Information-Economizing Organization of Legislatures." Unpublished manuscript on file with authors.

Rosenberg, David, and Steven Shavell. 1985. "A Model in Which Suits Are Brought for Their Nuisance Value." *International Review of Law and Economics,* 5: 3.

Rosenbluth, Frances McCall. 1989a. *Financial Politics in Contemporary Japan.* Ithaca: Cornell University Press.

———— 1989b. "The Political Economy of Financial Reform in Japan: The Banking Act of 1982." *UCLA Pacific Basin Law Journal,* 6: 62–102.

"Saibankan shin'nin kyohi wo dangai suru" [We Impeach the Refusal to Appoint Judges]. 1971. *Hōgaku seminaa* (June): 12–15.

Saikō saibansho jimo sōkyoku, ed. 1989. *Shihō tōkei nenkan: I minji-gyōsei hen [Annual Report of Judicial Statistics: I Civil, Administrative Edition].* Tokyo: Hōsōkai.

Saikawa, Chiyoko. 1984. "Suigai soshō" [Water Damage Litigation]. *Hanrei taimuzu,* 520: 50–52.

Saitō, Hideo. 1971. "Saikōsai no shihō gyōsei no arikata" [The Proper Method of Judicial Administration by the Supreme Court]. *Jurisuto,* 480: 66–71.

———— 1985. *Saibankan ron [The Theory of Judges].* 3d ed. Tokyo: Ichiryū sha.

Sakakibara, Eisuke. 1991. "The Japanese Politico-Economic System and the Public Sector." In Samuel Kernell, ed. *Parallel Politics: Economic Policymaking in Japan and the United States.* Washington, D.C.: Brookings Institution, pp. 50–79.

Samuels, Richard J. 1983. *The Politics of Regional Policy in Japan: Localities Incorporated?* Princeton: Princeton University Press.

Sanekata, Kenji. 1977. "Administrative Guidance and the Antimonopoly Law." *Law in Japan,* 10: 65–80.

Sasago, Katsuya. 1989. *Seiji shikin [Political Campaign Financing].* Tokyo: Gendai kyōiku bunko.

Sasago, Hiroto, Kazuyoshi Abe, and Katsuya Muraoka. 1990. *Seiji kenkin no kōzu [The Structure of Political Finances].* Tokyo: JICC shuppan kai.

Sasaki, Takeshi. 1991. "Postwar Japanese Politics at a Turning Point." *The Japan Foundation Newsletter*, 18 (5–6): 1–7.

Satō, Hideyoshi, Seiichirō Hayakawa, and Takashi Uchiyama, eds. 1984. *Kōmuin no seido to chingin* [*The System and Wages of Public Servants*]. Tokyo: Ōtsuki shoten.

Satō, Seizaburō, and Tetsuhisa Matsuzaki. 1986. *Jimintō seiken* [*The LDP Administration*]. Tokyo: Chūō kōron sha.

Seifu kankei tokushu hōjin rōdō kumiai kyōgikai, ed. 1981–91. *Amakudari hakusho* [*Government Reemployment White Paper*]. Tokyo: Seifu kankei tokushu hōjin rōdō kumiai kyōgikai.

Seifu zeisei chōsa kai, ed. 1986. "Zeisei no bapponteki minaoshi ni tsuite no tōshin" [A Report on Restructuring the Tax System]. Unpublished manuscript on file with authors.

Seinen hōritsuka kyōkai. 1969. "Seinen hōritsuka kyōkai kiyaku" [Bylaws of the Young Jurists League]. In Shisō (1969), pp. 58–61.

Seikei kenkyū sha, ed. 1990. *Yakunin no hōshū, shōyo, nenshū* [*Salaries, Bonuses, and Annual Compensation of Officers*]. Tokyo: Seikei kenkyū sha.

Seinen hōritsuka kyōkai. 1969. "Seinen hōritsuka kyōkai kiyaku" [Bylaws of the Young Jurists League]. In Shisō (1969), pp. 58–61.

Selton, Reinhard. 1978. "The Chain-Store Paradox." *Theory and Decision*, 9: 127–59.

Shapiro, Carl and Joseph Stiglitz. 1984. "Equilibrium Unemployment as a Worker Discipline Device." *American Economic Review*, 74: 433–44.

Shapiro, Martin M. 1981. *Courts: A Comparative and Political Analysis*. Chicago: University of Chicago Press.

Shavell, Steven. 1979. "Risk Sharing and Incentives in the Principal and Agent Relationship." *Bell Journal of Economics*, 10: 55–73.

Shepsle, Kenneth A., and Barry Nalebuff. 1990. "The Commitment to Seniority in Self-Governing Groups." *Journal of Law, Economics, and Organization*, 6: 45–71.

Shepsle, Kenneth A., and Barry R. Weingast. 1981. "Structure Induced Equilibrium and Legislative Choice." *Public Choice*, 37: 503–19.

"Shihō gyōsei to saibankan [Judges and Judicial Administration]. 1971." *Hōritsu jihō* (Jan.): 104–106.

Shindō, Muneyuki. 1986. *Gyōsei kaikaku to gendai seiji* [*Administrative Reform and Contemporary Politics*]. Tokyo: Iwanami shoten.

——— 1989. *Zaisei hatan to zeisei kaikaku* [*Fiscal Insolvency and Tax Reform*]. Tokyo: Iwanami shoten.

Shiomi, Kazuo. 1987. "Tamagawa suigai soshō hanketsu no ronri to haikei" [The Background and Logic to the Decision in the Tama River Litigation]. *Hōgaku seminaa* (Dec.): 18–21.

Shiota, Ushio. 1991. *Jimintō kabushikigaisha shachō sensō* [*The LDP, Inc. Presidential Wars*]. Tokyo: Tokuma Books.

Shioya, Kuniaki. 1991. "Saibankan no shogū ni tsuite no sairon" [A Reconsideration of the Treatment of Judges]. *Hōritsu jihō* (Jan.): 59–69.

Shiratori, Rei. 1986. *Nihon no naikaku (I)* [*Japan's Cabinets*, vol. I]. Tokyo: Shin hyōronsha.

Shisō undō kenkyū sho, ed. 1969. *Osorubeki saiban* [*Fearsome Decisions*]. Tokyo: Zenbō sha.

Shūgiin sōsenkyo ichiran [*Directory of Members of the House of Representatives*]. Various years. Tokyo: Shūgiin jimukyoku.

Silberman, Bernard. 1982. "The Bureaucratic State in Japan: The Problem of Authority and Legitimacy." In Tetsuo Najita and J. Victor Koschman, eds. *Conflict in Modern Japanese History: The Neglected Tradition*. Princeton: Princeton University Press, pp. 226–57.

Snyder, James M. 1990. "Campaign Contributions as Investments: The U.S. House of Representatives, 1980–1986." *Journal of Political Economy*, 98: 1195–1227.

Soma, Masao. 1977. *Kokusei senkyo to seitō seiji* [*National Elections and Party Politics*]. Tokyo: Seiji kōhō sentaa.

——— 1986. *Nihon senkyo seidoshi* [*A History of the Japanese Electoral System*]. Fukuoka: University of Kyūshū Press.

Sone, Yasunori, and Masao Kanazashi. 1989. *Nihon no seiji* [*Japanese Politics*]. Tokyo: Nihon keizai shimbunsha.

Spiller, Pablo T. 1990. "Politicians, Interest Groups, and Regulators: A Multiple-Principals Agency Theory of Regulators or 'Let Them Be Bribed'." *Journal of Law and Economics*, 33: 65–101.

Steiner, Kurt, Ellis Krauss, and Scott Flanagan, eds. 1980. *Political Opposition and Local Politics in Japan*. Princeton: Princeton University Press.

Sterngold, James. 1991. "A Japanese-Style 'Old Boy' Network." *New York Times*, June 7.

Steslicke, William E. 1973. *Doctors in Politics: The Political Life of the Japan Medical Association*. New York: Praeger.

Stigler, George S. 1971. "The Theory of Regulation." *Bell Journal of Economics and Management Science*, 2: 3–21.

Stigler, George S., and Gary S. Becker. 1977. "De Gustibus Non Est Disputandum." *American Economic Review*, 67: 76.

Strom, Kaare. 1990. *Minority Government and Majority Rule*. New York: Cambridge University Press.

Sunstein, Cass R. 1990. *After the Rights Revolution: Reconceiving the Regulatory State*. Cambridge, Mass.: Harvard University Press.

Suzumura, Kōtarō. 1990. "Ryūtsū kisei no keizaiteki kiketsu: 'Daitenhō shisutemu' no naniga mondai ka" [The Economic Conclusion to Distribution Regulation: Locating the Problem of the "Large Stores Act System"]. Hitotsubashi University, Institute of Economic Research Discussion Paper A-230.

Taagepera, Rein, and Matthew Shugart. 1989. *Seats and Votes: The Effects and Determinants of Electoral Systems.* New Haven: Yale University Press.

Tajima, Hiroshi. 1991. *Giin no tame no hōritsu sai jiki* [*An Almanac of Laws for Diet Members*]. Tokyo: Gyōsei.

Takayanagi, Kenzō. 1964. "A Century of Innovation: The Development of Japanese Law, 1868–1961." In Arthur Taylor von Mehren, ed. *Law in Japan: The Legal Order in a Changing Society.* Cambridge, Mass.: Harvard University Press.

Takeichi, Teruhiko. 1976. *Seiji shikin zensho: shomondai hen* [*Collection on Political Campaign Contributions*]. Tokyo: Nihon kokusei chōsakai.

Takeuchi, Naokazu. 1989. *Nihon no kanryō: Eriito shūdan no seitai* [*The Japanese Bureaucracy: The Ecology of an Elite Group*]. Tokyo: Kyōyō bunko.

Tan, Hong W., and Arthur J. Alexander. 1987. "Entry Restrictions and Japanese Lawyers' Incomes in International Legal Practice." Los Angeles: RAND Corporation.

Tanaka, Zen'ichirō. 1981. *Jimintō taisei no seiji shidō.* [*Political Leadership of the LDP Regime*]. Tokyo: Daiichi hōki shuppan sha.

———— 1986. *Jimintō no doramatsurugii* [*The LDP's Dramaturgy*]. Tokyo: University of Tokyo Press.

Tanakadate, Shōkitsu (trans. Jim Rosenbluth). 1986. "A Summary of the Limitations on Administrative Adjudication under the Japanese Constitution." *Law in Japan,* 18: 108–17.

Telser, Lester. 1982. "Voting and Paying for Public Goods: An Application of the Theory of the Core." *Journal of Economic Theory,* 27: 376.

Thayer, Nathaniel B. 1969. *How the Conservatives Rule Japan.* Princeton: Princeton University Press.

Tiedemann, Arthur. 1971. "Big Business and Politics in Prewar Japan." In James Morley, ed. *Dilemmas of Growth in Prewar Japan.* Princeton: Princeton University Press.

Tokyo bengoshi kai. 1970. "22-ki shūshūsei no ninkan sabetsu mondai chōsa hōkoku" [Report on the Problem of Discrimination in the Selection of Judges against Students in the 22d Class]. *Hōgaku seminaa* (Jan. 1971): 14–18.

Tokyo daigaku shimbun kenkyūjo, ed. 1988. *Senkyo hōdō to tōhyō kōdō* [*Election Media Coverage and Voting Behavior*]. Tokyo: Tokyo daigaku shuppan kai.

Tollison, Robert D. 1972. "Consumption Sharing." *Economica*, 39: 276–91.

Toma, Eugenia Froedge. 1991. "Congressional Influence and the Supreme Court: The Budget as a Signalling Device." *Journal of Legal Studies*, 20: 131–46.

Tsuji, Kiyoaki. 1969. *Shimpan: Nihon kanryōsei no kenkyū* [*New Edition: A Study of the Japanese Bureaucratic System*]. Tokyo: University of Tokyo Press.

Tsukada, Jitsuo. 1973. *Anami jiyūtō shimatsuki* [*A Record of Anami's Liberal Party*]. Tokyo: Shin jinbutsu jūraisha.

Tsukahara, Eiji. 1990. "Saibankan keireki to saiban kōdō" [Court Behavior and Judicial Biographies]. *Hōritsu jihō* (Aug.): 26–33.

Tsuruta, Hiromi. 1990. "Hojokin no kōzō to dōkō" [The Structure and Direction of Subsidies]. In Ken'ichi Miyamoto, ed. *Hojokin no seiji keizaigaku* [*The Political Economy of Subsidies*], pp. 39–84. Tokyo: Asahi sensho.

Tullock, Gordon. 1967. "The Welfare Costs of Tariffs, Monopolies, and Theft." *Western Economic Journal*, 5: 224–232.

────── 1990. "The Costs of Special Privilege." In Alt and Shepsle (1990), pp. 195–211.

Tsuruta, Toshimasa, and Toshiyuki Yahagi. 1991. "Daitenhō shisutemu to sono keigaika" [The Large-Stores Act System and the Development of Its Framework]. In Miwa and Nishimura (1991), pp. 283–324.

Tsūshō sangyō shō (MITI), ed. 1989. *90-nendai no ryūtsū bijon* [*A Distribution Vision for the 90s*]. Tokyo: Tsūhō sangyō chōsa kai.

Uchida, Mitsuru, ed. 1980. *Seiji no hendō* [*Political Change*]. Tokyo: Asakura shoten.

Uesugi, Akinori. 1986. "Japan's Cartel System and Its Impact on International Trade." *Harvard International Law Journal*, 27: 389–424.

Upham, Frank K. 1979. "After Minamata: Current Prospects and Problems in Japanese Environmental Litigation." *Ecology Law Quarterly*, 8: 213.

────── 1987. *Law and Social Change in Postwar Japan*. Cambridge, Mass.: Harvard University Press.

────── 1991. "Privatizing Regulation: The Implementation of the Large-Scale Retail Stores Law in Contemporary Japan." Unpublished manuscript on file with authors.

Urabe, Noriho. 1990. "Rule of Law and Due Process: A Comparative View of the United States and Japan." *Law and Contemporary Problems*, 53(1): 61–72.

Usaki, Masahiro. 1990. "Restrictions on Political Campaigns in Japan." *Law and Contemporary Problems*, 53(2): 133–56.

Ushiomi, Toshitaka. 1969. "Shihō gyōsei to saibankan no dokuritsu" [Judicial Administration and the Independence of Judges]. *Hōgaku seminaa* (Aug.): 2–8.

―――― 1971. "Shihō gyōsei no kempōteki kankaku" [The Constitutional Sense of Judicial Administration]. *Hōgaku seminaa* (June): 2–5.

van Wolferen, Karel. 1990. *The Enigma of Japanese Power: People and Politics in a Stateless Nation.* New York: Vantage Books.

Vogel, Ezra F. 1979. *Japan as No. 1: Lessons for America.* Cambridge, Mass.: Harvard University Press.

Wagatsuma, Sakae. 1983. "Wagatsuma Sakae shi no kōen" [Lecture by Mr. Sakae Wagatsuma]. In Kondan kai (1983), pp. 22–36.

Ward, Robert E., and Yoshikazu Sakamoto, eds. 1987. *Democratizing Japan: The Allied Occupation.* Honolulu: University of Hawaii Press.

Watanabe, Mutsumi. 1991. *Nihon chūshō kigyō no riron to undō.* [*The Theory and Practice of Japan's Small- and Medium-Sized Enterprises*]. Tokyo: Shin nihon shuppan kai.

Watanabe, Yasuo, Setsuo Miyazawa, Shigeo Kisa, Shōzaburō Yoshino, Tetsuo Satō. 1992. *Gendai shihō* [*The Modern Judicial System*]. Tokyo: Nihon hyōron sha.

Watanuki, Jōji, Ichirō Miyake, Takeshi Inoguchi, and Ikuo Kabashima. 1986. *Nihonjin no senkyo kōdō.* [*Japanese Voting Behavior*]. Tokyo: University of Tokyo Press.

Weinberg, Jonathan. 1991. "Broadcasting and the Administrative Process in Japan and the United States." *Buffalo Law Review,* 39: 615–735.

Weingast, Barry. 1979. "A Rational Choice Perspective on Congressional Norms." *American Journal of Political Science,* 23.

―――― 1984. "The Congressional Bureaucratic System: A Principal-Agent Perspective (with Applications to the SEC)." *Public Choice,* 44: 147–91.

Weingast, Barry, and William J. Marshall. 1988. "The Industrial Organization of Congress; or, Why Legislatures, Like Firms, Are Not Organized as Markets." *Journal of Political Economy,* 96: 132–63.

Weingast, Barry, and Mark J. Moran. 1983. "Bureaucratic Discretion or Congressional Control?: Regulatory Policy Making by the FTC." *Journal of Political Economy,* 91: 765–800.

Williamson, Oliver E. 1975. *Markets and Hierarchies: Analysis and Antitrust Implications.* New York: The Free Press.

―――― 1983. "Credible Commitments: Using Hostages to Support Exchange." *American Economic Review,* 73: 519–40.

―――― 1985. *The Economic Institutions of Capitalism.* New York: The Free Press.

―――― 1990. "Comparative Economic Organization: The Analysis of

Discrete Structural Alternatives." University of California Berkeley School of Law Working Paper no. 90–21.

Wilson, James Q. 1989. *Bureaucracy: What Government Agencies Do and Why They Do It.* New York: Basic Books.

Wood, B. Dan and Richard W. Waterman. 1991. "The Dynamics of Political Control of the Bureaucracy." *American Political Science Review,* 85: 801–28.

Wright, John W., and Edward J. Dwyer. 1990. *The American Almanac of Jobs and Salaries.* New York: Avon Books.

Yakunin no hōshū, shōyo, nenshū [*Salaries, Bonuses, and Annual Compensation of Officers*]. 1990. Tokyo: Seikei kenkyū sha.

Yamaguchi, Jirō. 1989. *Ittō shihaisei no hakai* [*The Demise of One-Party Dominance*]. Tokyo: Iwanami shoten.

Yamamoto, Shichihei. 1989. *'Habatsu' no kenkyū* [*Research on Factions*]. Tokyo: Yūhikaku.

Yamanouchi, Kazuo. 1974. "Administrative Guidance and the Rule of Law." *Law in Japan,* 7: 22–33.

Yanagisawa, Hakuo. 1985. *Akaji zaisei no jūnen to yonin no sōritachi* [*Ten Years of Deficit Financing and Four Prime Ministers*]. Tokyo: Nihon seisansei hombu.

Youn, Jung-Suk. 1981. "Candidates and Party Images: Recruitment to the Japanese House of Representatives, 1958–1972." In Campbell (1981), pp. 101–115.

Young, Michael. 1988. "Administrative Guidance in the Courts: A Case Study in Doctrinal Adaptation." In Haley (1988c).

Yuasa, Hiroshi. 1986. *Kokkai zoku giin* [*'Policy Tribes' in the Diet*]. Tokyo: Kyōikusha.

Zadankai [Panel Discussion]. 1959. "Shihō seido wo meguru shomondai" [Issues Relating to the Judicial System]. *Hanrei taimuzu,* 92: 1–18.

—— 1971a. "Shihō no kiki o dō haaku suruka" [How to Grasp the Crisis in the Judiciary]. *Hōgaku seminaa* (Spec. Feb. issue): 1–22.

—— 1971b. "Saibankan wa dokuritsu shite iruka" [Are Judges Independent]. *Hōgaku seminaa* (Spec. Feb. issue): 57–73.

—— 1971c. "Saiban to saibankan" [Courts and Judges]. *Jurisuto,* 469: 20–43.

—— 1990. "Hanken jinji kōryū kaidō kyōgikai to saibankan no dokuritsu o kangaeru" [Considering Judicial Independence and the Exchange of Prosecutors and Judges, Meetings, and Conferences]. *Hōritsu jihō* (Aug.): 6–25.

Zenkyoku shin'yō kinko kyōkai, ed. 1977. *Shin'yō kinko nijūgonenshi* [*A Twenty-five Year History of Credit Associations*]. Tokyo: Zenkyoku shin'yō kinko kyōkai.

ZSKS. See Nihon minshu hōritsuka kyōkai.

Zuckerman, Alan. 1979. *The Politics of Faction: Christian Democratic Rule in Italy*. New Haven: Yale University Press.

———— 1975. *Political Clienteles in Power: Party Factions and Cabinet Coalitions in Italy*. Beverly Hills: Sage Publications.

Zupan, Mark. 1990. "Local Benefit-Seeking in the Legislature: An Investigation of Congressional Staffing Decisions." *Economics and Politics*, 3: 163–76.

———— 1992. "An Economic Explanation for the Existence and Nature of Political Ticket Splitting." *Journal of Law and Economics*, 34: 343–369.

Index